T0361932

India's Contemporary Urban Conundrum

EDITED BY

SUJATA PATEL
AND OMITA GOYAL

Routledge
Taylor & Francis Group

LONDON AND NEW YORK

India International Centre

First published 2019
by Routledge
2 Park Square, Milton Park, Abingdon, Oxon OX14 4RN

and by Routledge
605 Third Avenue, New York, NY 10017

First issued in paperback 2020

Routledge is an imprint of the Taylor & Francis Group, an informa business

India International Centre

British Library Cataloguing-in-Publication Data
A catalogue record for this book is available from the British Library

Library of Congress Cataloging-in-Publication Data
A catalog record has been requested for this book

ISBN 13: 978-0-367-73239-4 (pbk)
ISBN 13: 978-1-138-32680-4 (hbk)

Typeset in Berkeley
by Apex CoVantage, LLC

India's Contemporary Urban Conundrum

This book lays out the different and complex dimensions of urbanisation in India. It brings together contributors with expertise in fields as varied as demography, geography, economics, political science, sociology, anthropology, architecture, planning and land use, environmental sciences, creative writing, filmmaking and grassroots activism to reflect on and examine India's urban experience. It discusses various dimensions of city life—how to define the urban; the conditions generating work, living and (in)security; the nature of contemporary cities; the dilemmas of creating and executing urban policy, planning and governance; and the issues concerning ecology and environment. The volume also articulates and evaluates the way Indian urbanism promotes and organises aspirations and utopias of the people, whilst simultaneously endorsing disparities, depravities and conflicts.

The volume includes interventions that shape contemporary debates. Comprehensive, accessible and topical, it will be useful to scholars and researchers of urban studies, urban sociology, development studies, public policy, economics, political studies, gender studies, city studies, planning and governance. It will also interest practitioners, think tanks and NGOs working on urban issues.

Sujata Patel is National Fellow at the Indian Institute of Advanced Study, Shimla, India. Earlier, she taught sociology at the Universities of Hyderabad and Pune and SNDT Women's University. Her work is influenced by Marxism, feminism, spatial studies and post-structuralism, and covers areas such as modernity and social theory, history of sociology/social sciences, city-formation, social movements, gender construction, reservation, quota politics and caste and class formations in India. She is also an interlocutor of teaching and learning practices, and has written on the challenges that organise its reconstitution within classrooms and university structures. She is the author of over sixty peer-reviewed papers/book chapters and the Series Editor of *Oxford India Studies in Contemporary Society* and Routledge's *Cities and the Urban Imperative*. From 2010 to 2015, she edited the *Sage Studies in International Sociology and*

Current Sociology Monographs. She is also the author of *The Making of Industrial Relations* (1997), editor of *The ISA Handbook of Diverse Sociological Traditions* (2010) and *Doing Sociology in India, Genealogies, Locations and Practices* (2011) and is co-editor of five books: *Bombay: Metaphor of Modern India* (1995), *Bombay: Mosaic of Modern Culture* (1995), *Bombay and Mumbai: The City in Transition* (2003), *Thinking Social Science in India* (2002) and *Urban Studies* (2006). She has been associated in various capacities with the International Sociological Association and has been its first Vice-President for National Associations (2002–6). She was the President of Indian Sociological Society from January 2016 to December 2017.

Omita Goyal is presently Chief Editor of the *IIC Quarterly*, the Journal of the India International Centre, New Delhi, India. She started her career in the voluntary sector with the Indian Social Institute, New Delhi, and then moved into academic publishing where she has spent over 27 years. She worked at Sage Publications India Private Limited for 20 years, leaving as General Manager, and thereafter was a consultant for the World Bank, UNICEF, UNDP, Voluntary Health Association of India, Centre for Women's Development Studies, WHO, Institute of Social Studies, The Hague, and TERI. In 2005, she was invited by Taylor and Francis Group to start a social science programme under the social science and humanities imprint, Routledge, as Publishing Director. She has a master's degree in Sociology from the Delhi School of Economics.

CONTENTS

CONTENTS

Illustrations by Pragnya Shankaran (pragmikan@gmail.com)

CONTRIBUTORS

AMITA BHIDE is currently Professor and Dean, School of Habitat Studies, Tata Institute of Social Sciences (TISS). Bhide's recent work at the School of Habitat Studies has been on urban governance reforms, and housing and land issues with a focus on small and medium towns. Her recent publications include *The Regularising State* and *Comparing Informalities*.

CHRISTIANE BROSIUS is Professor, Visual and Media Anthropology, Heidelberg Centre for Transcultural Studies, Heidelberg University. She has published widely on visual popular culture and politics in India, on social spatialisation in Delhi, and on the field of art production in India and Nepal. She is co-founder of www.tasveerghar.net. Currently, Brosius works on contemporary art events and activism in Delhi and Kathmandu, on questions of transcultural comparison and on urban disaster management in the context of the Nepal earthquake in 2015.

HIMANSHU BURTE has practiced architecture, and written extensively on the poetics and politics of the built environment since 1990. His book, *Space for Engagement: The Indian Artplace and a Habitational Approach to Architecture*, proposes an alternate conceptual framework for architecture centred on the act of dwelling. A former Fulbright Fellow, Burte teaches at School of Habitat Studies, Tata Institute of Social Sciences (TISS), Mumbai.

KAREN COELHO is Assistant Professor, Madras Institute of Development Studies (MIDS), based in Chennai. Coelho holds a PhD in Socio-Cultural Anthropology from the University of Arizona, Tucson. Her work critically explores urban governance and transformations, focusing on shelter policy, urban civil society and collective action, urban ecologies and informal labour. Coelho teaches courses in History of Development Thought and Qualitative Methods at MIDS, and Urban Studies at the Asian College of Journalism, Chennai.

ERIC DENIS is Research Director, French National Centre for Scientific Research (CNRS), currently at Géographie-cités Lab., Université Panthéon-Sorbonne University. Besides small towns, his research concerns urban land access and economy, and geo-technology and governance. Denis has authored about 60 articles on social geography and urban studies, and is the editor of several volumes, including *Popular Housing and Urban Land Tenure in the Middle East*; *Villes et urbanisation des provinces* égyptiennes; and the *Atlas of Cairo*.

RENU DESAI is Research Fellow, Centre for Urban Equity, CEPT University, Ahmedabad. She holds a PhD in Architecture from the University of California, Berkeley. Her research examines urban informality and urban transformation in Indian cities. Desai has published several articles in journals and book chapters based on her research, and is co-editor of *Urbanizing Citizenship: Contested Spaces in Indian Cities*.

RUPALI GUPTE is an architect, urban designer and artist based in Mumbai. She is currently Associate Professor, School of Environment and Architecture, which she co-founded. Gupte is also a co-founder of the urban research network, CRIT. Previous assignments were as Assistant Professor, Kamla Raheja Vidyanidhi Institute for Architecture; Consulting Urban Designer, Town Administration, Mendefera, Eritrea; and Architect, Kohn Pederson Fox Associates, New York. Gupte's works revolve largely around tactical practices in cities and their spatial implications.

SWASTIK HARISH is a Senior Consultant at the Indian Institute for Human Settlements (IIHS). He is trained as an architect and has 15 years of experience. Besides heading the design lab at IIHS, Harish conducts research and practises in the field of urban housing in India, with a focus on rental housing.

BARBARA HARRISS-WHITE drove to India from Cambridge in 1969 and has been studying India through fieldwork on-and-off ever since, resulting in 35 (co)authored or (co)edited books, over 250 papers and chapters, and 40 doctoral students. Originally educated in agriculture and economics, she is Emeritus Professor, Development Studies, Oxford University; Emeritus Fellow, Wolfson College; and Visiting Professor, Centre for the Informal Sector and Labour Studies, JNU. Harriss-White is currently interested in the economy as a system producing waste alongside goods and services.

AMITABH KUNDU is currently Visiting Professor, Institute for Human Development, and Consultant to the Government of Sri Lanka. Kundu was Professor of Economics and Dean of the School of Social Sciences, JNU. He has headed, and been a member of, several technical committees appointed by the Ministry of Statistics and Programme Implementation, Ministry of Housing and Urban Poverty Alleviation, among others. Kundu has been Visiting Professor at the Universities of Amsterdam and Kaiserslautern, and South Asian Institute, Heidelberg, Germany, among others.

DARSHINI MAHADEVIA is Professor, Faculty of Planning, and Director, Centre for Urban Equity, CEPT University. Specialising in urban development policies, Mahadevia has published on housing policy, urban poverty, human and gender development. She holds a Bachelor's in Architecture, a Master's in Urban and Regional Planning, and a PhD from Jawaharlal Nehru University. Mahadevia has collaborated for research with many national and international academic institutions and universities in India, Europe and China.

AJAY K. MEHRA is Director (Honorary), Centre for Public Affairs, Noida, and teaches Political Science at the University of Delhi. He has been a keen student of urban processes, public security, public institutions, and electoral and political processes in India for four decades. He has authored/co-authored and edited/co-edited 14 publications. Mehra has contributed research papers to prestigious refereed journals and over 200 articles to the national media.

DINESH MOHAN retired from the Indian Institute of Technology (IIT), Delhi, as Chair Professor for Transportation Planning and Safety.

Currently, he is Distinguished Professor, Shiv Nadar University, and Guest Professor, IIT, Delhi. Mohan is on the Board of the International Research Council on Biomechanics of Injuries. Mohan is the recipient of the Distinguished Alumnus award from IIT, Bombay, and the Distinguished Career Award from the University of Delaware.

PARTHA MUKHOPADHYAY is Senior Fellow, Centre for Policy Research (CPR), Delhi. Previously, he was part of the founding team at IDFC. He has also worked at the EXIM Bank of India and the World Bank in Washington, taught at IIM, Ahmedabad, and XLRI, Jamshedpur, and been associated with a number of government committees. Mukhopadhyay's research interests lie in urbanisation, infrastructure, and the development paths of India and China. His most recent book is *Power, Policy and Protest*.

SEEMA MUNDOLI is Research Associate, Azim Premji University, Bengaluru. Her research interests include the conservation of urban ecological spaces, concerns of equitable access to these commons, and the role of governance institutions in these processes.

HARINI NAGENDRA is Professor, School of Development, Azim Premji University, Bengaluru, and the author of *Nature in the City: Bengaluru in the Past, Present, and Future*. Her research focuses on questions of social-ecological sustainability in Indian forests and cities, with a long-term programme of research on biodiversity, green spaces and lakes in Indian cities.

VAISHALI PARMAR is Assistant Professor, R. K. University, Rajkot. She holds a Master's in Urban and Regional Planning from CEPT University, Ahmedabad.

HARSH RAMAN SINGH PAUL grew up fascinated by art's ability to make tangible his vivid imagination. His creativity manifests itself through art, graphic design, fashion, art direction and illustration. Prolific within the subculture that has redefined India's streets, Harsh's art takes many forms—from walls to canvases to installations and digital platforms, surrealist murals covering lifeless, concrete walls and vibrant painted cars driving around the streets—to bring about a positive change in the collective consciousness of our society, using the power of art.

TANUSREE PAUL is Assistant Professor, Centre for Women's Studies, Visva-Bharati University, Santiniketan. A geographer by training, she holds a PhD from the Centre for the Study of Regional Development, Jawaharlal Nehru University, Delhi. She has worked extensively on the complex issues of spaces, places and gender in the context of a globalising world. Paul's research interests also span gender questions in development, health, the labour market and natural resources. She has also published widely on these issues.

KANHU C. PRADHAN is Senior Research Associate, Centre for Policy Research (CPR), Delhi, and Research Scholar, Indian Institute of Technology (IIT), Delhi. His research looks at patterns of urbanisation, the interaction between rural and urban areas, and migration in India. Pradhan holds a Master's in Economics from Jawaharlal Nehru University and is pursuing a PhD at IIT, Delhi.

SARASWATI RAJU is a geographer whose interests relate to social development with a focus on gendered marginalities in the labour market, access to literacy/education/skills, empowerment, and gender and space. Raju recently co-edited *Women Workers in Urban India*. She is the recipient of the Janet Monk Service Award (2010) and the 2012 Distinguished Service Award for Asian Geography by the Association of American Geographers for exemplary contribution to the fields of Feminist Geography and Asian Geography.

SHARADINI RATH is Affiliate Fellow, Indian School of Political Economy (ISPE), Pune. The implementation of the 74th CAA at the municipal level and its impact on the structure of public finance of urban, local self-governments has been a long-term interest. Rath has also worked on urban economies, with a specific interest in patterns of industrial location and their relationship with urban agglomerations, including the role of the State in shaping the rapid developments in these areas.

RANABIR SAMADDAR belongs to the critical school of thinking and is considered one of the foremost theorists in the field of migration and forced migration studies. *The Politics of Dialogue* was the culmination of his long work on justice, rights and peace. His recent political writings, *The Materiality of Politics and The Emergence of the Political*

Subject, have signalled a new turn in critical postcolonial thinking. Samaddar is currently Distinguished Chair in Migration and Forced Migration Studies, Calcutta Research Group.

PRASAD SHETTY trained as an architect and specialises in urban management. Based in Mumbai, he currently teaches at the School of Environment and Architecture, which he co-founded. He is also co-founder of the urban research network, CRIT. Shetty has worked as Urban Manager, Mumbai Metropolitan Region Development Authority; Secretary, MMR—Heritage and Environment Society; Lecturer, Kamla Raheja Vidyanidhi Institute for Architecture; and as an Urban Management expert for Town Administration, Mendefera, Eritrea. His works centre round cultural dimensions of urban economy and property.

GAYATRI SINGH is an urban development specialist at the World Bank. As a Rhodes Scholar, she studied at Oxford University, earning degrees in Philosophy, Politics and Economics (BA Honours, senior status) and Forced Migration Studies (MSc). Trained as a demographer, she holds a PhD from Brown University. Singh's expertise spans areas of poverty and inequality, urbanisation and urban policy, migration, displaced populations, public health and application of mixed methods in development research using spatial, survey and qualitative approaches.

VIKRAM SONI is presently Emeritus Professor at Jamia Millia and JNU, and Advisor to the Delhi Jal Board. In Physics, he has made seminal contributions to our understanding of a whole range of phenomena. The conservation of the Aravalli biodiversity park in Delhi is mainly due his activism to protect living heritage. The protection and moratorium on building on the floodplain of the river Yamuna, and the pioneering natural storage and recharge, drinking water scheme in Delhi is authored by him and co-workers.

ASHIMA SOOD teaches at NALSAR Law University and is Affiliate Fellow, Indian School of Political Economy (ISPE), Pune. Sood's research and writings have appeared in *Urban Studies* and the *Economic and Political Weekly,* among others. In 2016, along with

Loraine Kennedy, she co-edited a special issue of the *Economic and Political Weekly's* Review of Urban Affairs on greenfield urban development. Sood is currently working with Sharadini Rath on an Azim Premji Foundation-funded project, 'City as Infrastructure: Private and Greenfield Urban Development in India'.

SANJAY SRIVASTAVA is Professor of Sociology at the Institute of Economic Growth, Delhi University. His publications include *Constructing Postcolonial India: National Character and the Doon School; Asia: Cultural Politics in the Global Age* (co-authored); *Sexual Sites, Seminal Attitudes: Sexualities, Masculinities and Culture in South Asia* (contributing editor); *Passionate Modernity, Sexuality, Class and Consumption in India; Sexuality Studies* (contributing editor); and *Entangled Urbanism: Slum, Gated Community and Shopping Mall in Delhi and Gurgaon*.

TRINA VITHAYATHIL is Assistant Professor of Global Studies, at Providence College. She holds a Master's and a PhD in Sociology from Brown University, an MPP from the Kennedy School of Government, Harvard University, and a Bachelor's from Carleton College. Vithayathil's research and teaching interests include Political Sociology, Social Inequality, Comparative Race, Urban Sociology, Political Economy, Sociology of Knowledge, and Globalisation and Development.

HITA UNNIKRISHNAN is a Post-doctoral Research Associate at Azim Premji University. Her recent doctoral research explores histories of lakes in Bengaluru and relates it to contemporary events, emphasising the voices of communities traditionally dependent on lakes.

JEEMOL UNNI is Professor of Economics, AM School of Management, Ahmedabad University. She was Director, and, earlier, RBI Chair Professor of Economics at Institute of Rural Management, Anand. She holds a PhD in Economics and was a post-doctoral Fellow at the Economic Growth Center, Yale University. She is a Director of BoG and Women in Informal Employment and Globalising and Organising (WIEGO), UK. Unni's recent publications include *Ecology Economy: Quest for a Socially Informed Connection*.

MARIE-HÉLÈNE ZÉRAH works with the Institute of Research for Development, Paris, and is currently visiting the Centre for Policy Research (CPR). Previous to her interest in small towns, she has worked in the areas of infrastructure, governance and democracy in Indian cities. Her books include *Right to the City in India* and *Water: Unreliable Supply in Delhi*. Zérah is on the editorial board of *Geoforum* and is Series Editor of the *Springer Series: Exploring Urban Change in South Asia*.

◆

FOREWORD

Urbanisation is a major concern as our population continues to grow exponentially, and the middle class is also rising. We have, of course, a long and rich tradition of planned cities, going all the way back to Harappa and Mohenjo-Daro in the Indus Valley/Sarasvati Civilisation, and also since Independence with Chandigarh, Bhuvaneshwar, and now Amravati. However, apart from the rare planned cities there is a proliferation of unplanned urbanisation in the metros and semi-rural areas. All of these raise a number of crucial issues which need to be frontally addressed.

How can we ensure that some sense of order and logic is brought into our urban development? The concept of the city itself has expanded, and Delhi for example is now a federation of many townships rather than an integrated city. Therefore, it is necessary to have a structure of Resident Welfare Associations to oversee the requirement of individual townships. Here our Corporations, Municipalities and Panchayats have to be motivated to try and ensure some degree of coherence in our urban expansion. Another question is with regard to the massive influx of population from rural to urban areas. Unless satellite towns are developed around the major population hubs, the whole structure is rapidly becoming clogged and dysfunctional. Central and state agencies need to become much more active and effective if the situation is to be reversed.

A third issue that faces our cities emerges from climate change which is beginning to produce, with startling regularity, extreme weather conditions that cause havoc. The latest phenomenon that we have witnessed is the drowning of entire cities. This has happened in Chennai, Bengaluru, Srinagar, Mumbai and elsewhere over the last few years. The Srinagar flood was a classic example of a climate crisis compounded by human error and ineptitude. It is difficult to believe that many parts of Srinagar were submerged under 30 feet of water for several days. With climate change speeding up, such ecological disasters are likely to increase. We need, therefore, on the one hand to re-structure our water management systems in the cities, and, on the other, to keep ecological factors closely in mind while planning new urban settlements.

Another area that has not received adequate attention is the structural aspect of unbanisation. I recall several decades ago there was a buzz regarding prefabricated houses which promised large-scale low-cost housing. However, subsequently, the concept seems to have vanished, although I understand that the technology has greatly improved and could now provide the possibility of massive construction, particularly in semi-urban areas. Green technology also needs to be developed instead of our increasing dependence on cement concrete. Structures that are environment friendly, such as those having solar panels, would help in reducing our carbon emissions. The whole technology of construction, therefore, needs a fresh survey and an innovative approach.

Finally, the importance of civic amenities in our cities has been gravely discounted. Waste management is still generally a disaster story. Potable drinking water is still not available in many areas and medical facilities fall far short of the growing requirements. These are areas upon which the central and state governments must concentrate their attention in the decades ahead. While the old concept of the city as a meeting place of people from different backgrounds has virtually disappeared, it is still necessary that areas for creative mingling should be provided within our urban conglomerations.

Taken together, these constitute a massive challenge to the country. This volume contains a number of insightful essays by people who have studied the problems in depth, and will surely be a valuable addition to the literature in this area. I commend it not only to directly involved organisations, but to concerned citizens without whose active interest the massive challenges that we face cannot be effectively met.

KARAN SINGH

◆

PREFACE

I t was the best of cities, it was the worst of cities.
(brutal misquote of the memorable opening lines from *A Tale of Two Cities* by Charles Dickens).

In the mid-1980s, urban studies found little space in academic publishing. Today, it is quite the opposite. Universities across the country include courses on urban studies, and there are a number of research institutes and think tanks that focus on contemporary urbanisation as part of larger centres for policymaking. This volume, with contributions by academics and academic-practitioners, lays out for us the different and complex dimensions of urbanisation and its impact on our lives. Urbanisation goes hand in hand with 'development', with little thought for the fallout in terms of a breakdown, not only of physical infrastructure, but also quality of life, as this volume shows. These essays were originally published as part of the *IIC Quarterly*, Winter 2016/Spring 2017 issue.

Despite this, however, we are passionate about our cities, even vociferously protective. We protest against malls being built in our colonies, or trees being sacrificed for development projects. We think nothing of polluting our environment, but we take pride in the metro. India Gate in Delhi is still a favourite place to walk on hot summer evenings when electricity fails. Marine Drive in Mumbai is another iconic space to walk, jog, or do nothing at all. The huge open space near Victoria Memorial in Kolkata is a blessing for the young who have dreams of becoming football or cricket stars.

We have to acknowledge that urbanisation is inevitable. And while we look to the state to provide not just basic amenities but better planning of cities, we have to ask how we, as citizens, can contribute to making our cities liveable today and for the future.

I will not hold you back from the brilliant contributions to this volume. It is our privilege that some of the best minds in the field agreed to come on board to make this a rich addition to the literature on urbanisation.

◆

OMITA GOYAL

INTRODUCTION
REVISITING URBAN INDIA

SUJATA
PATEL

I ndia is in the process of a revolutionary urban transition. The estimates of the size of the urban population vary with the Indian census pegging the level of urbanisation at 33 per cent in 2011, and the World Bank at 52 per cent in 2013 (The World Bank, 2013). Between 2014 and 2050, a UN report (Mehra, quoted in this volume) suggests that India will add 404 million to its urban population. Another information sheet suggests that the southern and western states of India are already more than 50 per cent urban.

The visual manifestation of this burgeoning urbanisation is apparent all across the country; we see new buildings rising, new roads being dug, new pipelines being laid. Our cities have become crowded and polluted with people jostling against hand carts, bicycles, motorcycles and cars, and negotiating potholes. In the midst of all this, there are broken pavements housing street markets and selling goods and food. Expanding urbanisation is now a way of life. This is true not only of big and large cities but also small and medium towns, and now increasingly of villages.

How do we understand, analyse and examine what this experience implies? One has to be cautious in answering this question. For there is of course the sheer size and numbers of those who have become urban and are becoming urban; India, as we know, will soon have the largest urban population in the world. But the answer is not related only to these numbers (though for many demographers and census analysts this is a key issue); the urban, as we know, implies an assessment of the continuously changing, complex and uneven patterns of physical habitat that are organised in distinct space–time processes. Thus to answer this question, it is necessary to comprehend the manner in which distinct geographies are constituted as a consequence of the intervention of economies, policies and ways of living, and how these have shaped the everyday lives of the people who inhabit them and who, in turn, have refashioned these in new ways as they organise and adjust their work, living and mobility within this habitat.

Most social scientists agree that they have only recently started assessing the urban experience in India critically, and that until the late 1990s, social scientific literature on cities and urbanism was at best banal. Although cities have traditionally nurtured critical knowledge about the world, generally, and about the urban, specifically, in India, intellectuals within the nationalist movement developed a strong social scientific orientation on the assessment of the rural and agrarian processes. In turn, this consciousness fuelled both policy and professional research on rural India. However, although almost all nationalist intellectuals were born and raised in major towns and cities of India, all of which were going through revolutionary transformations as they were growing up, their gaze was not on the nature of India's urban modernity but on the conditions organising village life and the agrarian processes that exploited the peasantry. Be that as it may, the implication of this trend has impoverished theoretical positions on the urban in India, both by policymakers and by professional social scientists.

The recent 'urban turn' has allowed for an intensive interrogation on urbanism in India, leading to the production of a significant body of critical empirical work. Contributors with expertise in fields as varied as the social sciences (demography, geography, economics, political science, sociology and anthropology), architecture, planning, environmental sciences, activism, and even creative writing and film making have reflected on India's urban experience, thereby contributing to its knowledge. These writings have assessed, examined and articulated the many dimensions of city life, and evaluated both the way Indian urbanism promotes and organises aspirations and utopias of the people, whilst simultaneously endorsing disparities, depravities and conflicts.

This volume enters into the discussion at this critical juncture. It brings together interventions from a group of thinkers who are shaping the contemporary debate and deliberations on the urban and the city today. The essays discuss and debate the various aspects of India's urban experience as assessed in the early 21st century. Of the many varied contributions by social scientists, we focus on five themes: the debate on how to define the urban; the conditions generating work, living and (in)security; the nature of contemporary cities; the dilemmas organising urban policy, planning and governance; and the issues concerning ecology and environment.

Our contributors have used their various disciplinary positions to present a synoptic view of the various dimensions that organise the urban experience in contemporary India. Their differing positions open up for debate various aspects of city life, presenting new concepts that may be used to study cities and urbanisation such as the shadow settlements (Sood and Rath); transactional spaces (Shetty and Gupte); the logistical city (Samaddar); rurbanisation (Kundu); subaltern urbanisation (Mukhopadhyay, et al.); engine urbanism (Burte); post-national urbanism (Srivastava); inclusive urbanisation (Unni); and sustainable urbanisation (Mundoli, et al.) We hope that together these essays and their perspectives challenge the reader to think about India's contemporary urban experience.

THE DEBATE ON HOW TO DEFINE THE URBAN

An analysis of the urban experience always starts with a discussion on numbers and this concern leads commentators to census figures. As mentioned earlier, the 2011 Census of India suggests that 33 per cent of the Indian population is urban, i.e., living in settlements designated urban by the Indian state. The urban is divided by the census into small and medium towns, and metropoles and megacities, on the basis of population figures. Towns and cities are also internally divided into sections and wards.

Demographers, geographers and planners have been puzzled by the 2011 Census data which, instead of indicating the phenomenal increase of urban populations, suggests a sluggish growth rate of urbanisation. The National Sample Survey data also suggests that the migration of male population into cities has declined. However, the census also suggests a growth in what it calls Census towns (settlements which have a population of more than 5,000, wherein 75 per cent males are employed in non-agricultural activities and there is a density of more than 400 per square kilometres). What causes this anomaly?

Two papers try to answer this question. The first hypothesis is that of rurbanisation (Kundu), which he defines as settlements with urban characteristics that at the same time retain a rural socio-economic base. Kundu suggests that India has a unique pattern of urbanisation and identifies three trends of rurbanisation. First, there is a real expansion in the periphery of highly developed regions because large cities have become exclusionary. This trend of peripheral rurbanisation is evident in satellite cities and large urban agglomerations.

Second, there is a decrease in migration and increasing out migration, with declining investments in small and medium towns in backward regions of the country. A large number of small and medium towns, with some exceptions, show sluggish growth, stagnation and a fluctuating agricultural economy. Their rurbanisation is linked to regional integration.

Third, there is a sharp increase in the number of Census towns (almost 2,500 more such declared) because these satisfy the demographic criteria, but many have not been given this statutory status by their respective state governments. As a consequence, they have not been provided with urban infrastructure and thus remain rurbanised. The census, it has been argued, has not been able to capture the complex diversities in urbanisation processes and has proved inadequate in comprehending them.

The second hypothesis, of subaltern urbanisation, defines it as being 'autonomous, economically vital and independent of the metropolis', and is a process that perceives cities as a system of interrelationships (Mukhopadhyay, et al.). The authors argue that subaltern settlements are those that have a significant population in cities just below Class 1. For example, about 41 per cent of India's urban population resides in small towns with a population of less than 100,000. The spatial spread of urbanisation can be located not only in the increase of Census towns but also in what it calls settlement agglomerations. These territories have emerged due to economic and historical reasons and whose developments have not been noted in the census. If these geographies are taken into account, the urban population may be pushed up by another

10 per cent, i.e., India may declare that its population is at least 39 per cent plus urban, if not more.

Both these perspectives have attempted to capture the complex set of forces associated with the urbanisation unleashed in India in recent times. Both attest to the rapid rise of urbanisation in the form of the expansion of roads, transport and communication networks, and of economic activities, social infrastructure such as housing, health and education, and new lifestyles. They suggest that these processes are leaving a deep imprint on all the regions of the country. As a consequence, it is extremely difficult to delineate what is non-urban. They also attest to the fact that the urban is patterned in complex, uneven and unequal manner, and thus constitutes variegated geographical and spatial hierarchies.

As a consequence, some demographers and geographers suggest caution in using census data uncritically and argue that in all likelihood the urban exists extensively, if not completely, outside officially designated towns and cities, and within what is called rural. In other words, official data has not been able to capture the urban when it has folded itself into villages and into what the census describes as rural. Social scientists are thus suggesting that urbanisation in India is in all probability highly variegated and complex. To understand it, we need to support census definitions with other conceptual terminologies that give us an entry to an assessment of the specific attributes governing Indian urbanisation. So what should be these be? Is one of them the slum?

CONDITIONS GENERATING WORK, LIVING AND (IN)SECURITY

What is the slum? S. Harish uses the UN-Habitat definition to conceptualise the slum. The slum is defined generally as an informal and non-legal settlement of dense population, characterised by substandard housing, little-to-no-services in the form of water, sanitation and other infrastructure, and a lifestyle of squalor (UN-Habitat, 2003). The 2001 Census states that 43 million (i.e., 23 per cent) of India's urban population lives in slums and by 2011 this number had increased to 93 million, with more than 50 per cent of Mumbai's population living in slums, with megacities such as Chennai and Delhi having 19 per cent. If we match this information with another bit of information in government records that show that more than 30 per cent of those who live in slums have no tenure (legal right) over their land and house, then we can understand the extreme vulnerability and insecurity in which this population lives.

This has allowed some social scientists to argue that slums house the poor and thus represent urban poverty. If this argument is accepted, then it seems about a quarter of the urban houses the poor of the country. However, recent interventions by social scientists suggest the need to look beyond the slum to understand poverty and vulnerabilities. Commentators contend that an analysis of poverty, and thus of exclusions, needs to combine housing with access to services such as water, sanitation and electricity. They also suggest the need to go beyond official definitions of slums to understand these vulnerabilities and exclusions.

As a consequence, literature on this theme has moved on to an assessment of spatial inequalities and segregation. Vithayathil, et al. follow this argument in affirming that contemporary Indian urbanisation can be distinguished for its spatial segregation of marginal groups. To understand this spatial segregation, the authors use census data, and correlate housing and access to services with the social affiliation of groups. Having established that SCs and STs, together with migrants, live in the outer wards of cities, they plot their access to services and indicate the nature of their deprivation. Their analysis confirms the findings of another study that suggests that caste and tribe segregation increases when plotted against access to in-house drinking water and in-house latrines, each of which is a basic public good. Although urbanisation and modernity are supposed to filter pre-modern social affiliations, such as caste and religiosities, in India these are increasing, especially in small and medium towns.

Inequalities, exclusions and the resultant segregation also need to be understood in terms of the employment structure in cities and, in turn, the access of workers to transport facilities, and thus to safety, in order to access such employment. This becomes particularly significant in the case of women workers whose work starts in the household and then extends to informal markets. Given that a number of these households do not have legal tenure, the vulnerabilities and insecurities of women working in households, and accessing transport for work and markets, increases in geometric proportion. In this section we include papers on transport and women's work, safety, and their differential access to public spaces within cities.

Economists have highlighted how the Indian economy has not transited towards industrial manufacturing and that a significant part of the Indian work force—almost 85 per cent—labours as informal workers. Studies of increasing informalisation and casualisation of the work force in the manufacturing sector, together with other studies that evaluate occupations being practiced by various members of slum households, draw our attention to the fact that most slums house workers who labour in urban informal low-end service economies, such as garbage collection and waste picking, small-time retailing or as domestic servants. About one-third of the informal workers are also self-employed, a large number of them being women.

Jeemol Unni discusses the informal sector in Ahmedabad. She notes the range of informal work being done by women; women may be employed in informal wage employment, self-employment in informal enterprises and in informal employment in formal enterprises, and within households. Women who are employed in the informal sector are thus engaged in 'pluri-activity, multiple job-holding and secondary activities', all of which do not capture completely the many ways women work to create assets and incomes.

Desai and Mahadevia focus on the vulnerabilities experienced by women living in resettled areas in the peripheries of the city. They give examples to show how increasing transport costs, long-distance travel, intermittent frequencies of bus services, overcrowded conditions of public transport, sexual harassment, and the use of intoxicants, alcohol and drugs by men create a hostile urban environment and promote insecurities. They suggest that the gamut of difficulties being faced by women relates to the way the planning process has been executed in cities.

This issue of planning is also discussed by Dinesh Mohan, but through a different perspective. He argues for proper transport planning of cities, given that there is high ownership of personal vehicles, leading to pollution and global warming, overcrowding, dense traffic, increased decibel levels and resultant health problems.

CITIES OF CONTEMPORARY INDIA

What are the characteristics of Indian cities? The papers in this section highlight their attributes: the use of real estate and the private sector in developing cities; the digitilisation of service delivery and of the planning process; the privatisation of municipal governance; migrants as key to an assessment of cities; the reproduction of transactional spaces; and the gendered reconstitution of private and public spaces.

Gurgaon, according to Sood and Rath, is the model of private urban development now institutionalised in Special Economic Zones (SEZs) and Special Investment Regions (SIRs), and in the Greenfield part of the Smart City Policy. Gurgaon was initially developed by Delhi Land and Finance (DLF) which constructed residential, business and commercial buildings, and now houses the headquarters of some of the most important multinationals and IT industries of the region. But despite its prominence as a city of shopping malls, golf courses and five-star hotels, Gurgaon's growth has been termed a 'failed experiment', given that it could not establish city-wide services of electricity, water and sewerage, and thereby created zones of spatial and class exclusions.

The authors argue that this seems to be the trend in other company towns that have sprung up around manufacturing towns. An earlier experiment at Jamshedpur, which has been discussed as an ideal model, indicates the flaws that can be generated when governance of public services is privatised. Jamshedpur started as a company town around the manufacturing unit of Tata Steel. The company provided superior services to its upper-echelon staff and was not able to cater at all to the increasing number of migrants entering the city to gain employment. The town, thus, was organised in terms of spatial and class divisions which were further aggravated given the ethnic/tribal bias in the recruitment of employees, creating new kinds of ethnic identities in the city. Instead of industrialisation and urbanisation giving access to new modes of living to reproduce new concepts, company towns, according to the authors, have promoted 'shadow settlements' where the excluded population lives without access to services in the peripheries of such cities.

Ranabir Samaddar presents a new theory to examine and assess Greenfield cities (such as Gurgaon and Rajahart, which he has studied) being developed today, He calls this kind of city 'logistical city'. According to him, the contemporary neo-liberal model allows the city to become an infrastructural hub by engaging in all forms of extraction and thereby accumulating capital through rent. It is logistical because it continuously extracts from the physical aspects of the city—air, water, soil, waste—and uses rent as a means to accumulate. The key to the logistical city, according to Samaddar, are the conflicts that are generated as a consequence of the need to use migrant labour for extraction. This labour cannot be settled and provided services; if this happens then profits accumulated through rent will decline. The city, according to Samaddar, in the present neo-liberal context cannot become bourgeois but has become 'a contentious place marked by groups fighting for resources, space, rights, claims and justice'.

Spatial, class and ethnic exclusions are also the focus of the next two papers in this section. Christiane Brosius describes how artists understand and explore the constant thirst for land in the city, which destroys nature and creates consumerist cultures, while Shetty and Gupte glorify the indigenous innovations that create its habitat. They initiate their discussion of 'smartness' with an exploration of the growing digitilisation of planning and service delivery processes in contemporary cities. While critically interrogating the way the term 'smart' is used in the contemporary discourse, they argue that cities have their indigenous ways of being 'smart'. Cities, according to Shetty and Gupte, create 'unclear geographies, unstable forms' and bring together contradictions of spaces, practices and relationships. While the authors wish to celebrate these transactions as innovative ways of living the urban, for many commentators these crowded spaces represent the most depraved aspect of the city. Usually it is equated with a settlement called the slum and is associated with poverty.

The next paper discuss how economists, geographers and sociologists have analysed inequalities and exclusions in housing and work in contemporary India. Raju and Paul open up a new dimension when they assess the framing of public–private places in India. They suggest that the public–private needs to be defined anew in case of countries such as India, and highlight the fact that industrial legislation has not been pro-women and has not encouraged conditions for them to work night shifts. They also examine new work cultures (e.g., in the IT industry) and show

how the legitimation of traditional gender roles in the form of household duties (the private domain) affect women's involvement in their work, leading them to accept secondary positions at work by enhancing their 'feminine' attributes. These work cultures do not challenge nor enhance women's socio-economic and political status, nor provide equal participation in work.

Does urban policy reflect these concerns? Has it indicated a sensitivity to assess and examine the complex patterning that structures urban problems in India?

URBAN POLICY, GOVERNANCE AND PLANNING

The papers in this section highlight the dissonance of policy from realities that organise the urban worlds in India. Mehra calls it a 'policy disconnect', while Bhide highlights the continuous changes in thought and ideas making urban policy infructuous. Other commentators have described it as opaque, myopic, chaotic and, at best, formulated in fits and starts. Harriss-White describes the policy on waste economy as constituted by 'discursive incoherence'; this term can be applied more generally to all urban policy.

Mehra gives an overview of the concerns that have dominated the formulation of urban policy and shows how these have changed continuously. Dividing the Five-year plans into three phases, he argues that there have been three contradictory principles on which policy has been enunciated over the last seven decades: (i) in the initial years there was focus on solving immediate problems of housing for migrants and refugees, and an expectation that subsidies by the state government through the instrument of planning would suffice; (ii) this concern for subsidised housing for the poor declined with the acquisition of land for new towns as private-sector corporate players were roped in to develop towns; and (iii) new private–public partnerships were promoted through central schemes of upgrading urban services (such as JNURRM), while simultaneously asserting decentralisation, participative democracy and corporate governance.

Bhide continues by asking whether urban policy has increased democratisation and decentralisation within local bodies. This question is important because, for Bhide, it is only through local bodies that services are delivered to the people. She assesses the history of the institutionalisation of local bodies in India and suggests that since colonial times it has been rooted in elite control. After independence, even though democracy flourished in villages, this was not true regarding urban bodies and the state government continuously determined functions, power and finances of the municipalities. Elections to the latter became a matter of choice. Second, the states set up parastatal institutions, such as slum boards and sewerage and water supply boards, to deal with growing informal housing within cities, diluting the role of local bodies in management and administration. It is in this context that the 74th Constitutional Amendment is discussed. Although it implied decentralisation and democratic participation, its implementation has remained selective, especially in the case of transfer of powers regarding its functions, powers and finances.

S. Harish examines another aspect of policy framework—the lack of a clear understanding of what constitutes the problem and the manner of implementation. In order to understand this, he takes the case of affordable housing. The first problem is the lack of clarity of what constitutes affordable housing. The state believes that affordable housing is what is available to medium-income groups. Another definition is five times a household's annual income. Given that those who need housing are from economically weaker sections or are female-headed households, there exists an anomalous situation in which affordable housing is inadequate, and adequate housing is unaffordable, leading a large number of people to continue to live in slums. Again, as described earlier, housing is related to employment transportation and security, both of residence and of safety. Given that investments needed for new affordable housing are huge, Harish suggests the need to upgrade the existing slum settlements, providing permanent tenure, elevating infrastructure, and providing sustainable economic and social relationships.

Unfortunately, such an approach to create affordable housing is not attempted by those who govern. Burte cites the case of the Slum Redevelopment Scheme of Bombay city (1991/1995) that promised free housing to owners of slum tenements from the profits of the private development of land on which they lived. Burte calls this kind of urbanism 'engine urbanism', i.e., when a city is built as a machine and urban policies are implemented in a mechanistic manner. It is characterised by the twin processes of rationalisation and integration, and by four adjectives that organise urban spatiality: formal, big, private and networked. These adjectives describe the processes unleashed by liberalisation in the country.

This section ends with a paper by Srivastava on how attempts at democratic decentralisation, instead of empowering the poor, have been used by Delhi's middle classes to confront the urban poor, and thus redefine the relationship between the citizen and the state. An experiment in local democracy in Delhi was attempted through the formation of the institution of the Resident Welfare Association (RWA), a body representing mostly middle-class housing societies. The RWAs were given powers to govern certain public sites such as parks, community halls, roads and sanitation facilities, and question the lack of governance by local bodies. But this attempt at decentralised democracy has been seized by the middle classes who use nationalist language and its politics to legitimise their consumerist cultures.

Post-nationalist cultures, according to Srivastava, are common in the middle-class gated community in Delhi, which has now reconstituted an idea of itself as the new 'people', who are constituting a new discourse for themselves. It is also associated with the questioning of subsidies to the poor, alleging that the poor are constantly accessing illegally public resources. In this new political culture, the slum-dweller is perceived as a criminal and a threat. It is not surprising that the RWAs have moved courts to remove slums from around their localities, terming the poor encroachers.

ECOLOGY, ENVIRONMENT AND WELL-BEING

Four papers combining different perspectives introduce the ecological and environment issues of urban habitats. Mundoli, et al. affirm the need to analyse the necessity of examining urban commons as ecosystems that have environmental functions, such as purification and replenishment of water sources, and regulation of climate, but also as sites that provide employment to people living in urban areas, those who can use water, eat food like fish, graze their livestock, and cultivate vegetables and flowers for sale. Because the urban commons sustain the urban poor, the continuous degradation of this environment in cities becomes a cause of concern. This paper makes an assessment of changing land use in the urban commons in Bengaluru to examine how it impacts the environment and the urban poor.

Given that Bengaluru was located in a semi-arid region, the city grew by constructing reservoirs to conserve rainwater through tanks and lakes. In and around these lakes wooded groves emerged, together with grazing land, supplying the needs of the local population and their livestock for water, fuel wood, fodder and food. However, in the last few decades as Bengaluru has expanded, these urban commons have become dilapidated and their role in generating employment has declined. The authors suggest that Bengaluru's case shows that the loss of commons not only affects those who live by it, but also has larger environmental implications: the loss of flood control, the maintenance of micro-climate and replenishing water tables.

The next paper by Harriss-White presents a stark narrative on the waste economy in a small town in Tamil Nadu where most of its waste is left to sink, creating extensive pollution and damaging the ecology of the region. The paper looks not only at the environmental implications of the waste economy, though the problem is huge given that India is the third-largest producer of waste in the world, but also at the organisation of waste disposal and its impact on its workers.

The focus of the paper is on the informal labour that manages the waste economy in the town, describing the conditions under which the labourers, both men and women, dispose waste. Given that this is informal work, wages are low and there is little-to-no security of service. In addition, there are occupational hazards and health problems. Associated with the work, more significantly, is stigma. It is unfortunate that the waste economy is not thought of as a problem of caste and pollution, but rather as something that can be solved through technology, planning and management—as in the policies of Swach Bharat and Amrut.

The interlinkages between ecology, human organisation and lives of people form the discussion of the Buckingham Canal of Chennai. Coelho discusses how, when it was built in the 19th century, its main function was to transport commodities through the eastern districts of Madras Presidency and thereby link the city's three major rivers. But beyond this function, the canal nurtured on its banks new settlements and communities. Thus, if the analysis shifts from the canal to its banks it is possible to perceive the canal as a generator of new settlements of primarily low-caste workers around which they built new livelihoods and diverse communities.

The last paper thus suggests that it is imperative that as citizens we rethink our priorities regarding ways to live and to reproduce ourselves. Soni argues that in the next 50 years, 60 per cent of our ecosystems would have been degraded and about 60 per cent of animals extinct. Cities have become invasive; they are destroying the air, polluting the rivers and depleting the water table. The need of the hour is to create natural cities, to create a 'quality of life with minimum consumption and habitat wear and tear'. Soni gives a blueprint for creating such a city in the case of Amravati, the new capital for Andhra Pradesh.

We hope that this volume will trigger a debate on the many issues raised here and will help to create a consciousness of the paradoxes and contradictions that organise India's urban conundrum.

◆

DEBATE ON DEFINING THE URBAN

RURBANISATION
An Alternate Development Paradigm

AMITABH
KUNDU

Projections by the UN system, as also global development-cum-banking agencies, suggest that India, along with China, will lead world economic recovery in the next couple of decades by registering a growth rate of about 7 per cent per annum in GDP, in real terms. A critical assumption built into their models is that India will experience rapid urban growth in the coming years. Many of the policy documents of the World Bank, as also the Asian Development Bank, claim that the epicentre of urbanisation would shift to Asia, and that an urban avalanche is likely to hit India. The process of urbanisation is implicitly or explicitly linked to the metropolitan cities (with a population above a million) that account for, on an average, about 70 per cent of the urban population in Asian countries. The urban world has, thus, been analysed through the perspective of a few metropolitan cities, posited in competition with each other.

The Population Division of the United Nations (UNPD) had issued an alert that global urban population would touch the 50 per cent level by 2006–7. With some hiccups, this was finally achieved, but only in 2009. The actual growth of urban population in the developing world, particularly India, turning out to be less than the figures projected could well be responsible for this delay. It can be attributed to the deceleration in metropolis-based urbanisation, linked partly to the Euro-zone crisis and the global economic slowdown.

THE METROPOLITAN BIAS IN URBAN STUDIES IN INDIA
The urbanisation process in India since Independence has favoured metropolitan and larger cities, with small and medium towns

tending to stagnate. Importantly, the percentage of urban population in million-plus cities is higher than in most other large countries of the world, and has gone up relatively faster in the five decades since Independence. The share of cities with a population above 5 million to total urban population is 24 per cent compared to the global average of only 17 per cent. An increasing concentration of urban population in Class I cities (those with a population above 100,000) too can be observed in the percentage share of these cities in the total urban population going up from 26 in 1901 to over 70 in 2011. This has often been attributed, and rightly so, to the faster growth of large cities. However, the other factor responsible for the increasing dominance of these cities is the graduation of lower-order towns into the Class I and metropolitan category, without a corresponding increase in the base of smaller towns. The main body of research, therefore, has understandably been focused on large cities, as is the case in the Global South.

Indian researchers have, thus, looked at urban processes mostly through the prism of large cities. Urban research has remained centred on these cities and their interrelationships, besides a few success stories of smaller towns, undertaken within the livelihood framework. Urban structure is envisioned through, or in comparison with, a set of global cities and, more recently, smart cities that can compete with the iconic megalopolises of New York, London, Paris and Shanghai. The key concern is to design infrastructure and public services supported by modern technology in select large cities so as to attract capital from within and outside the country for realising agglomeration economies and building cities as engines of growth. Several international agencies, explicitly and implicitly, proposed that the success of globalisation and livelihood strategy in India would depend on the speed with which modern production, trading and banking institutions in all urban centres can be linked with metro cities, and global values injected into the business behaviour of the former.

It is also important to note that there has been stability, and even deceleration, in urban growth during the past couple of decades, as against the accelerated growth scenario predicted by UNPD. This can hardly be explained in terms of a fall in the natural growth of population. Largely, it is due to the slowing down of growth in metropolitan cities because of the slump in the global capital market. Of the 25 largest cities, all except five report a decline in growth, much more than can be attributed to natural factors. More important is the realisation that the decline would have been much sharper had there been no alternate processes outside the metropolises compensating for the loss.

The critical process that has helped in sustaining overall urban growth is 'rurbanisation', which may be described as a process of settlements acquiring urban characteristics while retaining their rural socio-economic base. A number of micro-level studies suggest that the socio-political environment created in several small and medium towns with a strong, rural economic base have been able to attract investments in small-scale and agro-processing industries. These demonstrate that formal and informal institutions, along with their norms and practices, play an extremely useful and supportive role in the organisation of production, skill formation and industrial development. There is an urgent need to build up an alternate macro-economic framework for understanding the economic geography in the country by recognising the process of rurbanisation.

A NEW ECONOMIC GEOGRAPHY OF RURBANISATION

It would be important to rescue urban studies from the paradigm of metropolis-based urbanisation, a paradigm which envisions urban processes in the developing world responding only passively to compulsions of global capital. A large part of contemporary urban growth occurs outside of the hegemonic power structure of globalisation. Therefore, instead of confining urban research to global and national markets, state-level institutions, formal programmes, missions and legal systems, it is important to build a 'history of urbanisation from below' and explore the role of common people as actors and agencies in this process. A section among researchers has described this as *subaltern urbanisation*, conceptualising this as an attempt to build the voices emerging from smaller places and their inhabitants. It is a new narrative and constructed through an analysis of situations and processes that are considered of marginal importance within the framework of metro-centric urbanisation.

An attempt must be made to analyse the extent to which urban growth in the developing world reflects the hegemony of global capital, often rationalised in the name of economic efficiency and maximisation of growth. Or, alternately, one may enquire if local economic forces and institutional structures are able to do a functional stage-setting for global capital, partially outside the dependency framework. Do these diverse urban territories, constituted through complex webs of historicised arrangements, reflect some form of resilience or robustness of local economic systems? It is only by studying the context of urbanisation within such a framework that one can hope to understand the plurality of development in a developing country, participate meaningfully in public debates, and provide analytical inputs for policy making.

It must be noted that simple dualistic formulations and postulating categories, such as rural and urban, small and big cities, mainstream and subaltern urbanisation, etc., are inappropriate in order to understand the dynamics of urban development. The spatial pattern of development continuously blurs their distinctions, and one must focus on the relationships emerging across both the hierarchical as well as non-hierarchical arrangement of the settlements.

THE DIVERSE MANIFESTATIONS OF PROCESSES OF RURBANISATION

Given the fact that Indian urban reality stands up robustly as a refutation of the global models of explanation and prediction, an attempt is made to analyse three diverse processes of rurbanisation with empirical rigour. These operate (i) in and around large cities; (ii) in small and medium towns; and (iii) in rural settlements exhibiting urban characteristics, many of these being identified as Census towns. These three processes are not completely insulated from the functioning of global capital, but have their own dynamics and specificity emerging from their local economy. These, nonetheless, provide definite evidence of in situ urbanisation—expansion of cities into rural territories and transformation of villages into urban settlements.

THE EXCLUSIONARY TRENDS OF LARGE CITIES AND DEGENERATED PERIPHERALISATION

There has been a significant change in the pattern of urbanisation in the past couple of decades. Many among the metros and Class I cities have tended to be exclusionary in character by not absorbing rural migrants who do not have the capacity and the skills suitable for metropolitan labour markets. The large industries have, therefore, located themselves in neighbouring villages. This is also because land, labour and environment-related problems and administrative controls are less exacting. The entrepreneurs, engineers and executives associated with these industries often reside within the central city and travel to the periphery through rapid transport corridors. For poor and unskilled migrants, the high cost of access to land and basic amenities works as a strong disincentive. Generally, they move to neighbouring towns and villages in the hinterland, since housing and basic amenities are affordable, but commute to the city to work. The process of 'sanitisation' in these cities is expedited by the capture of prime urban space by the upper and middle class, leading to small-scale pollutant industries and other land-intensive activities being pushed to the periphery.

As a consequence, the growth rate of population in metropolitan cities has gone down with a corresponding increase in that of the peripheries, ushering in a process of rurbanisation. Unfortunately, a part of this growth is not counted as urban in official statistics. Many of these cities have, however, been able to maintain a high demographic growth despite a decline in fertility and immigration rates because of the expansion in their area. They report the emergence of satellite centres in their vicinity that eventually become a part of the agglomeration. Industrial units tend to get located or pushed out of the municipal limits because of environmental concerns reflected in laws and byelaws emanating from the City Master Plans. What is regrettable, however, is that peripheral rurbanisation, a large part of which is driven by the people's struggle for survival, has received scant attention in its literature.

THE RURBAN CHARACTER OF SMALL AND MEDIUM TOWNS
Class I cities (with a population over 100,000) in India exhibit a distinctly higher demographic growth compared to lower-order towns, except those belonging to Class VI. This large-city-centred urban growth may be observed during the entire second half of the last century. Even in the period from 2001 to 2011, Class I cities maintained their edge in their growth rates over the lower-order towns. The urban structure has, therefore, become more and more top-heavy over time, as earlier discussed.

In recent decades, the rate of deceleration in the population growth of small and medium towns has been higher than that of large cities. This can be attributed to their weak economic base and deficiency in infrastructure and basic amenities, leading to the declassification of many, particularly from 1991 to 2000. It is possible to explain the stagnation, decline and declassification of small and medium towns, dependent on agriculture and agro-processing activities, in terms of the low and fluctuating base of the agrarian economy. Many of these towns survive by building trading and business relations within the region. They facilitate ancillarisation, attract labour and encourage the commute from their hinterland, thereby blurring the boundaries between rural and urban areas. Their less-than-modest levels of infrastructure and basic services prompted a few researchers to describe them as manifestations of 'subaltern development'. The Registrar General of India, while collecting slum statistics from these towns as supplementary work for the 2001 Census, at the behest of the Ministry of Housing and Urban Poverty Alleviation, had held that in many cases entire townships could be declared slums.

However, the demographic and economic growth rates in a few of these small and medium towns are very impressive, making a mark on the national map. These towns have their linkages with neighbouring large cities and benefit from the spillover of industries and, in turn, cater to their requirements. Other towns owe their origin and growth to historical and institutional factors, away from the zones of influence of large cities. Their linkages with neighbouring villages do not operate within the traditional framework since they obtain a part of their supply of foodgrains, milk, vegetables, raw materials, etc., from the national market. In this sense, they are not totally excluded from the global or national market system. Notwithstanding growth dynamics in a few of these towns, the large majority of them with a population of less than 20,000 are overgrown villages, providing trading and basic services to their own population and those in neighbouring villages.

The manifestation of the rurban character, however, is strongest in Class VI towns with a population below 5,000. These towns constitute a special category, as many are part of an expanded city or agglomeration, or have come into existence through the establishment of a public or private sector unit or a public utility.

A few have emerged with a university or a residential suburb as their core. They stand apart since their demographic growth rates are higher as compared to the towns in higher size classes—even the metro cities. Their relatively stronger economic base may partly be attributed to exogenous investment. Many of these towns are neither district nor *taluka* headquarters. Taking advantage of the demand-support from adjacent industrial or commercial units and personnel employed there, the local rural population is able to build a modest production and service sector base. It struggles to find livelihoods for itself but the quality of life is poor, with serious inadequacies in terms of access to basic amenities. The non-hierarchical linkages of these towns with other urban centres, however, help in maintaining a stable livelihood pattern, even during the global economic crisis.

THE EMERGENCE OF NEW TOWNS AND IN SITU URBANISATION

Over the 19th century, the total number of urban settlements (Census and Statutory towns) in the country shows sluggish growth from 1,827 to 4,368. The emergence of very few new Census and Statutory towns on the urban scene has resulted in a top-heavy urban structure. In general, it reflects the lack of growth dynamics in the rural economy and settlement structures. The 2001 Census had reported the declassification of as many as 445 towns (the number was only 93 in 1991). Consequently, the total number of 'Census towns'—identified on the basis of population size, density and share of workers outside the primary sector—had shrunk from 1,693 to 1,363. Understandably, in situ urbanisation was marginal during the 1990s, which should be a matter of anxiety for the country. Given such trends, McKinsey Global Institute (MGI) predicted the emergence of only 1,000 towns between 2008 and 2030.

The recognition of this problem, and of the urgency to promote the emergence and growth of new urban centres through decentralised governance, led to the adoption of the 74th Constitutional Amendment Act in 1993. This created a policy environment which resulted in a significant increase in the number of Statutory towns in several states, mostly belonging to Class V and VI, in the 2001 Census. The Eleventh Five Year Plan (2007–12) also took note of the problem as it observed that 'the growth of rural settlements which are acquiring urban characteristics is very slow'.

Fortunately, the number of towns has increased by 2,774 in the very first decade of the 21st century. The increase in the number of 'Census towns' from 1,352 to 3,894 is unprecedented in the history of the Indian Census. It may be premature to conclude that the Census has gone overboard to identify over 2,500 new settlements that are essentially rural in character, as towns. Almost all of them satisfy the three criteria of the Census and, hence, should legitimately have been elevated to urban status in 2011. Most of them, however, met these criteria even in 2001. It is therefore evident that there has been a growth in population and density in several large villages during the past two, and even earlier, decades that can rarely be attributed to the developments in the global market. These, unfortunately, have mostly gone unnoticed by urban researchers.

An analysis of the locational pattern of new Census towns confirms that there is considerable randomness in their spatial distribution. There is no empirical evidence to suggest a strong process of sectoral diversification or growth of non-agricultural employment behind the emergence of these towns, as a large number of them are outside the hinterland of large urban centres. As a relatively small number of these towns falls within the metro region, or around the industrial corridors, the hypothesis that they have emerged under the shadow of metropolitan cities can be dismissed. In West Bengal, reporting the largest number of new towns, it is observed that the level of urbanisation at the district level negatively affects the emergence of these towns. This questions the trickle-down theory, or the theory that the industrial base of these towns is linked to the regional/national market.

A large section of the country's urban population, thus, lives in Census towns that are governed by rural administrative set ups, as they have not been given urban status by their respective state governments. These towns, therefore, have very different demographic and economic characteristics, low levels of infrastructure and basic amenities. All these could adversely affect their future growth, as also the overall process of regional and urban development, unless major interventions are initiated at the central and state levels.

IMPLICATIONS OF THIS ALTERNATE PARADIGM

The inter-settlement linkages and socio-economic contexts noted in the rural hinterland of metropolitan and other large cities are different from those of small towns away from metropolises. Also, growth dynamics, or their absence, in small and medium towns vary enormously, depending on cultural and economic histories of their own, in addition to their proximity and linkages with large cities. Most of these towns languish with low levels of sectoral diversification and poor infrastructural facilities, stuck in a vicious circle of the structural under-development and feudal relations of an agrarian society. There are a few towns, however, that exhibit the high growth of modern globalised activities by being strategically located near a large city or on a major national highway.

More important, some small towns, despite not having such locational advantages, have maintained a certain level of economic activity by cashing in on the middle-class demand for housing and multifarious services, including repair and maintenance work. They have exhibited a fairly high rate of demographic growth in recent years, despite receiving no support from public agencies. This dynamism can be attributed to strong local factors, delinked from the global or national economy. Furthermore, the new Census towns that have emerged around large cities, many constituting parts of existing built-up areas of the agglomerations, would have certain specificities not found in others. Their growth too cannot be linked to any metropolis and, consequently, does not reflect the relationship of dependency observed in the metropolitan hinterland. All these can be considered as important manifestations of rurbanisation.

These diverse patterns of urbanisation and rurbanisation under discussion question the advocacy of a uniform system of governance as a solution to urban problems. Despite the general trend of de-industrialisation and economic stagnation in most small towns, innovative arrangements, operationalised at the local level through social and financial institutions here, attract investments in small-scale manufacturing and real-estate development in a few urban centres. The alignments in these arrangements often follow caste and community ties that are linked with social networks operating at a larger territorial scale, complementing the local processes of economic growth.

Regrettably, the national government and development-cum-banking agencies at the global level have paid scant attention to cultural and institutional factors determining the process of rurbanisation. It is extremely important to understand these factors and their linked problems, and, more important, to address them at the micro level to promote sustainable development. The economic and demographic growth in these towns must be supported with specific interventions because, if left to market forces, it would take decades to be transformed and get linked with the national market. There is an urgent need to make them 'a part of India's future urbanisation'. Strengthening their infrastructural and institutional base, and establishing linkages with an agglomeration and through that to national and global markets, is one alternative. The analysis in the present study suggests that alternatives to the dominant development model of linking to global markets do exist. These need to be understood and promoted, necessitating the designing of a strategy to identify the diverse forces of livelihood generation and growth at ground level. Since the socio-economic implications of each of these three processes are varied, policy initiatives for mainstreaming these would be very different.

WHERE DO WE GO FROM HERE?

The process of urbanisation at the grass-roots level has possibly gone unnoticed because of the system of data generation by the Census organisation, which identifies towns by employing three demographic criteria to the data available from the last Census and conservative discretionary judgement. This has resulted in the systematic under-reporting of the level of urbanisation. A proper identification, however, may not increase the growth rate in urban population (since both initial- and terminal-year figures would have to be revised). Also, there has been an increase in the number of workers with no fixed all-time location and who commute on a daily basis, which helps them find a survival strategy in off-peak seasons. This, too, has slowed down the pace of urbanisation. These processes are very different from those of the dominant paradigm of urbanisation in the country.

The basic question one must ask, however, is whether the growth of industry and the emergence of 'self-made engineers' in many of these small towns can be attributed to local-level institutions and entrepreneurship of the people. Could the informal institutional arrangements and governance system supporting industrial growth in these towns be strengthened and deficiencies corrected so as to provide sustainable livelihoods to the local population and immigrants? Is it possible to scale up such success stories to the national level?

The answer, indeed, is yes. A strong case has been made on paper for larger assistance from the central government to small towns for addressing the deficiencies in their infrastructure and revenue-generating capacity through Missions similar to that of JNNURM and Smart Cities. There is an urgent need to build an understanding of the functioning of local-level institutions for designing effective strategies for policy intervention. Unfortunately, the S. P. Mukherjee Rurban Mission, designed to address these issues, has proved to be a non-starter. The state must step in to ensure that marginalised sections of the population, which do not belong to any caste or other social network and are therefore likely to get excluded from the traditional/informal institutional set up, are brought into the mainstream. Public intervention could go a long way in promoting such an inclusive system and strengthening sustainable urbanisation.

The thesis of rurbanisation is, thus, rooted in the proposition that the market-based urban system, dependent on a few metropolitan cities, is not the only paradigm of development for India, as also many other countries in the developing world. The ongoing process of urbanisation has created an extremely top-heavy urban structure, leading to a slowdown of the pace of urbanisation, as has been officially recognised. This is adversely impacting on the developmental process. An alternate strategy for more balanced urban economic development in the country can be devised through an understanding of developmental dynamics at the local level, and strengthening growth potentials of a large number of small and medium towns. For this, it would be important to identify the geographical and socio-economic factors, including the cultural contexts that characterise and determine their growth potential. It is only then that a strategy, utilising these potentials, can be designed. Addressing the constraints and strengthening appropriate institutions and practices at the local level can promote sustainable urbanisation in the country. The focus on *rurbanisation* would help in making the bottom section of the urban hierarchy visible and intelligible, and mainstream the problems of the vulnerable and marginalised.

◆

SUBALTERN URBANISATION REVISITED*

PARTHA
MUKHOPADHYAY

MARIE-HÉLÈNE
ZÉRAH

ERIC DENIS

INTRODUCTION

When we used the phrase 'subaltern urbanisation' (Denis, et al., 2012), we were quite up front about it being as much a literary device to focus attention on our area of inquiry as to acknowledge a link, possibly tenuous, with the wide literature on subaltern studies, particularly in Guha of the 'contribution made by the people *on their own* that is *independently of the elite*' (1982: 39). Four years later, as we publish results of the initial project (Denis and Zérah, 2016), it is a matter of some satisfaction to see the phrase travel a little—even to a documentary featuring four residents of Guwahati.[1]

To recall, subaltern urbanisation refers to the autonomous growth of settlement agglomerations—large clusters of people living in close proximity (which may or may not be classified as urban by the Census of India or the relevant state government)—that are generated by market and historical forces, and which are not dependent on large, traditionally important settlements or planned cities like Chandigarh and Bhubaneswar, or industrial townships like Mithapur or Bokaro. The attempt is to investigate the growth of settlements beyond that driven by the economics of large agglomerations as advanced by new economic geography, or directly orchestrated by the state or private corporate enterprise. The object is to focus on the autonomy of the settlement, not in the sense of autarchy, but in the ability to affect its growth process and interact autonomously with other settlements, whether local or global. In essence, therefore, subaltern urbanisation is about vibrant smaller settlements—spaces outside the metropolitan shadow—sustainably supporting a dispersed pattern of urbanisation. Concomitantly, subaltern urbanisation refers to an unseen, and often unspoken, process of myriad form, effected by local actors, far from the major metropolitan areas and outside urban schemes.

In doing so, the intent is not to put forward a claim in opposition to large cities. Rather, it is to present a fuller picture, especially in India, where the share of urban population (as defined by the Census in 2011) living in settlements of less than 100,000 people has grown slightly since 2001. In this, we are in agreement with Bell and Jayne, that what is

> lost as a consequence of the bias towards large cities is a full picture of urban form and function: the urban world is not made up of a handful of global metropolises, but characterised by heterogeneity. Studying small cities enables us to see the full extent of this (2009: 683).

Smaller settlements need to be studied not in contrast to large cities, but for themselves, as sites of urbanity, economic activities and social transformations, and for their place in the process of urbanisation, as rural–urban links and as a part of global economy.

In this brief reprise, we interrogate their role in India's development trajectory. We first focus on the diversity, agency and socio-economic transitions of these spaces. Next, we discuss the different scales and implementation processes of governance and policy, interrogating the relevance of the rural–urban dichotomy in theory and practice. Finally, we relate our findings in the context of a broader reappraisal of urban transition in India.

THE PROCESS OF TRANSFORMATION

Indian urbanisation, such as it is, is more about morphing places than moving people. From 2001 to 2011, of the 90.9 million freshly minted urban population, approximately 40 million were added through natural growth, 19.1 million by migration, and the remaining 31.8 million came from this phenomenon of morphing places. Small towns account for a growing share of even the officially urban. As of 2011, 41.1 per cent of the urban population lives in small towns of less than 100,000—up from 40.3 per cent in 2001. However, much of this growth took place in the small towns without administrative urban status—Census Towns—whose share of urban population nearly doubled from 7.4 to 14.6 per cent, whereas that of small towns with urban administrative status dropped from 32.9 to 26.5 per cent.[2] But, even this does not fully reflect the situation. In 2011, when 31.2 per cent were officially urban, another 23.5 per cent of the rural population, i.e., a total of 47.4 per cent of the population, lived in settlement agglomerations of more than 5,000 people.

This kind of morphing creates a level of dispersion that makes it harder to maintain a clear—'bright line'—distinction between rural and urban. Figure 1a shows the spread of villages over 1991–2011, where a majority of the male workforce has moved away from agriculture. As one can see, such villages cover large portions of the country. There were 34,998 such villages in 1991, comprising 8.4 per cent of the rural population. In 2011, this had risen to 23 per cent of the rural population in 116,430 villages. In many of these places, individuals start self-providing services. Figure 1b highlights areas where villages have better sanitation (higher proportion of households with septic tanks) than the average for small statutory towns (with a population of 50,000 or less) in the state. In many areas, this reflects the lack of services in formal urban areas, political choices to provide status but not services and, in other cases, it points to the lack of information inherent in classifying a settlement as a village or a town, and an inadequate and outmoded system of statutory governance classification.

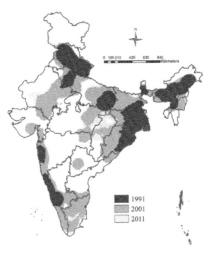

Figure 1a: *Spread of villages with a majority of non-farm workers*

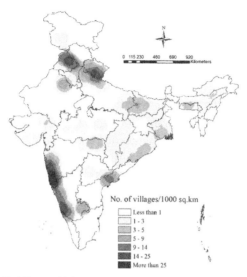

Figure 1b: *Villages with better sanitation than small statutory towns (2011)*

Source: The authors acknowledge the support of Shamindra Roy and Kanhu C. Pradhan
in preparing these maps. Any remaining errors are our responsibility.
Note: Figure 1a shows areas with at least one village per 1,000 sq km with majority
non-farm workers.

It is perhaps useful at this stage to separate, at the risk of over-simplified dichotomy, two broad types of settlements. One is a more nationally and globally connected settlement, often, but not always, somewhat larger and statutory, while the other is a locally connected settlement—census town, small statutory town, large village with many non-farm workers, etc. These two types of settlements contribute to the growth of the economy in different ways.

In many respects, several of the first type of settlements possess the qualities associated with large metropolises—like innovation, global connectivity, etc., albeit at much smaller scales. This can be observed in localities like Tiruchengode and Ranipettai in Tamil Nadu, which have been reinventing themselves over decades, adapting their entrepreneurial endeavours to local demand, as well as global market transformations. The first excels in the drilling truck industry, while the other predominates in leather and shoemaking. Today, companies from Tiruchengode are able to export their low-cost bore-well drilling trucks to Africa, where their adaptation to local needs is much appreciated, especially their ease of repair and maintenance. These manufacturers developed the ability to satisfy markets neglected by large truck makers of Europe and the United States, which produce over-sophisticated vehicles that are too expensive. Furthermore, these large firms are able to provide the individual customisations requested by the customers. In all Indian states, such small and medium towns based on a long tradition of craft—e.g., textile and furniture—and developing low-cost products, often starting from reverse engineering a prototype, are flourishing. These products are adapted to the frugal needs of a non-metropolitan population in transition to their urban environment.

In some places, these innovative environments extend beyond individual settlements, to specialised clusters of towns and villages with a long tradition of manufacture and trading. This is the case, for instance, in Udupi, coastal Karnataka, where an assemblage of towns' and villages' role in the fishing industry is known up to Japan for supplying fishnets, as well as for the quality of their fish products. These traditional activities have been able to cope with globalised trading. Since the beginning of the last century, local private actors engaged in development initiatives to further this strong and open regional economy. From the 1930s, investments were geared to build an integrated and affordable bus network, and from the 1960s, syndicated banks were set up (such as the well-known Canara Bank) to facilitate local investments. But, despite this, planners, consultants and private corporates conceive of this coast as a *tabula rasa*, well suited for SEZs, power plants, tourism and real estate investments, ignoring its current existing global economic presence and its importance for employment.

Compared to these first type of 'micro global settlements', the second type of settlements fulfil a much more banal but very necessary function. While they are often not sites of production—except for construction—they are service towns, markets, private health and education, and local transit hubs. They are spaces of change, where people drift in and out between non-farm and farm work. Some of the spread and depth of this phenomenon is made possible by the density of India as a country, and now by the rapidly improving rural transportation networks.[3] In these small census towns, the nature of economic transformation can be grouped into three categories: (i) the everyday economy; (ii) settlement-specific activities, which may reflect historical function; and (iii) new activities. Almost all of these are largely financed through non-formal sources. It is important to stress that these banal but necessary functions can often provide incomes much higher than traditional agricultural activities.

The everyday economy, which is geared towards servicing the demand of surrounding areas, benefits from higher levels of connectivity and better transport possibilities. Local markets, or bazaars, are at the centre of this everyday economy. However, in spite of its resilience in providing employment and trade in the surrounding villages, its scale of activity is usually insufficient to generate surplus capital. Some of these settlements also benefit from external investment in their area, such as the road to the Dhamra port project in Erein, Odisha, or the public hospital and college in Bishnugarh, Jharkhand.

The bazaar economy benefits from the rising incomes of rural areas, and their demand for diverse consumer goods which are supplied through an intricate, locally specific logistics chain. Few of these consumer goods would be produced locally but the logistics chain does generate local employment.

Activities that are specific to settlements can differ considerably, but tend to be small scale and often linked to traditional caste occupations, such as the yoghurt industry in Gopalpur, West Bengal, and small-scale foundries in Cherra, Jharkand. The ability of such specific activities to scale up and provide more income and employment improves with better connectivity, as transport networks increase the market for such products. The markets for these goods can be quite far-flung, especially for handloom and handicrafts, or bidi manufacturing, which has well-developed supply chains. These settlement-specific economic activities may also be linked to local natural resources, such as stone crushing in Domchach, Jharkhand (entrepreneurs adjusting to a loss of traditional mica mining), or cold storages for potato farmers in Garbeta, West Bengal (Sircar, 2015).

In addition to these channels, five new activities appear to be present at many of these small census towns. Two of these, which are major in scope in terms of employment and/or local impact are construction and para-transit services. Construction is driven by the continuous process of shifting to brick and mortar (*pucca*) housing that appears to be taking place in rural India, while the para-transit services for both freight and passengers lubricate the everyday economy mentioned earlier. In addition to these two, three other common activities are services around cell phones (sale and recharge of SIM cards, loading of multimedia, sale and repair of instruments, etc.), private education and private healthcare.

It is possible to identify three main drivers of growth in para-transit transport, viz.: (i) public investment in rural roads; (ii) increased demand for travel, e.g., for education and general consumption; and, critically (iii) manufacturers and/or banks providing financing to purchase these vehicles. There are also spin-off benefits, such as repair and maintenance services for these vehicles, and in some places like Gopalpur, there is also local manufacturing of vehicles like battery-powered electric rickshaws. People engaged in para-transit activity can often be migrants returning from large cities, where they acquired finance and the skills required for driving vehicles.

A factor that is often common across both types of settlements is the centrality of the land-based economy that is supporting the financing of the urban transition, especially in the more developed states, in a context of poor access to institutional banking and credit. Everywhere, the rapid and extensive conversion of land, often fertile, into popular real estate, educational institutions and factories, as well as the sprawl of idle lands backing the access to loan support the monetisation, and diversification of local economies. It blurs the frontiers of urban and rural environments, and questions the effectiveness of present regulations.

POLICY AND GOVERNANCE

It is important to recall that the definition of urbanisation in India is unique. Statutory towns are recognised by state municipal acts. They are all full-fledged urban local bodies, whose governance structure and delegation of responsibilities are defined by the 74th Constitutional Amendment on decentralisation for urban areas. Census towns are considered urban by the Registrar General of India and included in the measurement of urbanisation. However, they remain under rural governance with village panchayats. In other terms, census towns can avail of rural government schemes, such as the Mahatma Gandhi National Rural Employment Guarantee Scheme (MGNREGS) and Indira Awas Yojana (IAY), while small statutory towns can benefit from urban programmes.

Consequently, there is a complicated relationship between the governance of small towns and service provision. The limited work on basic services in small towns points towards low levels of both infrastructure services and administrative capacity. These small statutory towns are a neglected layer of development as exhibited in the bias of the Jawaharlal Nehru National Urban Renewal Mission (JNNURM) that focused on large agglomerations (Khan, 2016). Thus, though service delivery varies, depending on the effectiveness of local governance, there is, controlling for size, little measurable difference in service provision between census and statutory towns (Mukhopadhyay, 2016).

Regardless, in census towns, service provision remains a major axis of mobilisation related to the form of governance (rural vs. urban). Whether a census town should remain a village or become a small town is a matter of vigorous discussion at the local level. Our qualitative inquiries show that, on the ground, proposals for alternative administrative formations (which are developed at different scales such as redefinition of boundaries, demand for urban status or reversal to rural status) can be traced, in varying degree, to four axes of contestation, the first of which is service provision itself.[4]

The nature of non-farm activity and related land-use changes benefits from public schemes like the IAY, and costs of new taxes and local socio-political formations form the three other axes of contestation. In particular, social grouping and local conflicts of the area often influence the debate on governance in a 'politics of classification'. In some areas, the aspirations for urban status appear to be pushed by local elites and resisted by poorer groups, reflecting an economic divide between the bazaar (including traders and members of the local elite) and the basti (residential area). In others, it is the opposite, since the landed elite see rural status as offering more freedom in monetising land and the increase in taxes, and the enforcement of building bye-laws is seen as a constraint on local development. In states where access to welfare schemes is poor, such schemes, in and of themselves, are not a strong argument to remain rural. Social elements, such as caste, can feature prominently within political coalitions resisting or advocating the transition from rural to urban status. In more developed states, a more central role is played, inter alia, by the monetisation of land. This could lead to the appearance of a capital surplus, which could be invested in productive activities at the same, or different, place and time.

This grounded view of the politics of classification underlines the limits of claims that 'all is urban', as in the recently coined notion of 'planetary urbanisation' (Brenner and Schmid, 2014). From an operational point of view, such a posture wishes away a reality where binaries (here urban vs. rural) are inscribed in legislations and public policies. Although we question the relevance of these binaries in the face of contemporary urban transition, they are performative: they guide investments of private actors, development initiatives of national and regional governments, as well as shape ordinary practices of inhabitants.

URBAN TRANSITION IN INDIA

At the start of this project we had stated that India seemed intent, as Nijman (2012: 18) put it, on 'writing its own script', a story of urbanisation based on 'contribution[s] made by the people *on their own*' (Guha, 1982: 39). We had said that understanding how agents make a world no state or theory could imagine was critical for comprehending the ongoing Indian transformation. In this endeavour, we tried to shed light on unseen and neglected non-metropolitan transformations.

A first learning that bears reiteration is the complexity of the urban transformation process and the violence that is done by analytical over-simplification into dichotomous categories. The spatial pattern of development and the relationships across settlements come in various hues, rather than distinct colours, and one must focus as much on the similarities as on the differences. Posited against this, a binary constitutional framework of governance is proving inadequate to the task at hand.

Initially, we were guilty of these attempts at sparse categorisation, e.g., trying to characterise subaltern urbanisation on two axes, viz., spatial proximity and administrative recognition. On the spatial proximity axis, we considered two types: peripheral, where the settlement is located in the periphery to the metropolis, and non-peripheral, i.e., all other settlements. We have since come to realise that a more nuanced measure of transport connectivity is perhaps more important as a metric. Similarly, on the administrative recognition axis, we posited four types of settlements: (i) invisible, or not recognised as urban by either the census or the state; (ii) denied, or classified as a census town; (iii) recognised, as a statutory town; and, finally (iv) contested, where the settlement is contesting its administrative status (Denis, et al., 2012). Here, we learnt that while classification often has little measureable effect, there are myriad local reasons to prefer one classification over another, that vary by context, and often, there is active politics around this issue.

Put simply, we now increasingly question the relevance of focusing on a poorly articulated *urban* transition, rather than studying the myriad changes in settlements across the country.

Second, it questions the pre-eminence of metropolitan areas in fashioning the transition from agriculture (and the transition of agriculture) and the broader development process. The effects that smaller settlements have on their neighbourhood are diverse and durable, making for a broader, if more deliberate, process of change. The autonomous global connections of settlements like Tiruchengode or the Udupi cluster, as well as many other settlements and clusters of villages and towns, also brings into relief the manner in which global influences are rapidly becoming scale-free, chipping away at the indispensability of 'global cities'. The same forces that activate business networks through the diaspora can also, however, make these urban spaces (as in the guilds of early global cities) closed to people outside particular social and caste groups, a feature that militates against the—possibly oversold—conception of cities as socially open spaces compared to rural India.

These findings provide textured detail about the connections that underpin the findings of Himanshu, et al. (2011: 38), who found a statistical relationship between rural non-farm diversification and rural poverty reduction with growth in consumption in neighbouring urban centres. They found a stronger association when the urban centre was a small one as compared to a large city. Given that the overwhelming majority of the urban poor live in small and medium towns (Lanjouw and Murgai, 2010), the implications for a broad-based development transition are obvious.

Third, land use change or spatial transformation in a census town is not confined within the administrative boundaries of the village. In all the settlements, expansion occurs outside the census town (village) boundaries, a process also observed in many of the statutory towns studied, and as indeed is the familiar experience with larger settlements. In the statutory towns, this spatial spillover may be partly driven by the lack of building regulations and lower taxes outside the boundary of the town, but in the census towns this may be simply the inability to contain growth within a small settlement area or because the locus of activity is at the edge of the settlement. In such a situation, the recent initiative of the Union Ministry for Urban Development to get states to convert census towns into statutory urban local bodies[5] is probably not a good idea.

Instead, this points to the need to plan at a more aggregated level, like the panchayat or sub-district, and not at the level of the settlement. The arrangements under the Shyama Prasad Mukherji Rurban Mission[6] are a first step in this direction. There is a dissonance between the existing administrative separation of rural and urban, which affects all public interventions, and the spatial and economic reality of smaller settlements. There are many ways to imagine a different approach requiring more or less intervention. For example, a start could be made by effectuating district planning committees. The existing administrative framework accounts for them and they have been implemented more or less successfully in Kerala. Eventually, one could consider the radical solution of ending the rural–urban binary present in the 73rd and 74th Constitutional Amendments. These are just some of the discussions provoked by a detailed study of subaltern urbanisation.

CONCLUSION

But, is subaltern urbanisation about urbanisation at all? It is a question of some interest—one that goes back to Wirth (1938): Are these census towns or even these small statutory settlements urban in any sense, or are they merely overgrown villages? One way of answering this question would be to say that they are not visibly different from other, if slightly larger, small statutory towns that are designated as urban by the state government. Their claims of recognition as urban stand, as it were, on a comparable footing.

One can then, of course, question the urbanity of these small statutory towns, too. This is a debate worth having, one that comes into contention once we move away from metrocentricity (Bunnell and Maringanti, 2010), but it is not one with which we choose to engage.

Neither is our proposition of a continuum of the urban beyond the metropolitan novel. A well-known precursor is the concept of *desakota* (McGee, 1991). Indeed, the recent trope of 'planetary urbanisation', which is being increasingly used, can also be seen as a reflection on the morphing of places, the blurring of rural–urban boundaries, and on the encompassing process of urbanisation, both from a morphological point of view (the physical spread of the urban) and from an economic point of view (the role of the urban footprint in the shaping of places). However, our less aerial and more grounded approach leads us to articulate two main reservations.

The first, already mentioned, is that such an approach wishes away a reality where legislations and public policies are inscribed with such binaries (here urban vs. rural), which, even if irrelevant, are performative, affecting the actions of governments, corporates and individuals.

The second relates to the very nature of the subaltern urbanisation process that interrogates deeply the nature of the economic transformation. While Brenner and Schmidt (2014) argue that the emerging urban forms are to be understood in their dependence and exploitative relationships to the larger cities, we consider that subaltern urbanisation is imbued with agency, it is not necessarily linked to a metropolitan hierarchy, and that both local and external factors are at play.

At this time, though a primate top-heavy urban structure prevails in many states of India, the national urban system remains more dispersed and balanced (Swerts and Pumain, 2013). Such an urban system may actually be more future ready, in a world that is moving away from large-scale Fordist manufacturing to more mass customisation of products. In such a future, the scale of viability for towns could rapidly diminish. While it is as yet unclear at what city scale the benefits from interaction with other individuals and increasing diversity of consumption start to peter out, it is likely to be less than that needed for purposes of production. Better understanding of local development dynamics can provide insights into the future potential of smaller settlements and a more complete understanding of the system of human settlements. This, in essence, was one of our goals of advancing the notion of subaltern urbanisation.

* The authors would like to thank Ayan Meer for his assistance.

◆

NOTES

1. *Little City, Blues* directed by Pranom Datta Mazumdar, produced by Public Service Broadcasting Trust, available at: https://www.youtube.com/watch?v=5d6iulgPfwohttps://www.youtube.com/watch?v=5d6iulgPfwo

2. Census towns are settlements designated as urban by the Registrar General of India, but which do not have statutory urban status. They are villages with a population of more than 5,000, density of more than 400 per sq km, and where more than 75 per cent of the male main workforce is engaged in non-farm occupations.

3. Almost half a million kilometres of rural roads have been added under schemes such as the Pradhan Mantri Gram Sadak Yojana and its state counterparts in the last 15 years.

4. Much of the subsequent discussion in this section draws from Mukhopadhyay, *et al.* (2015).

5. For details see http://pib.nic.in/newsite/ParintRelease.aspx?relid=145405.

6. For details see http://pib.nic.in/newsite/printrelease.aspx?relid=126934.

REFERENCES

Bell, David and M. Jayne. 2009. 'Small Cities? Towards a Research Agenda', *International Journal of Urban and Regional Research*, 33 (3): pp. 683–99.

Brenner, Neil, and Christian Schmid. 2014. 'The "Urban Age" in Question', *International Journal of Urban and Regional Research*, 38 (3): pp. 731–55.

Bunnell, Tim and A. Maringanti. 2010. 'Practising Urban and Regional Research beyond Metrocentricity', *International Journal of Urban and Regional Research*, 34 (2): pp. 415–20.

Denis, Eric, P. Mukhopadhyay and M-H. Zérah. 2012. 'Subaltern Urbanisation in India', *Economic & Political Weekly*, 57 (30): pp. 52–62.

Denis, Eric and M-H. Zérah (eds.). 2016. *Subaltern Urbanisation in India: An Introduction to the Dynamics of Ordinary Towns*. Berlin: Springer.

Guha, Ranajit. 1982. 'On Some Aspects of the Historiography of Colonial India', *Subaltern Studies I: Writings on South Asian History and Society*. Delhi: Oxford University Press.

Himanshu, P. Lanjouw, A. Mukhopadhyay and R. Murgai. 2011. 'Non-Farm Diversification and Rural Poverty Decline: A Perspective from Indian Sample Survey and Village Study Data.' Asian Research Centre Working Paper 44. London: London School of Economics.

Khan, Sama. 2016.'The Other Jawaharlal Nehru National Urban Renewal Mission: What Does it Mean for Small Town India?' in E. Denis and M-H. Zérah (eds.), *Subaltern Urbanisation in India: An Introduction to the Dynamics of Ordinary Towns.* Berlin: Springer, pp. 333–66.

Lanjouw, Peter and R. Murgai. 2010. 'Size Matters: Urban Growth and Poverty in India, 1983–2005.' Development Economics Research Group Working Paper. Washington, DC: World Bank.

McGee, Terence Gary. 1991. 'The Emergence of "Desakota" Regions in Asia: Expanding a Hypothesis', in N. Ginsberg (ed.). *The Extended Metropolis: Settlement Transition in Asia.* Honolulu: University of Hawaii Press, pp. 3–26.

Mukhopadhyay, Partha. 2016. 'Does Administrative Status Matter for Small Towns in India?', in E. Denis and M-H. Zérah (eds.), *Subaltern Urbanisation in India: An Introduction to the Dynamics of Ordinary Towns.* Berlin: Springer, pp. 441–67.

Mukhopadhyay, Partha, M-H Zérah and A. Maria. 2015. *India—Understanding India's Urban Frontier: What is Behind the Emergence of Census Towns in India?* Washington, DC: World Bank Group.

Nijman, J. 2012. 'India's Urban Challenge', *Eurasian Geography and Economics,* 53 (1): pp. 720.

Sircar, Srilata. 2015. 'You Can Call it a Moffusil Town, but Nothing Less: New Narratives of Urbanisation and Urbanism from Census Towns in West Bengal', presentation at CSH–CPR urban workshop, Delhi, 25 February.

Swerts, Elfie and D. Pumain. 2013. 'Approche statistique de la cohésion territoriale: le système de villes en Inde (A Statistical Approach to Territorial Cohesion: The Indian City System)', *L'Espace géographique,* 1/2013 (Tome 42), pp. 77–92.

Wirth, Louis. 1938. 'Urbanism as a Way of Life', *American Journal of Sociology,* 44 (1): pp. 1–24.

❖❖

II
CONDITIONS GENERATING WORK, LIVING AND (IN)SECURITY

ONLY 'GOOD PEOPLE', PLEASE

Residential Segregation in Urbanising India*

TRINA
VITHAYATHIL

GAYATRI
SINGH

KANHU C.
PRADHAN

The first time, I went with an upper-caste colleague. The landlord said about five times that he wanted 'good people'. I took that to mean I qualified, as I don't drink or party; we are quiet people and I am an academic researcher. But the questions my wife faced from the landlady, when we said we were Buddhist, persisted, and one day my wife said we were from a Scheduled Caste. We were asked to leave. My mother insisted we go and ask the landlady again, who told us clearly that her God doesn't allow her to rent house to a 'low-caste' family. She gave us a month to find another place.[1]

This narrative, shared by a research scholar in India's capital, is not an isolated incident. It is the reality faced by more than 13 per cent of urban Indians, or 47.5 million individuals, whose life opportunities are structured by their ex-untouchable identity.[2] Over the last several months, triggered by the brutal flogging of Dalits by cow vigilantes, the media has been ringing with news stories, debates and discussions about the violent atrocities against Dalits in rural areas of Gujarat, Uttar Pradesh, Bihar, Andhra Pradesh and other parts of India. Most of these accounts speak of severe, persistent, and deep-seated discrimination and violence against Dalits by upper castes in India's villages. But the nature and impact of the discriminatory treatment of Dalits in India's cities has largely gone unacknowledged over the decades. At a time when the absolute increase in population in urban areas is greater than in rural areas for the first time in the post-colonial era, it is imperative that we no longer turn a blind eye to persistent caste-based prejudice and discrimination in rapidly urbanising India.

Discrimination against urban Dalits is insidious, often violent, and widely acceptable, although sometimes more coded in its expression than the discrimination and violence faced by Dalits in rural India. Caste-based discrimination is often beneath the surface, as landlords and rental agents may use seemingly caste-neutral language to describe their preferred renter: 'good people', 'vegetarians' or 'people like us'. In actuality, neither the language nor the underlying belief system is caste neutral. Migrating from Deora district in eastern Uttar Pradesh, Kanaklata, a young post-graduate scholar in Delhi University, was brutally assaulted by her upper-caste landlords when they discovered that she and her siblings had been hiding their Scheduled Caste (SC) surname:

> These people (the landlord and his wife), whom we once shared food with, said things like 'first, you are Biharis and then you are Chamars, you have made our house impure'. For the past three days, we haven't had water to either cook or drink. When we were being beaten up, not one person in the neighbourhood came to our rescue.[3]

In this account, Kanaklata's urban mobility is not transformed into social mobility, but into experiences of discrimination and violence, like so many other Dalit university students searching for rental housing in urban markets. Accumulating evidence from previous social research highlights the pervasive role of caste-related barriers in urban India that constrain opportunities and outcomes for Dalits and Muslims in accessing jobs, housing and education.[4] As India urbanises, the caste and religious dimensions of exclusion persist and interact with other forms of discrimination in terms of class, gender and region to produce new forms of urban inequality.

Before moving forward, it is important to emphasise that Muslims also face severe experiences of discrimination while searching for housing in Indian cities. Recent research in five metropolitan cities in the NCR indicates clear evidence of homeowner prejudices in renting homes to both Muslims and Dalits, with Muslims facing more severe censorship (Thorat, et al., 2015). The barriers due to these prejudices do not simply result in mere inconveniences but have tangible economic and psychological consequences for those at the receiving end, including higher payment for substandard housing, longer commute times and increased transportation costs to work, exorbitant annual rental hikes, forced exits and, sometimes, violence. In our own research using Indian census data, we have been unable to quantify the level of residential segregation that Muslims experience in urban India. The Office of the Registrar General of India has refused to make data on religion available at the urban ward level, which is needed to analyse spatial inequality by religion in cities.

This paper discusses key findings with regard to the residential clustering of Scheduled Castes (SCs) and Scheduled Tribes (STs) populations in Indian cities. Our research indicates that residential segregation by caste/tribe is prevalent throughout urban India and is persisting over time. In addition, there are important differences by city size. In smaller cities, inequalities by caste are more severe than in larger ones (Desai and Dubey, 2011), and on average the degree of residential segregation by caste is higher. Finally, the degree of spatial inequality by caste in urban India also varies across region (Singh, et al., forthcoming).

MEASURING RESIDENTIAL SEGREGATION BY CASTE

We borrow methods from scholars of race in the United States to explore the degree of residential segregation by caste in India's cities. We use the index of dissimilarity, which is a measure of evenness that requires categorising the total population of a geographical area into two groups. Dissimilarity has an easy-to-comprehend verbal interpretation: 'the fraction of one group that would have to relocate to produce an 'even' (unsegregated) distribution' (White and Kim, 2005: 405). Values for the dissimilarity index range between zero and one, with higher values (i.e., those closer to one) indicating a greater degree of residential segregation by caste. To illustrate how the dissimilarity index is interpreted, we look at the case of a hypothetical city with a 15 per cent SC population (and 85 per cent population that is 'non-SC') and a calculated dissimilarity value for the residential segregation of SCs of 0.40. As such, 40 per cent of SCs (or non-SCs) would have to move wards within this city to create an even distribution of SCs (or non-SCs) across the city. In an 'even' or 'unsegregated' distribution, the population of each ward in the city would consist of a 15 per cent SC population and 85 per cent non-SC population—similar to the citywide proportions for each group.

In our analysis, we have used caste data from the 2001 and 2011 Indian decennial Census. Census data on SCs and STs are publicly available at the ward level. The last six postcolonial censuses have limited the census enumeration of caste/tribe to SCs, STs and 'other'. We combine the SC and ST populations in our analysis and compare this group's residential distribution with the non-SC/ST population. Given that, historically, the location of residences in villages has been highly influenced by the practice of untouchability, and that STs have lived in relative social isolation, comparing SCs/STs with 'others' can be seen to capture a distinction that is relevant to patterns of residence in India. In 2011, SCs accounted for 16.6 per cent of the population in India, while STs made up 8.6 per cent of the population.

Our analysis includes statutory towns that fall under the 74th Constitutional Amendment of India and are available in Census data of 2001 and 2011. We exclude cantonment boards and other specially notified industrial areas. We highlight results from two papers (Vithayathil and Singh, 2012; Singh, et al., forthcoming): the first that calculates residential segregation in India's seven largest metropolitan cities in 2001, and a second paper (under review) that examines residential segregation by caste over time in India's large cities (population of 100,000–1 million) and small cities (population of 25,000–50,000).

TRENDS IN RESIDENTIAL SEGREGATION BY CASTE

Residential segregation by caste/tribe in urban India is high, with negligent improvement from 2001 to 2011; the dissimilarity value for all cities was 0.47 in 2001 and 0.45 in 2011. These aggregate numbers underestimate important interstate variation; e.g., a socio-economically advanced state in India with a history of anti-caste politics like Tamil Nadu houses some of the most spatially unequal cities by caste/tribe (like Madurai in Tamil Nadu). We provide a more nuanced picture of patterns of residential segregation by caste in urban India by highlighting four trends.

First, looking at India's seven largest cities, the level of segregation by caste/tribe is greater than segregation by class in 2001 and 2011 (Sidhwani, 2015). In comparison, as a baseline measure, residential segregation by gender is negligible in these cities.

Against a backdrop of liberalisation and the rapid growth of Indian cities, we might expect class to explain patterns of residential segregation above and beyond caste. However, these findings illustrate that even in India's largest and most cosmopolitan metros, caste continues to structure where people live in the 21st century.

Second, we find the degree of residential segregation by caste varies across city size. On average, the degree of residential segregation is smaller in larger cities. This trend holds true at the all-India level and across most major states in the country. For example, the average dissimilarity index for small cities (with a population of 25,000– 50,000) in 2011 is 0.45; while at the same time the dissimilarity index for large cities (with a population of 100,000–1 million) is 0.37. As the growth of small and medium cities starts to play an increasing role in India's urbanisation story, the discrimination and structural inequalities that lead to higher levels of residential segregation by caste in smaller cities is particularly problematic.

We also find important regional variations in the level of residential segregation by caste, which a forthcoming paper details. Four states that account for nearly half of India's Dalit population, viz., Uttar Pradesh, West Bengal, Bihar and Tamil Nadu, highlight the regional variations in the level of residential segregation by caste/ tribe in urban India. In 2011, Tamil Nadu and Uttar Pradesh have the highest levels of residential segregation by caste for small cities (0.55 for Tamil Nadu and 0.53 for Uttar Pradesh) and large cities (0.45 for Tamil Nadu and 0.39 for Uttar Pradesh). In contrast, West Bengal has one of the lowest levels of residential segregation by caste (0.31 in small cities and 0.32 in large cities). Bihar falls in the middle with a dissimilarity value of 0.41 for small cities and 0.36 for large cities in 2011. Socio-economic development indicators do not provide straightforward explanations for the observed trends. We found no meaningful correlation between levels of residential segregation by caste/tribe and levels of human development (Human Development Index) or economic development (Gross Domestic Product per capita) at the state level. Rather, a more complex story is underway, which signals that durable inequalities deeply embedded in historical forms of discrimination and entrenched in social practices are not easy to displace through advances in education, health and income.

Finally, perhaps most troubling, many Indian cities are not experiencing improvements in the level of residential segregation by caste/tribe over time. Looking at a sample of small and large cities for which the number of wards remains constant in 2001 and 2011, nearly 60 per cent of cities are remaining stagnant (44 per cent) or getting worse (15 per cent) with regard to their levels of residential segregation by caste/tribe over time.[5] Forty per cent of cities experience an improvement in their levels of residential segregation by caste/tribe. While we limited our analysis to cities with a consistent number of wards across successive decennial census rounds, the population increase in these cities over time means that the median ward size is larger in 2011. The index of dissimilarity is sensitive to the size of underlying area units, i.e., the size of urban wards in our analysis, such that as the median ward size increases, the dissimilarity index is likely to decrease even with no change in the patterns of residential segregation by caste. As such, our longitudinal findings are likely to underestimate the degree to which residential segregation by caste/tribe is remaining stagnant or getting worse in our sample of cities.

POLICY IMPLICATIONS OF FINDINGS

The research presented here indicates that residential segregation by caste/tribe is a persistent problem in urban India. Looking ahead, we have four preliminary recommendations to begin to address the mechanisms that lead to segregation by caste in Indian cities.

PASS LEGISLATION TO MAKE CASTE-BASED DISCRIMINATION IN RENTING OR PURCHASING HOMES ILLEGAL

The central government is set to introduce an anti-discriminatory clause under the Real Estate (Regulation and Development) Act, 2016 (RERA) to curb the practice of builders refusing to sell their apartments based on a buyer's caste, ethnicity, gender, religion, or dietary preferences, among other things. This legislation needs to be passed to end discriminatory practices in the selling of new homes. While this is an important step in the right direction, it does not address overt and coded discriminatory practices in rental markets, which have been conclusively established by previous social science scholarship and highlighted through anecdotes in this paper. Nor does RERA cover the sale of privately owned homes.

In order to tackle the prevalent forms of caste-based discrimination in the housing sector, legislation must also be passed to specify that these practices are also illegal during the sale or rental of privately owned homes, whether by homeowners, real estate agents or lending institutions. Developing a legal framework that makes caste-based discrimination—both overt and coded—illegal in renting or purchasing homes is a first step towards changing a culture where housing discrimination is pervasive.

ANTI-CASTE AND ANTI-UNTOUCHABILITY CAMPAIGN TO SHIFT PEOPLE'S WAY OF THINKING

A public awareness campaign to publicise and challenge the common discrimination and violence Dalits experience in finding housing in urban areas is important. Through TV, newspaper and billboard advertisements, the experiences of discrimination faced by Dalits in urban areas could be illustrated and shown to be morally and legally wrong. Using prominent Dalits such as public intellectuals, authors, social and political leaders, and entertainers in the public campaign could help to raise the visibility of this issue. In addition, these messages could also educate urban Indians on new legislation, such as the Real Estate Regulation and Development Acts, 2016, which has paved the way for setting up a regulatory authority and tribunal to regulate all transactions between buyers and sellers, with specified punitive measures in case of violations of existing anti-discrimination laws. Raising awareness of coded or subtle discrimination as well as overt forms of discrimination, and their implications for those at the receiving end and society-at-large, could be an especially powerful tool to confront the deep-seated prejudices that influence thoughts and actions in everyday urban life.

ENFORCEMENT OF ANTI-DISCRIMINATION LAWS IN PUBLIC AND PRIVATE HOUSING

Legal change must be accompanied by efforts to change the status quo, both by shifting how people think and feel (second recommendation) and having consequences for those who continue to discriminate based on caste. Without an enforcement mechanism, anti-discrimination laws have limited consequence in helping to change widespread practices. To create an effective mechanism, sufficient separate resources must be allocated toward the enforcement of legislation to end discrimination in rental markets and home sales. These enforcement mechanisms could include undertaking housing audits or undercover operations, and setting up of fast-tracked judicial processes to ensure a quick resolution of discrimination cases in order to encourage reporting of discriminatory acts, among other things.

HEAVILY SUBSIDISED LOANS FOR HOME OWNERSHIP BY DALITS

Given the historic and continuing discrimination that Dalits face, they on average have much lower rates of home ownership. Programmes to make low-income loans available to Dalits could increase home ownership, reduce fear and violence, and create a mechanism for securing intergenerational wealth. A linked intervention would be to increase the financial inclusion and ease of banking for low-income urban residents, especially migrants to the cities who are often unable to benefit from subsidised loans and other grants, given their lack of ability to produce sufficient forms of identification and proof of residential address for membership to formal banks. The introduction of the Aadhar Card may aid this process, but more needs to be done to enhance the financial inclusion of Dalits and low-income urban migrants.

As mentioned earlier, existing research also finds that Muslims face considerable discrimination in urban housing markets. Due to the limitations of publicly available census data, our analysis and policy recommendations focus on SCs and STs; however, several of our recommendations are also likely to be applicable to address housing discrimination experienced by Muslims in urban India. In order to fully understand the forms and trends of discrimination in urban spaces, the Indian government must release ward-level religion data across multiple census rounds.

CONCLUSION

While upper-caste, educated urban residents believe that caste is a problem of rural India or of earlier generations of urban residents, we find clear evidence for the persistence of residential segregation by caste in 21st-century urban India. Although there are notable differences over time and by region—some of which are highlighted here—the most surprising and worrisome of our findings is that in many cities throughout the country, the level of residential segregation by caste is not improving over time.

Rather, caste-based prejudice constrains equitable access to housing markets as caste identities shape patterns of urban residence and reproduce social inequality in Indian cities. While there is an increasing body of evidence to conclusively establish the presence of caste discrimination in urban India, more work is needed to understand the specific mechanisms through which exclusion and discrimination by caste occur and persist in order to design interventions. Money alone is not enough to socially integrate, as experiences of inequality concentrate along caste lines and often lead to a residential clustering of families by caste or religion within a specific socio-economic class.

At this juncture in India's post-colonial history, when the absolute increase in population is greater in urban areas than in rural India, our findings are of considerable concern. Deep-rooted, everyday behavioural patterns are unlikely to change without considerable and concerted efforts by local communities and the Indian government to design interventions that address persistent discrimination in multiple spheres, including access to housing and employment. Indian civil society and the intelligentsia must be an integral part of the efforts to increase awareness of caste prejudices in urban India, and be open to examining our own unconscious biases in everyday talk and action. We hope that our preliminary recommendations reinforce the dedicated work of anti-caste, anti-untouchability and anti-housing discrimination activists throughout India, and seek to foster a broader conversation about building equitable and just urban communities.

◆

*This research received support from the Population Studies and Training Center (PSTC) at Brown University. The PSTC receives core support from Eunice Kennedy Shriver National Institute of Child Health and Human Development (R24HD041020, T32HD007338). The Office of Academic Affairs at Providence College also provided research and travel support for this project. Funding from National Science Foundation Graduate Research Fellowship Program (DGE-0228243) provided support during the early stages of data analysis for this project. The findings, interpretations and conclusions expressed here are only those of the authors, and do not represent the views of their organisations or any other organisations that have provided institutional, organisational or financial support for the preparation of this paper.

NOTES

1. This narrative by Dr. Nitin was published in *The Indian Express*. See Chishti (2016).

2. The 2011 census finds that SCs make up 12.6 per cent of the urban population of India. The administrative classification of SCs includes those Dalits who identify as Hindu, Jain or Buddhist. Dalit Muslims and Christians, who are likely to face similar experiences of discrimination and violence while finding a place to live, are not in the official count.

3. This quote by Kanaklata was published in *The Telegraph*. See Sengupta (2008).

4. For some examples of recent research on discrimination of Dalits in urban India, see Thorat, et al. (2015) on housing markets; Thorat and Attewell (2007); and Madheswaran and Attewell (2007) on labour markets.

5. In our analysis, we define 'no difference' in the level of residential segregation by caste/tribe over time when the difference in dissimilarity values for a city between 2001 and 2011 is less than or equal to +/– .03.

REFERENCES

Chishti, Seema. 2016. 'In Nation's Capital, Housing Bias Research Turns Real for Dalit Academic', *The Indian Express*, 23 January.

Desai, Sonalde and Amaresh Dubey. 2011. 'Caste in 21st Century India: Competing Narratives', *Economic and Political Weekly*, 46 (11), pp. 40–49.

Madheswaran S. and Paul Attewell. 2007. 'Caste Discrimination in the Indian Urban Labour Market: Evidence from the National Sample Survey', *Economic and Political Weekly*, 42 (41), pp. 46–53.

Sengupta, Ananya. 2008. 'A Dalit Student in Delhi? Hide your Surname', *The Telegraph,* 5 May.

Sidhwani, Pranav. 2015. 'Spatial Inequality in Big Indian Cities', *Economic and Political Weekly,* 50 (22), pp. 55–62.

Singh, Gayatri, Trina Vithayathil and Kanhu C. Pradhan. Forthcoming. 'Recast(e)ing Inequality: Residential Segregation by Caste across City Size and Over Time in Urban India.'

Thorat, Sukhadeo and Paul Attewell. 2007. 'The Legacy of Social Exclusion', *Economic and Political Weekly,* 42 (41), pp. 41–45.

Thorat, Sukhadeo, Anuradha Banerjee, Vinod K. Mishra and Firdaus Rizvi. 2015. 'Urban Rental Housing Market: Caste and Religion Matters in Access', *Economic and Political Weekly*, 50 (26–27), pp. 47–53.

Vithayathil, Trina and Gayatri Singh. 2012. 'Spaces of Discrimination', *Economic and Political Weekly*, 47 (37), pp. 60–66.

White, M. J. and A. Kim. 2005. 'Residential Segregation', *Encyclopaedia of Social Measurement*, 3, pp. 403–9.

INCLUSIVE URBANISATION
Informal Employment and Gender

JEEMOL UNNI

G lobalisation has brought about increased competition, new technology, and the reorganisation of production in the form of global production chains. This restructuring has led to the proliferation of irregular forms of employment and outsourcing in the informal economy. As a result, 'core' formal jobs (with security, opportunities to advance and social security benefits) have decreased in size and proportion, and work in the informal economy (comprising non-standard forms of work) has grown rapidly in both developed and developing countries. The gendered effects have not been uniform. Rapid urbanisation is posing a further challenge to inclusive growth. The article begins with a brief introduction to the UN Habitat III, Draft 'New Urban Agenda', which gives urgency to urbanisation as an engine of economic growth, investment, and prosperity and job creation in the coming years. It is followed by an account of urban informal employment in India and the gender concerns arising from it. In conclusion, the possible ways to inclusive urbanisation are discussed.

THE NEW URBAN AGENDA

Discussions on urbanisation are now not complete without reference to the UN 'New Urban Agenda', Habitat III. The United Nations Conference on Housing and Sustainable Urban Development in Quito, Ecuador, adopted the New Urban Agenda in October 2016.[1] The 'agenda will provide guidance to nation states, city and regional authorities, civil society, foundations, NGOs, academic researchers and UN agencies in their thinking about cities, urbanization and sustainable development, but is not binding'.[2]

The Zero draft of the New Urban Agenda recognises and recommends the inclusion of the informal sector, informal workers, informal economy and the urban poor 'in the way cities and human settlements are planned, developed, governed and managed' (Policy Paper I: Right to Cities).[3]

> We commit to recognize the working poor in the informal economy as contributors and legitimate actors of the urban economies, including the unpaid and domestic workers. A gradual approach to formalisation will be developed to preserve and enhance informal livelihoods while extending access to legal and social protections, as well as support services to the informal workforce.[4]

The New Urban Agenda thus appears inclusive of the informal economy and the urban poor. The direct reference to, and inclusion of, informal workers as contributors to the urban economies in the agenda is a major victory for representatives of the organisations of these workers. However, an international policy advocacy group, WIEGO (women in informal employment, globalising and organising), noted that 'within the draft document, there are no mentions of self-employed or own-account workers' who constitute a large segment of the informal worker in urban India. It proposes to include in the section:

> Leave no one behind, urban equity and poverty eradication: Recognising that all forms of work, including informal work in formal and informal sector enterprises, self-employed work, own-account workers and contributing family workers, and the care economy, contribute to the urban economy....Recognition of the job-creation and economic potential of the informal economy, and its links to wider economic processes, can enable informal workers to realise their full potential contribution to urban productivity (addition of a new sentence at the end of Paragraph 47).[5]

The article presents empirical evidence of the large size of the informal workforce and components of the self-employed and own-account workers in urban India. It emphasises the need to recognise job creation and the potential of the informal economy for creating an inclusive urban agenda for India.

GENDER DIMENSIONS OF INFORMAL URBAN EMPLOYMENT

WORKFORCE PARTICIPATION

It has been a matter of concern that workforce participation of women, in general, and in urban areas, particularly, has been rather low. It is an even greater puzzle that the participation rates of women have been falling over the past decades, particularly in rural areas (Figure 1). This poor participation is partly due to the women's double burden of work, and partly to their invisibility and consequent lack of recognition in the statistical system. The consequence of the latter two factors is that gender issues in women's work do not find the requisite space in the policy domain, further weakening their economic empowerment.

Figure 1: Work Participation Rates, 1993–94 to 2011–12
(Principal + Secondary)

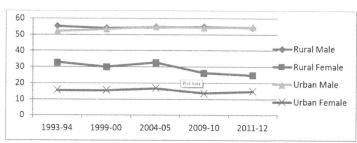

Source: Various rounds of the Employment and Unemployment Survey, National Sample Survey Organisation (NSSO), Ministry of Statistics and Programme Implementation, Government of India.

Women are often engaged in pluri-activity, multiple job holding and secondary activities, contributing to higher levels of invisibility in the labour force and to the undervaluation of their contribution to production. In many societies, a woman's right to own land is not recognised by law or custom. As a consequence, her work may be captured as 'unpaid family worker' in labour-force surveys. More often than men, women are involved in non-market and home-based secondary activities, such as the processing of agricultural and food products. Thus, the following characteristics of their work contribute to their invisibility in agricultural and related activities: they do not own the land, they work as unpaid family workers, and their secondary activities are home-based and non-market oriented.

Figure 1 shows that urban female employment was as low as nearly 15 per cent in 2011–12, while male employment was about 54 per cent. Further, nearly 20 per cent of all urban women workers were in a subsidiary status of employment in 2011–12, growing from about 13 per cent in 2009–10, i.e., they worked for less than 180 days a year, as compared to 1 per cent of urban male workers in 2011–12. In fact, during this period, self-employed women in subsidiary work in urban areas grew from 10 to 17 per cent. This increased invisibility, a second important feature of women's work, and further downgraded their status as workers.

The literature is divided on reasons for the decreasing work participation of women. One argument is that it is because of the 'income effect', i.e., as economic growth occurs and household incomes grow, women tend to withdraw from the workforce, partly because they consider themselves as subsidiary workers contributing only additional income. The household decides that the woman's 'additional income' is no longer necessary for survival; and the family improves its social status if women opt out of the labour force. Another argument is that the decline in work participation is a consequence of the 'discouraged worker effect', i.e., women offer themselves for work if there is a demand for it. Therefore, in years of boom their work participation grows and in times of recession, it falls. The interpretation of these trends has important implications for policy, as the idea that women respond to the demand for work would make them more visible to policymakers. The first interpretation of 'income effect' implies that women are not available for work and, hence, there is a need to focus on their economic contribution to the economy.

INFORMAL EMPLOYMENT

Informal employment can be defined broadly to include informal wage employment, self-employment in informal enterprises, and informal employment in formal enterprises and households. Informal enterprises are those that are not incorporated or registered with the concerned authorities and constitute employment in the informal sector.

In urban India, in 2011–12, only about 20 per cent of all the employed of the working population above the age of 15 were in formal employment; 80 per cent were informally employed—either self-employed or with no social security cover from the employer.[6] The percentage of women in informal employment was just a little higher at 82 per cent. Even among those in the formal sector, 25 per cent of the men and 30 per cent of the women were informally employed, i.e., without the social security cover of the employer and often without access to paid leave or other benefits.

In the informal sector, women's invisibility is greater than men's, although the number of women involved is relatively higher. Again, much of their informal self-employed work is in the form of unpaid family labour. The urban self-employed men and women formed nearly 46 per cent and 51 per cent, respectively, in 2011–12.[7] Nearly 77 per cent of men and 59 per cent of women operated 'own-account' enterprises, i.e., with only family labour and without hired workers. Further, while nearly 40 per cent of women were contributing family members, and hence invisible, men formed only 16 per cent, i.e., a much smaller proportion of women independently operated enterprises.

In many cases, women's informal economic activities begin at home and then extend into the informal marketplace. For example, they manufacture garments at home which are sold in the market either by them or their male counterparts. The manufacturing sector constitutes approximately 22 and 28 per cent of urban men's and women's work, respectively. However, in 2011–12, nearly 68 per cent of these women were home-based, and hence invisible, while men constituted only 16 per cent.

The ILO Convention 177, 1996,[8] singles out those working from home as a vulnerable group requiring special protection. Homeworkers are sub-contracted workers in manufacturing industries, a category which is under-declared by employers, and under-recorded by administrative rosters and enquiries. Women may seek this kind of work, even though the remuneration and conditions of work are bad, because it allows them to simultaneously do their unpaid housework (caring for children, cooking, etc.), and save time otherwise spent commuting. This phenomenon was earlier referred to as the double burden of work.

Homeworkers constituted nearly half of the women workers in the manufacturing sector in 1999–2000. According to the National Commission for Enterprises in the Unorganised Sector (NCEUS),

> Homeworking in the manufacturing sector is what can be clearly identified as a system of production often within a global or domestic value chain. Among the nearly 22 million manufacturing sector workers about 32 per cent are homeworkers, while among the 9 million women manufacturing workers, nearly 50 per cent are homeworkers.[9]

Trade is a major component of urban employment, constituting 23 and 10 per cent of urban men and women's work in 2011–12. However, within the trade sector, 21 per cent of women and 17 per cent of men are involved in street trading. They may process their own foods or other products and sell them on the street. Thus, the full value of their economic activity is often missed as they may only be captured as 'participants in trade activities', whereas they have actually contributed more to the value-added process.

The service sector—other than trade—including transport, banking and communications, constituted about 38 per cent of urban employment in 2011–12—36 per cent for men and 46 per cent for women. While transport constituted the majority (77 per cent of non-trade services), women worked mainly as domestic workers (58 per cent of non-trade services). Urban women domestic workers grew from nearly 20 per cent in 1999–2000 to 26 per cent in 2011–12. Domestic workers are hired by households and form part of informal employment. Their security, both physical and of service, is a major source of concern.

VULNERABLE GROUPS

Besides these broad groups of workers, certain occupations in the urban space are more vulnerable. These include the street vendor, home-based worker, domestic worker and waste picker. Their vulnerability stems partly from their place of work. The most visible among this group is the street vendor who operates in public spaces. She is subject to daily harassment and taxed by the local police and goons for occupying public space, whether designated by the municipal authorities or not.

Home-based women workers are vulnerable as they are dependent on the agency or their male counterparts for market access and sale of their goods. They are relatively less subject to physical harassment, but would be squeezed by lower prices for their goods or higher rates for inputs.

Domestic workers are confined to the premises of the households that hire them. If not recruited from an agency, they have no one to turn to if faced with physical and/or sexual harassment. They also do not have much bargaining power to negotiate wages and other terms and conditions.

Waste pickers form a much smaller component of the workforce. They contribute significantly to the mitigation of climate change by directly reclaiming and recycling waste. Besides harassment from the police and the local population, they are exposed to hazardous material and work in highly unhygienic conditions while collecting and sorting waste.

Of the total male urban employment in 2011–12, street trade constitutes about 4 per cent, home-based work about 10 per cent, domestic work about 2 per cent, and less than 1 per cent in waste work. Together, men in these four vulnerable groups constitute 17 per cent of urban employment.

In contrast, these four vulnerable groups constitute nearly 50 per cent of the female urban workforce. Of the total female urban employment in 2011–12, 3 per cent are street traders, 13 per cent are domestic workers, 32 per cent are engaged in home-based manufacturing, and about 2 per cent are waste pickers. Clearly, women workers in urban India are crying out for recognition of their contribution to the urban economy. They very urgently require policy focus and support in the urban planning and development agenda of the future.

INCLUSIVE URBANISATION

In June 2015, the Government of India declared the flagship 'Smart Cities Mission' with a focus on dissemination of information, communication and technology. Smart cities may refer to new cities (Greenfield projects) or existing cities (Brownfield projects) made smart through investment in technology and infrastructure. The smart city features the promotion of mixed land use in area-based development projects. It endorses housing, the preservation of open spaces and parks, walking spaces to reduce congestion and air pollution, and the development of an integrated transport system.

The AMRUT (Atal Mission for Rejuvenation and Urban Transformation) programme is meant to help rejuvenate urban areas by the development of infrastructure. The Delhi–Mumbai Industrial Corridor (DMIC) is another ambitious project involving the development of this corridor and also envisages the development of four new cities in Gujarat, Maharashtra, Madhya Pradesh and Uttar Pradesh. Similar such ambitious corridors are being visualised in other parts of the country too.

All these programmes will help the development of infrastructure in urban areas. The programme which directly addresses these concerns is the National Urban Livelihood Mission (NULM). It seeks to address multidimensional urban poverty and the vulnerabilities of the urban poor, identified as residential, occupational and social. The Mission document states that 'occupational and social (vulnerabilities) can be best addressed by creating opportunities for skill development leading to market-based employment and helping them to set up self-employment ventures'.[10]

Given the complexity of urban employment and development in India, it is necessary to identify the challenges relating to the establishment of such smart cities, and new corridor and township developments that can include the large proportion of informal workers and, particularly, the vulnerable groups identified earlier. These challenges include urban laws and regulations; the role of finance; integrating a public transport system; land use planning that allows for the needs of the street vendor; infrastructure such as water, sanitation and electricity for all, but particularly for the home-based worker; and recognition of the role played by the waste picker. As the home doubles up as workplace for the home-based worker, the development of housing that allows for work space, storage facility, water and sanitation is crucial. Innovative urban planning in the smart and new cities, and in rejuvenated towns, is required to allow for street vending, and space for the collection and sorting of recyclable waste.

Much of these activities take place in and around the slums, and low-income housing in existing cities and towns. For urbanisation to be inclusive, the new Urban Agenda and urban renewal programmes must visualise plans that are innovative. These developments occur along the periphery of the towns and cities, leading to peri-urban growth. Most of the new programmes and plans have focused on the development of infrastructure. But inclusiveness also derives from laws, rules and regulations, including urban zoning patterns and other design policies. Urban rules and regulations can create 'illegalities' by refusing water and electricity connections to such 'slum' dwellers. Hawking and non-hawking zones, or merely the lack of their definition, creates illegality for vendors who are undertaking a very legitimate economic activity—selling goods in public spaces.

Another challenge faced by urban India is the incorporation of a large proportion of semi-permanent migrants, mainly male, who send remittances back to their villages. The housing needs of these workers are currently met by informal landlords in dorm-like housing situations, often unhygienic and ghettoised. Given the needs of urban residents and the service industry, new cities have to plan for ways to house such short-term migrants which remain safe both for them and the rest of the urban population. Commuting to cities from the suburban areas and nearby villages is another major phenomenon that requires attention. Poorer informal workers are likely to bicycle to the city, which necessitates cycle paths and parking spaces. Or they require cheap transport services, which must also legitimately allow the transport of goods. Some form of identification or identity cards for all workers, particularly migrants, street vendors, waste pickers and domestic workers (who are also often female migrants), would add to their safety and reduce vulnerability.

Inclusive urbanisation thus faces many challenges. The majority of workers in urban India and more than half the women workers who work in unconventional places, or in those not 'designated', require imaginative urban policies to make their economic activities legitimate. This is only one of the many challenges faced by the new phase of growth and constructed urbanisation in India.

◆

NOTES

1. http: //unhabitat.org/new-urban-agenda-adopted-at-habitat-ii:/
2. http://citiscope.org/habitatIII/explainer/2015/06/what-new-urban-agenda (accessed on 2 October 2016).

3. http://www.csb.gov.tr/db/habitat/editordosya/file/POLICY%20PAPER-SON/PU1-right%20to%20the%20city%20and%20cities%20for%20all.pdf

4. https://www2.habitat3.org/bitcache/462d74cfb2e04878ff43c8fcca48037daf73d84f?vid=582559&disposition=inline&op=view (accessed on 2 October 2016: para 32).

5. http://wiego.org/blog/response-zero-draft-new-urban-agenda-women-informal-employment-globalizing-and-organizing-wiego (accessed on 2 October 2016).

6. The figures quoted in the paper are from the Employment Unemployment Survey, 2011–12, of the National Sample Survey Organisation (NSSO) computed from raw data by G. Raveendran and Marty Chen, http://wiego.org/sites/wiego.org/files/publications/files/Chen-Urban-Employment-India-WIEGO-WP7.pdf

7. Computed by the author from unit level data of NSSO, Employment Unemployment Survey, 2011–12.

8. http://www.ilo.org/dyn/normlex/en/f?p=NORMLEXPUB:12100:0::NO::P12100_ILO_CODE:C177

9. http://dcmsme.gov.in/Condition_of_workers_sep_2007.pdf, p.57.

10. http://nulm.gov.in/PDF/NULM_Mission/NULM_mission_document.pdf (accessed on 4 November 2016).

RESETTLEMENT, MOBILITY AND WOMEN'S SAFETY IN CITIES*

RENU DESAI

VAISHALI
PARMAR

DARSHINI
MAHADEVIA

INTRODUCTION

Over the past few years, triggered by the 2012 gangrape in Delhi, we have seen an expanding public and policy discourse around violence against women. Nested within these discussions are questions about women's safety and mobility in Indian cities. At stake here is no less than women's right to the city. However, an engagement with the varying experiences of different groups of women in public spaces and their differentiated vulnerabilities to violence continues to remain on the margins of these discussions. As Shilpa Phadke (2013) points out, 'the question, who can afford to speak and who will be heard is an important one that we must not forget'. This article, therefore, focuses attention on the everyday experiences of violence and safety in the city among a segment of women—those from impoverished and low-income households resettled on the city's periphery. It does so by asserting that their experiences are intricately intertwined with their physical mobility patterns and practices which are forged in the context of their spatiality in the city—a spatiality that is changing as Indian cities transform and expand in exclusionary ways.

The past decade or two have seen such households being pushed to the peripheries of many Indian cities because of the speculative rise in land prices in the central parts of these cities. This has led to peripheries developing as informal and affordable neighbourhoods, and also as spaces to relocate those displaced by urban development projects. By drawing upon research focused on a cluster of resettlement colonies located in Ahmedabad's south-eastern periphery, this article shows how these geographies of peripheralisation have created greater mobility challenges for the city's poorer residents, especially women, creating profound challenges with regard to their safety.

What do we mean by women's safety? In both public and policy discourse in India, women's safety in the city continues to refer largely to sexual assault and harassment and not, as for men, all types of violence, even though women also experience robberies and road accidents (Phadke, et al., 2011). This circumscribed perspective that focuses only on sexual safety arises from a preoccupation with controlling women's bodies in order to safeguard the 'honour' of their families. Phadke argues that

> the insistence on sexual safety actively contributes to not just reducing women's access to public space but also to compromise their safety when they do access public space, by focusing more on women's capacity to produce respectability rather than on their safety. The discourse of safety then does not keep women safe in public; it effectively bars them from it (2007: 1512).

In this article, not only do we move away from the protectionist approach to safety and equate safety with women's right to the city, but we also seek to broaden the definition of women's safety to include all forms of violence faced by her in the context of her mobility in the city, as well as ask what makes cities safe or unsafe for (different groups of) women.

Numerous studies from around the world reveal that women's experiences and practices of mobility in the city through various transport modes and public spaces are linked to their gendered roles (Cresswell and Uteng, 2008; Hanson, 2010; Turner and Fouracre, 1995). Worldwide, women are also found to use more public transport or paratransit services as compared to men, leading to lower mobility (Mahadevia, 2015). For low-income women, mobility is further constrained because of residential locations and resources at their disposal (Anand and Tiwari, 2006; Venter, et al., 2007). Further, Ali (2010) found that the experiences of safety of impoverished women in Karachi are intricately tied to the kinds of public spaces and transport infrastructures they must traverse in their daily struggles to earn a livelihood. NGO studies in some Indian cities have observed that living in a slum or resettlement area poses very different challenges to safe movement as compared to living in a middle-class residential area, and safe mobility is linked to struggles for livelihood, water and sanitation, etc. (Jagori, 2010). Drawing from these studies, this article looks at women's safety in the public realm by examining the interlinkages of gender, poverty and resources, city structure and residential location, and the nature of public spaces traversed and transport modes used in their daily lives. It pays attention to sexual assault and harassment, other types of crime like robbery, vulnerability to road accidents, as well as fear of these. Furthermore, paying close attention to our research participants' narratives and the meanings of *suraksha* (a word that encompasses notions of both safety and security) articulated by them, we also consider the social, economic and psychological insecurities that women experience because of the mobility constraints they face in accessing livelihood, urban infrastructures and amenities as integral aspects of women's safety (UN-HABITAT, et al., 2008).

LOCATING THE VATWA RESETTLEMENT COLONIES

Many informal neighbourhoods located in the central areas of Ahmedabad have been demolished for urban development projects over the past decade and their residents resettled in public housing constructed by the Ahmedabad Municipal Corporation (AMC). Most of these resettlement colonies have been built in eastern Ahmedabad as opposed to the more developed western part of the city, and almost half of the total resettlement flats, as of 2015, were constructed across seven adjacent colonies in Vatwa, an industrial and residential area located on the city's south-eastern periphery. This article draws upon research carried out over 2014 and 2015 at the three Vatwa colonies inhabited at the time: VGG Nagar, Sadbhavna Nagar and KBT Nagar.[1] These three colonies have a total of 156 four-storey buildings comprising 4,992 flats. At the time of our research, an estimated 4,000 were occupied.

Most of the residents were relocated here between 2010 and 2012 after a fraught resettlement process. Moving to Vatwa entailed moving 7 to 15 km from their former neighbourhoods. While Ahmedabad Municipal Transport Service (AMTS) buses plied along three routes from the Vatwa colonies, residents faced problems of infrequent service on one route, and delays and affordability on all the routes (the bus fares were increased substantially in the city in 2012). Moreover, the three routes provided connectivity only to a limited area of the city. Gaps in public transport were filled by 'shuttles'—the three-wheeled auto-rickshaws that operate as shared transport on fixed routes—which are based on informally fixed fares and illegally take up more than three passengers, the permissible number by law. Although shuttles plied along several routes from the colonies, they also posed problems related to frequency and affordability.

This distant relocation and inadequacy of transport options impacted the women's mobility in profound ways, producing insecurities and violence in their lives. Furthermore, the often hostile environment of the colonies compounded these insecurities and violence. Two main dynamics created this hostile environment. One was referred to by residents as *kharaab* or *boora mahol* (bad environment) at the colonies created by the distant resettlement, which negatively impacted livelihoods as well as the resettlement allotment process, leading to deep social disruptions. The other was a built environment, shaped by planning and governance in and around the colonies, which allowed opportunities for activities and behaviours that threatened women's safety.

GENDER, TRANSPORT AND TROUBLED MOBILITIES

Women living at the Vatwa resettlement colonies travelled for a range of reasons. Many women were domestic workers, as well as vending and manual labour, travelling to areas near their former neighbourhoods on a daily basis. Some travelled to work in factories in various parts of the city. Many others were home-based workers, stitching garments, making imitation jewellery and kites, and were likely to travel once or more in the week to buy raw material and deliver the finished product. A large number of women worked as vendors in the colony, and would travel intermittently to procure wares to sell. Some also did 'double-*kaam*', working outside the home, and pursuing home-based work or vending near the home. Both employed and unemployed women travelled intermittently to avail of medical care and subsidised commodities from the public distribution system (PDS), while many girls commuted regularly to school and tuition class. A small number of girls also attended college. Since the Vatwa colonies are not at walking distance from most women's workplaces and sources of home-based work, public hospitals, secondary schools and colleges, PDS shops and trusted private clinics, women had to use AMTS buses or shuttles. The long distances travelled and time taken because of the distant relocation, and the dependence on inadequate bus and shuttle services led to significant shifts in their mobility patterns, practices and experiences. For many women, increased insecurity and violence was part and parcel of these shifts.

First, Vatwa's distance from workplaces put a tremendous burden of travel costs on residents, deepening their economic insecurity. For many women who did not have to incur travel costs in their previous neighbourhoods since they could walk to work, the bus/shuttle fares substantially reduced their effective income. Many others, working as domestic help 14 km away in central city areas near where they had once lived and earning ₹3–6,000 per month, had to spend from one-third to one-sixth of their income on transport. For many women with low earnings, especially daily wagers, the high transport fares to central city areas—sometimes coupled with other factors like bus delays, crowded buses and shuttles, etc.—resulted in a loss of mobility and consequent loss of employment. Women tried to find domestic work in nearby middle-class areas but this often involved walking 2.5–3 km from their Vatwa home. Some like Saroj could not sustain this beyond a year or two as they found it difficult to walk half-an-hour each way and could not afford to switch to paid transport. While many women shifted to home-based work to eliminate daily travel costs, they had to travel by metered rickshaw to buy raw material and deliver the finished product, which was expensive. Many like Reshma and Nasreen could not bear these costs, which forced them to depend on middlemen who gave home-based work in the colonies at low piece-rate wages. The exorbitant travel costs of accessing social infrastructure (schools, hospitals, PDS shops, etc.) further heightened economic insecurity among women.

Second, this distance in itself created a loss of mobility for many women, deepening economic insecurity. This was because their mobility was dependent on the gendered roles that they performed in the household, such as taking care of children and chores. The long distances did not allow them the flexibility to intersperse their paid work outside the home and household chores. Many had, in fact, found it impossible to do both, preferring inescapable household chores, thereby leading to the loss of employment. Moreover, many mothers wanted to be able to intermittently check on their children, or were reluctant to leave female children alone at home because of the unsafe environment. However, the long commute made this impossible, causing some women to quit work. Travelling long distances for just a few hours of work was not an option since one had to earn enough to justify high travel expenses. Mobility practices were thus forged through a constellation of considerations.

Third, travel time had increased because of the colonies' distance from workplaces combined with the inadequacies of bus and shuttle services—the infrequent service of buses on certain routes, delays, the lack of direct connectivity to certain destinations; long waits for shuttles, which operated to no fixed timings as shuttle drivers commenced the journey only with a full vehicle, resulting in penalties issued by the traffic police because of illegal numbers of passengers. For many women, long working days led to greater challenges and stress, juggling paid work outside the home and unpaid household work.

Fourth, given the long commute, along with the unsafe environment at the colonies, women experienced daily anxiety over their own safety as well as the safety of their young children and teenage daughters. Farida explained that because it took longer to return home, she remained tense about the children until she got home. Suman and Amreen both articulated a sense of fear and anxiety, a foreboding, experienced on the return journey, especially as darkness descended. They worried about the bus arriving on schedule, and then if they would reach home on time. These anxieties about their own safety were in the context of sexual assault, harassment and theft.

Fifth, women pointed to the overcrowded conditions in buses, which led to sexual harassment. Especially targeted were girls, as young boys took advantage of the crowded conditions to touch them. Women pointed out that while seating was not ensured in packed buses, the shuttles at least provided them a seat; a seat, however, did not guarantee safety. Amreen, employed in an NGO, explained that on the return journey, if the bus was too crowded, she would get off midway to complete the commute by shuttle. But often the shuttles were equally crowded. There were frequently four passengers each, both in the front and rear, giving male co-passengers a chance to misbehave. Nafisa, a resident in her mid-30s who often took the shuttle to get home quickly, explained that if the shuttle was full, then 'jaan ghabrata hai', thus expressing the deeply embodied fear she felt in such situations (focus-group discussion, January 2014). Women also pointed out that shuttle drivers often played music loudly and stared at female passengers through the rearview mirror. Sometimes drivers were drunk, or high on *charas* or *ganja* (cannabis), and in such circumstances women felt harassed by their rash driving which could result in road accidents. Many women, including girls, stated that they would not share a shuttle with male co-passengers because they feared harassment. Women were often delayed in the wait for a shuttle with a trustworthy driver. Overcrowding also led many elderly women, like 60-year-old Noorjahan Bano, to quit work because the distance and discomfort of such travel took a toll on their health.

HOSTILE URBAN ENVIRONMENTS AND GENDERED INSECURITIES

Women moved in and around the locality by foot in order to access bus stops and shuttle stops, and shop for groceries from nearby vendors. Although jobs in the vicinity were hard to come by, some of them managed to find domestic or factory work within walking distance. The urban environments they traversed on foot within their resettlement colony and on nearby roads were hostile, leading to different types of risks, insecurities and violence.

Many women expressed fear of sexual harassment and theft in the locality, especially while walking on the main road between VGG Nagar and Sadbhavna Nagar, and at bus stops and shuttle stops, particularly those located on the main crossroads (where a police *chowky* was later built, making women feel safer once it was functional). Many women felt threatened walking on the internal roads of the colonies, particularly in Sadbhavna Nagar. The feeling of insecurity was greater after dark. The lack of safety was attributed to the presence of men high on cannabis and 'powder', and drunks in and around the locality. They referred to these men as *lukkhas* (idle men who are up to no good). Suman, a domestic worker from

Sadbhavna Nagar, explained that she made it a point to return from work before dark as such men loitered on the streets of the locality, often threatening and robbing people at knifepoint. Teenaged girls and young women expressed a fear of *cheddkhaani* (harassment) in and around Sadbhavna Nagar. Rubina, a 24-year-old resident, explained that she did not venture out alone in the locality, fearing a man might even grab her hand. The sale and consumption of alcohol in some of the locality's open spaces, mainly in Sadbhavna Nagar, also made many women feel vulnerable, especially since it often led to inebriated men fighting with each other and passers-by, as well as goons battling each other to control the illicit liquor business.

Illegal activities like selling alcohol and drugs, the consumption of these intoxicants (which women associated with increased possibility of sexual harassment) and theft had partly emerged from the negative economic and social impacts of resettlement to the periphery. While alcohol *addas* had existed in many of their previous neighbourhoods, residents of the Vatwa colonies repeatedly narrated how, after resettlement, the lack of appropriate employment opportunities nearby and the prohibitive costs of transport had led to unemployment and under-employment among men, which further led to more men participating in illegal activities or resorting to theft in the locality. They believed that the consumption of alcohol and drugs had increased due to the negative psychological impact of resettlement among adult men, youth and even adolescent boys. In Pramila's words, men who previously drank once a week before resettlement now drank thrice a week. Many residents pointed to drug users resorting to theft to fund their addictions. Moreover, a faulty resettlement process and poor governance at the resettlement sites resulted in many flats at the Vatwa colonies remaining unallotted and unmonitored, some of which were taken over by goons to house illegal activities. The police's complicity often came up in women's narratives.

Additionally, the resettlement allotment process also contributed to creating a *mahol* (environment) at the colonies that was rife with theft, illicit activities, *gundagardi* (bullying) and sexual harassment. This process, in which flats were randomly allotted at each resettlement colony to residents from several demolished slums without any consideration of the communities that they had forged in their previous localities, created social disruptions that led to a lack of trust and respect amongst the residents as well as the loss of authority of those who were relatively well-respected local leaders in their previous localities. This caused a loss of internal social control within the community and locality, allowing these activities and behaviours to flourish. Residents pointed out that the colony would have been safer if people of a single locality had been resettled together. This would have maintained long-standing community ties, ensuring a measure of internal control. In KBT Nagar, a male tenant had raped a three-year-old girl whose parents had left her alone at home while they went to work. The cause of the incident was explained as being the result of people not knowing their neighbours, and unfamiliar men living in their buildings as tenants. Ramila used the term 'parchuran basti' (roughly translated as 'miscellaneous population') to refer to the social composition of her Vatwa colony, explaining:

> In our old neighbourhood, people had a sense of shame and propriety in front of neighbours. Now everyone has been separated and the neighbours we have here are useless. Like, you are living next to me, but I do not trust you, and you do not trust me. At any time any incident can take place; that is the environment here. We cannot leave our children alone here. We have to take them with us [if we go out] (focus-group discussion, February 2014).

Further, the nature of planning and governance in and around the colonies created an environment conducive to harassment. Women and girls identified desolate areas like bus stops at the crossroads, with vacant plots on two corners and few vendors. These areas were contrasted with the more populated streets of VGG Nagar, where there were more vendors, and people sitting on their cots in the open and the bazaar area, on one of the main roads. Thus, the nature of land and street use created safe or unsafe environments in different parts of the locality. Infrastructural deficiencies also created an environment conducive to incidents of harassment and theft, making women feel less safe. Women talked about intermittently functioning streetlights on the main road and at bus stops, shuttle stops and inside the three colonies, which made them feel unsafe.

Roshan from VGG Nagar said that while in the daytime she was *befikr* (untroubled), she was afraid to walk within VGG Nagar after dark as streetlights did not function properly. In KBT Nagar, women felt that a solitary girl would be molested by drunks and, therefore, did not allow their daughters out alone after dark. Shabana, a 17-year-old schoolgirl, expressed a sense of fear while walking to the bus stop and waiting there on dark winter mornings. As the area around was desolate, streetlights did not always work and men loitered there, she was afraid of being robbed at knifepoint or harassed.

CONCLUSION

The mobility of impoverished and low-income women, and their related experiences of safety are interconnected with their daily struggles in the city for livelihood, water, sanitation, health and education. In the resettlement colonies at Vatwa, the factors contributing to women's practices and patterns of mobility, and the types of violence and insecurity they face in relation to this, are related directly to urban planning and governance. The distant relocation and the inadequacy of transport services with respect to frequency, connectivity and affordability have resulted in troubled mobility, deepening socio-economic insecurity for many and day-to-day anxiety about safety as women commute long distances. The nature of resettlement—distant relocation on the periphery with its economic and social impacts such as under-employment/ unemployment, social marginalisation and stress, as well as the resettlement allotment process with its social impacts of loss of internal social control and stability within the community—has created a local environment rife with alcohol and drug sale and consumption, sexual harassment and theft. Poor street lighting, as well as the nature of land and street use in many parts of the colonies, points to the more locale-specific planning and governance issues that create opportunities for these activities and behaviours which are threatening to women.

Urban planning and design contribute to the lack of women's safety, not only through the hostile localised environments created because of certain kinds of land-use patterns in these peripheral areas, the absence of women-friendly street corners and activities, and the absence of infrastructure like streetlights in/around the locality, but also through urban planning and governance dynamics beyond the micro-level, by socio-spatial transformations in cities and the manner in which this profoundly reshapes people's economic and social lives, and women's mobility. Many women compared their experiences of mobility for work, education, etc., at Vatwa to experiences in their previous neighbourhoods. For instance, women in our focus-group discussions, who had been displaced by the riverfront project, unanimously agreed that they had never experienced harassment while travelling in and around their previous residential localities. They explained that they could walk everywhere and most of them never had to take the bus or shuttle to work or for other purposes. Walking had been a safe experience, even at night, as there were diverse people and activities on the streets. All the school-going girls who were part of our focus-group discussions had felt no fear of harassment or theft while living in the central city areas which supported a multiplicity of people; whereas, here they were in danger of being robbed and harassed by drunks. Men talked about leaders in their previous neighbourhood, some of whom had indeed been musclemen, who controlled the activities and behaviours there. At the Vatwa colonies, the loss of their authority and tussles for power between themselves, and with new entrants into these local power games, made the colonies unsafe for many residents, especially women.

Behavioural factors linked to structures of patriarchy and sexism are certainly at the crux of instances of sexual harassment and assault. However, we believe that it is essential to bring in questions of urban planning, design and governance into the debates around violence against women, and their safety.

◆

ACKNOWLEDGMENTS

This paper is part of a larger research project entitled 'Dynamics of Poverty, Inequality and Violence in Indian Cities: Towards Inclusive Policies and Planning', funded from 2013 to 2016 at the Centre for Urban Equity, CEPT University, Ahmedabad, by the International Development Research Centre, Canada, and the Department for International Development, UK. Nupur Joshi provided valuable assistance in writing a draft paper on women's mobility and safety in Ahmedabad, upon which this paper draws.

NOTE

1. Between January and March 2014, Vaishali Parmar (2014) carried out gender safety audits at the colonies for her master's thesis which was supervised by Darshini Mahadevia. The audits included mapping of land use, infrastructure and street activities, and 10 focus-group discussions covering 46 women. Subsequently, Renu Desai carried out focus-group discussions, 7 unstructured group discussions and 35 semi-structured interviews—covering 51 men and 53 women—to examine a range of conflicts and violence.

REFERENCES

Ali, Kamran, Asdar. 2010. 'Voicing Difference: Gender and Civic Engagement among Karachi's Poor', *Current Anthropology,* vol. 51, pp. S313–20.

Anand, Anvita and Geetam Tiwari. 2006. 'A Gendered Perspective on the Shelter-Transport-Livelihood Link', *Transport Reviews,* vol. 26, pp. 63–80.

Cresswell, Tim and Tanu Priya Uteng. 2008. 'Gendered Mobilities: Towards an Holistic Understanding', in Tanu Priya Uteng and Tim Cresswell (eds.), *Gendered Mobilities.* Farnham: Ashgate, pp. 1–12.

Hanson, Susan. 2010. 'Gender and Mobility: New Approaches for Informing Sustainability', *Gender, Place and Culture,* vol. 17, pp. 5–23.

Jagori, 2010. *A Handbook on Women's Safety Audits in Low-income Urban Neighbourhoods: A Focus on Essential Services.* New Delhi: Jagori.

Mahadevia, Darshini. 2015. *Gender Sensitive Transport Planning for Cities in India.* Copenhagen: UNEP DTU Partnership, Centre on Energy, Climate and Sustainable Development, Technical University of Denmark.

Parmar, Vaishali. 2014. 'Gender Safety Audits in a Rehabilitation Site: A Case of Ahmedabad'. Unpublished master's thesis. Ahmedabad: Faculty of Planning, CEPT University.

Phadke, Shilpa. 2007. 'Dangerous Liaisons—Women and Men: Risk and Reputation in Mumbai', *Economic and Political Weekly,* April, pp. 1510–18.

Phadke, S., S. Khan and S. Ranade. 2011. *Why Loiter? Women and Risk on Mumbai Streets.* New Delhi: Penguin.

Phadke, Shilpa. 2013. 'Two Years Later... The Changing Terms of Debate around Women's Safety', *DNA,* 16 December.

Turner, Jeff and Philip Fouracre. 1995. 'Women and Transport in Developing Countries', *Transport Reviews,* vol. 15, pp. 77–96.

UN-HABITAT, WICI, SIDA, Huairou Commission, CISCSA. 2008. *The Global Assessment on Women's Safety.* Nairobi: UN-HABITAT.

Venter, Christoffel, Vera Vokolkova and Jaroslav Michalek. 2007. 'Gender, Residential Location and Household Travel: Empirical Findings from Low Income Urban Settlements in Durban, South Africa', *Transport Reviews,* vol. 27, pp. 653–77.

CITIES FOR HEALTHY PEOPLE

**DINESH
MOHAN**

grew up in small and mid-sized cities of India in the 1950s. My father worked for the government and the family would move every three years or so. Every time we moved, we would despair over losing friends but would very quickly get involved with the logistics of the move and look forward to settling down in the new city. As young boys, it was not so difficult to make friends in the new place as we would cycle to school and explore our neighbourhood, walking or cycling around. Quite soon, we would come to know the local grocer, the book and stationery shop owners and a number of street vendors. If my memory serves me right, when we did business with them we believed we were adults and haggled over prices and the products we bought. It was great to be independent and be able to buy ice-cream or snacks without parental supervision or teachers' disapproval. I even remember sneaking out of the house in 45°C midday heat to play with friends as soon as our mother retired for her siesta.

I recall all this not only with nostalgia (common with people my age), but also with concern about the motorisation of our cities. Motorisation has made our streets unsafe for children and the elderly. Living in Delhi, we denied the pleasure of independence to our daughter who was not allowed to venture out on a bicycle on the road in front of our house. It was too unsafe, we thought. While at work, I write and lecture about the merits of bicycling and walking. This just about sums up the dilemma most of us are confronted with while imagining the future of our urban spaces.

The problems of dealing with transportation policies have to include issues thrown up by the threat of global warming.

While technological solutions will be available for reducing emissions from motor vehicles, there is also a need to reduce the demand for motorised travel as incomes increase in our countries. This will not be easy unless we understand the underlying factors associated with the increasing demand for personal modes of motorised travel. Systems have to be put in place that help people choose less harmful modes of travel and reduce the need for long trips. The desired behaviour patterns need to be rewarded and harmful actions discouraged by negative feedback, socially and financially.

DEALING WITH URBAN TRANSPORT

Most of us are struggling with the threat of global warming and attend unending seminars on sustainable development. Almost all the discussion revolves around conserving energy and finding cleaner fuels. But more technology and less carbon dioxide (CO_2) alone will not bring more liveable cities for our grandchildren. The threat of crime and traffic accidents will not reduce with reductions in CO_2 after the Intergovernmental Panel on Climate Change (IPCC) meetings. Nor will the need for people to travel long distances for work, shopping and entertainment. Concepts like transit-oriented development (TOD) are the fashion.[1] But the evidence suggests that TOD on its own does not reduce travel distances, nor does it result in major shifts in transportation modal shares (Carlton, 2007: 30; Olaru, et al., 2011). A recent paper by Edna Murphy (2009) suggests that it is the density of public transportation networks that are critical in attracting riders in addition to mixed land use planning.

Some of these findings are self-evident if we look at how people move around cities in India. I believe that Indian cities are in the very enviable position of evolving into the most sustainable habitats in the world with human-scale living environments, if we change our mind-set and start looking at their positive attributes along with their shortcomings. A soft state and frequent elections have ensured that Western-inspired master plans of the 1960s could not be implemented in totality. This has made it possible to have mixed land use in our cities and the possibility for the poor to live interspersed with the rich (although 'illegally')—a development in line with the prescriptions of modern urban planners. Our cities have grown somewhat organically due to the pressure of people's needs in spite of the short-term vision of bureaucrats and businesspersons.

The result is that most people tend to live close to their places of work except the rich, and those poor families evicted by whims of city planners and land mafias. Recent data from the Census of India, 2011, shows that a majority of trips are less than 5–6 km in length, even in large cities. A sprawling Delhi is not like Los Angeles in the United States of America. In Los Angeles, everyone goes long distances from anywhere to everywhere, whereas Delhi functions as a conglomeration of a large number of 'cities' in a city. Most people work, live and socialise within their own 'city'. This is an ideal situation to work toward a very sustainable future by embracing policies that do not force people to travel long distances.

Most Indian cities have expanded after 1960 and all have planned for multiple business districts. In the second half of the 20th century, most families in Indian cities did not own a personal vehicle and so all leisure activity revolved within short distances around the home. In the past two decades, vehicle ownership has increased substantially in Indian cities. Delhi has by far the highest ownership levels, with 15–20 per cent of Delhi's families owning a car and about 35 per cent a motorcycle, at a very low average per capita income level of about ₹50,000 per year. Such high levels of private vehicle ownership (including motorcycles) did not take place until incomes were much higher in Western cities. Car ownership in all other cities of India is less than half that in Delhi. The high ownership of motorcycles, non-availability of funds to build expensive grade-separated metro systems, and official plans encouraging multi-nodal business activity in a city has resulted in the absence of dense high-population central business districts (CBD). Our cities have developed urban forms that encourage sprawl in the form of relatively dense cities within cities. The absence of systems like metros (grade-separated rail systems) that encourage long-distance travel have helped in this form of development in most Indian cities until recently.

There are two factors at work here. Low- and middle-income people do not require a very large pool of activities to find work. If businesses are mixed with residential areas, and lower-income people allowed to live everywhere, then those less skilled are more likely to find work closer to home. For example, a carpenter does not need a specialised work place to find a job. Only highly skilled people do, and they have to opt for work locations wherever available. It is this latter minority that needs long-distance travel and so they force policies for their own benefit.

All large Indian cities are growing around the periphery and will not have dense centres in the future either. So our public transport policies would have to be different from the 19th-century European cities that developed very important CBDs and required people to come to the centre. The latter were cities of empires and colonisers where magnificent buildings, theatres, opera houses and parks could be built with income from the periphery—peasants and colonies. We cannot indulge in this luxury as our villages are the only periphery. The magnificence of the central European city invoked a great deal of pride among its citizens and they have ensured its pre-eminence to the current times. There is no such social pressure in Indian cities and most upper-class citizens have already abandoned the city centre. This is one of the factors that does not favour very high-capacity radial transit systems bringing people to the centre.

Changes in car technology are also deciding how people behave in Indian cities. Brand new, quiet, stereo-equipped, air-conditioned cars are now being sold in India at prices lower than ₹300,000, and used cars for a third that price. This has made it possible for the middle-class, first-time car owner to travel in cars with comfort levels Europeans had not experienced until the late 20th century. Now, air-conditioned, comfortable, safe and quiet travel in cars with music in hot and tropical climates cannot be matched by public transport. Owners of such vehicles would brave the congestion rather than brave the climate on access trips and the jostling in public transport. If public transport has to be made more appealing, it has to come closer to home, reduce walking distances, be air-conditioned and be very predictable. These conditions would favour high-density, lower-capacity surface transport systems (to reduce walking distances) with predictable arrival and departure times aided by computers and modern information systems.

Wide ownership of motorcycles has never been experienced by Western cities. This is a new phenomenon, especially in Asia. The efficiency of motorcycles—ease of parking, high manoeuvrability, ease of overtaking in congested traffic, same speeds as cars and low operating costs—make them very popular in spite of motorcycle travel being very hazardous. Their availability has further reduced middle-class demand for public transport. In addition, it has pegged fare levels that can be charged by public transport operators. It appears that public transport cannot attract these road users who can afford motorcycles unless the fare is less than the marginal cost of using a motorcycle. At current prices, this amounts to less than ₹1 per km. The only option available is to design very cost-efficient public transport systems that come close to matching this price.

Higher education and trade obviously have a reasonable amount to do with the size of cities and form of urbanisation. The more educated we are, the larger the pool of resources we need, both for work and human contact. Therefore, a large city becomes essential for a reasonable section of the population for finding optimal employment and friends. The inverse of the same issue is that trade and industry need a large pool to select employees. This forces Indian cities to become larger than Western cities. This is because for each rich person a larger number of poorer people are required to serve them as compared to high-income economies. So the same number of professionals in an Indian city will coexist with a much larger number of poorer residents than in rich countries. This will make Indian cities much larger than the mature cities of Europe in the foreseeable future. The existence of large numbers of low-income people pursuing informal trade and income-generating activities places different political pressures on the rulers, increasing the demand for low-cost mobility and short-distance access to jobs and trade.

This is offset by the middle and upper classes wanting to live away from the poor, forming gated communities at the periphery of the city. These developments set up a powerful political demand, aided and abetted by contractors and consultants, to provide infrastructure. The upper-middle classes of post-colonial nations mainly have the United States of America as a model for the good life. All Asian, African and South American cities are more influenced by the United States than by any other society. For example, American town planners were sitting in Delhi helping us plan our cities in the 1950s (Breese, 1963). So, all cities have tried hard zoning, and broad avenues and highways running through them. If it has not happened here, it is due to our inefficiency and shortage of finances. In the face of all these changes and constraints, the Indian upper class and policymakers still seem to think that just the provision of flyovers, elevated roads and few lines of a metro will solve all our problems.

Indian cities at present have a very high proportion of people walking, bicycling and using public transport. If we include those who use company-provided buses and vans, and those who travel by shared three-wheeled taxis and other modes of private 'public' transport, then the actual share of public transport (among motorised modes) would be higher in *all* Indian cities than almost all European or American cities. This is an ideal situation in which to plan for a sustainable future. The problem is that most Indian citizens adopt these modes out of economic compulsion, not out of choice, because it is not a pleasant or safe experience doing so. The challenge before us is to understand the needs and desires of the city dweller, the options available, and then chart a new path for our future.

UNDERSTANDING URBAN TRAVEL

The modes of travel used by people in cities is decided by a balancing of economic compulsions, comfort and safety. Studies of travel behaviour around the world suggest that people do not necessarily minimise time spent on trips. Most seem to have a personal travel time/budget preference and utilise it fully except when circumstances do not permit them to do so (Knoflacher, 2007). If provided faster modes of travel, people live further away from work. Public transit is used mainly by those who do not have a vehicle for personal use or when car use is very inconvenient (irritating driving conditions, very long-distance travel), time wasting, impossible (no parking at destination) or very unsafe. At the very least, public transport should not take more time than car travel. This means that buses on main routes cannot be mixed with car traffic, as that will always make them slower than cars.

Door-to-door trip time by public transit is always greater than by car if there is no congestion. It is hardly surprising that it is so difficult to move people from cars to public transit. Therefore, it is surprising that all public transit projects justify the expense by claiming reductions in congestion. If you reduce congestion and make traffic smooth, there is little reason why a car driver would leave an air-conditioned space to spend more time travelling.

For short trips of up to 3 km, door-to-door time walking is about the same as by metro and up to 6 km a bicycle trip compares favourably with a metro trip. You are better off travelling by bus on a dedicated lane than a system that is grade separated for trips of up to 12 km. This is because any transit system operating underground or on elevated corridors requires you to climb or go down stairs/escalators and walk around inside the station. This extra time is about 6–10 minutes per trip in grade-separated systems around the world, including the Delhi metro. In one round trip, there are four such events, and so the time lost in underground or elevated systems of any kind amounts to 12–20 minutes.

SAFETY AND SUSTAINABLE FUTURES

Safety on access trips also emerges as a very important issue, especially for women and children. Unless the walking trip is safe from accidents, harassment and crime, people avoid using public transport. Therefore, safety emerges as a precondition for promoting public transport use (Mohan and Bangdiwala, 2013).

In addition to traffic safety, safety from crime and harassment is a major concern for parents, children and women. Forty-seven years ago Jane Jacobs suggested that crime could be reduced by having 'eyes on the street' (1961). By this, she meant shops on ground floors abutting the sidewalk, an abundance of kiosks and cafes, and a vibrant walking atmosphere. She was quite clear policing alone could not do it. We are again fortunate to have these 'eyes' on all our streets (except in very rich neighbourhoods) in the form of hawkers and vendors. Without them, our streets would not provide the relatively crime-free atmosphere we have. These vendors then become essential as a part of our transportation planning process. It is not very difficult to plan for them, as every road needs a treeline that occupies a corridor of 1–1.5 m of space on the pedestrian path. Vendors only need 1–1.5 m and they can occupy spaces between trees without bothering pedestrians.

TRANSPORTATION, HEALTH AND SOCIAL DISRUPTION

Enough has been written on the deleterious effects of vehicle emissions on the health of urban citizens. Action has been taken on these issues through regulation, and fuel and emission standards.

These are important avenues of action as the vehicle fleet is bound to grow for some time to come. On this front, it is important to understand that the most stringent standards must be placed on new models, as they will be around for 15–20 years. To ensure cleaner air quality we will also have to place a much greater emphasis on changes in modal shares of travel than we have up to now. A small shift from cars and motorcycles to walking and cycling has a much greater impact than change in engine quality because you go from a polluting mode to a zero-polluting mode. A vendor using a non-motorised mode coming to your home to sell vegetables does more to prevent global warming than you driving a less-polluting car to a supermarket. Some of these issues have to be understood in greater detail by all residents of a city to allow healthier policies to be put in place.

For example, very few people know that children living on wide, noisy roads tend to do less well in school than those who live in quieter neighbourhoods, all else being equal (Dora and Phillips, 2000). In addition, children living on wide, busy roads tend to have far fewer friends than those living on streets with less traffic. The effect on the elderly is similar. Senior citizens are reported to live lonelier lives on wide, busy and noisy streets, and suffer greater health problems with elevated blood pressure, etc. This is partly because they cannot cross the street easily and lose half the population for socialisation, shopping and other human needs. This means we should prevent any urban artery from being more than 45 m wide, of which not more than 25 m should be available for motorised traffic and the rest devoted to bicycle and pedestrian paths, the tree line, etc. This is because pedestrians cannot walk more than 25 m in one pedestrian phase of the traffic signal cycle. Cities with wider roads in general have a high pedestrian fatality rate.

The elimination of wide and elevated transportation corridors reduces noise and pollution and makes a city more liveable. Statistical data from many cities shows that rentals for residential accommodation have a distinct relationship with noise levels— noisier streets have lower rentals than quieter ones. This why many residents occupying prestigious plots in our cities shift out when the road in front of their homes is widened. Their residences end up as commercial establishments, legally or illegally. The evidence is clear, but the question that bothers everyone is, what to do when traffic volumes increase.

We cannot answer this without a vision of the kind of city we want. If we want liveable, quieter and healthier cities, then we need to decide the widest road we can tolerate. Having done that, we optimise it for carrying the maximum number of people by giving safe choices for all modes—walking, cycling, cars/two-wheelers and buses. After that, if it starts getting crowded, we should not widen it thereby inviting more people to come, but wait for less people opting to come there eventually.

THE WAY FORWARD IN THE FACE OF GLOBAL WARMING

In nature, stable and sustainable systems have two characteristics: all species, including human beings, grow to maturity and then stop growth, and all have negative feedback systems to maintain homeostasis. At present, no nation is contemplating limiting its economic growth, no matter how rich it is. This is clearly not sustainable. As an important component of these economic systems, the transportation sub-system must have negative feedback control to provide disincentives for excess travel by individuals. At present, the transportation system is driven largely by positive feedback, encouraging people to drive longer distances at higher speeds. A longer drive gets you a larger house at lower prices. Even public transport systems like metros that focus on higher speeds encourage long-distance travel and sprawl. In addition, elevated and underground transit systems further discourage short-distance travel because of large door-to-door trip times. Flat fares, instead of distance-based fares, reward long-distance travel and penalise those taking short trips. There are very few negative feedback loops in the system to provide stability and minimum use of energy.

Unless our transport systems build in negative feedback loops against excess consumption and positive feedback for emissionless travel, we are unlikely to see much progress. This would mean providing facilities that make walking and bicycling more pleasurable, healthier and safer than motorised travel. It is assumed that just the provision of good footpaths and bicycle lanes would encourage people to walk and bicycle. This is a necessary condition, but not a sufficient one. Fairly good footpaths are available in Lutyen's Delhi and Chandigarh, but you hardly see them crowded with pedestrians. One of the reasons is that pedestrians probably find them to be very sterile environments. All they can see are high boundary walls and barbed wire fences. The architecture of buildings is not visible; there are no shops, restaurants, kiosks, offices or human activity to make their walk pleasant and interesting. There are no places to sit or loiter with friends or socialise with acquaintances. Unless we allow a great deal of social activity along our urban streets, walking cannot be a preferred option. All the city neighbourhoods in the world, where you see a large number of people walking around by choice, have these characteristics.

All these issues can only be tackled if we give more importance to non-tailpipe concerns. Engine and emission technology will improve whether we give it importance or not—it is in the interest of the large corporations to do so. However, we will have to focus on safety, urban form, and systems providing negative feedback for bad behaviour for any chance of survival.

◆

NOTE

1. TOD is a concept to promote mixed residential and commercial areas around public transport nodes designed to encourage transit ridership, especially in low-density areas.

REFERENCES

Breese, G. 1963. 'Urban Development Problems in India', *Annals of the Association of American Geographers,* 53, pp. 253–65.

Carlton, I. 2007. *Histories of Transit-oriented Development: Perspectives on the Development of the TOD Concept: Real Estate and Transit, Urban and Social Movements, Concept Protagonist.* Berkeley, CA: Institute of Urban and Regional Development, University of California, Berkeley.

Dora, C. and M. Phillips. 2000. *Transport, Environment and Health.* Copenhagen: WHO Regional Office for Europe.

Jacobs, J. 1961. *The Death and Life of Great American Cities.* New York: Random House.

Knoflacher, H. 2007. 'From Myth to Science', *Seminar,* 579, pp. 40–44.

Mohan, D. and S. Bangdiwala. 2013. 'Urban Street Structure and Safety', in D. Mohan (ed.), *Safety, Sustainability and Future Urban Transport.* New Delhi: D. Eicher Goodearth Pvt Ltd., pp. 125–40.

Murphy, E. 2009. 'Excess Commuting and Modal Choice', *Transportation Research Part A: Policy and Practice,* 43, pp. 735–43.

Olaru, D., B. Smith and J. H. E. Taplin. 2011. 'Residential Location and Transit-oriented Development in a New Rail Corridor', *Transportation Research Part A: Policy and Practice,* 45, pp. 219–37.

◆◆

III

CITIES
OF
CONTEMPORARY
INDIA

THE PLANNED AND THE UNPLANNED
Company Towns in India

ASHIMA
SOOD
SHARADINI
RATH

INTRODUCTION

If Gurgaon is a problem city, can Jamshedpur be the solution? Both cities built by private capital, Gurgaon and Jamshedpur represent the widely disparate outcomes of the greenfield urban development project in India. On the one hand, marred by potholed roads, contaminated water sources and groundwater levels in precipitous decline, Gurgaon has increasingly come to be seen as a 'failed experiment' (Polanki, 2012) in private urban development.

On the other hand, India's first masterplanned company town Jamshedpur appears to stand out as an urban success story, emblematic of a model of benevolent 'welfare capitalism' (Kling, 1998: 70). Part of the United Nations Global Compact Cities programme, the company town boasts high quality of life indicators. Standards of basic services, such as water supply through the Town Division of Tata Steel and now the Jamshedpur Utilities and Services Corporation (JUSCO), have received recognition both in India and internationally.

Not only have Jamshedpur's basic services come in for growing approbation from urban commentators, the Jamshedpur model has found strong echo in an emerging policy architecture for greenfield town development, whether in the Special Economic Zones (SEZs), Special Investment Regions (SIRs) or the integrated industrial townships proposed along the Delhi–Mumbai Industrial Corridor (DMIC). Are we witnessing a rediscovery and revival, on a far larger scale, of the company town ideal? And what does this ideal portend for India's urbanisation trajectory? This essay will attempt to answer these questions through a close examination of the company-town model and its historical imprint on India's urban landscape.

MODELS FOR THE PRIVATE CITY?

On the face of it, there would appear to be few grounds for comparison between Gurgaon and Jamshedpur, the first constructed on Delhi's border through a process of accretion by a multiplicity of actors, and the second, the result of sustained investment over a century in a remote corner of what was then British India, by a single corporate visionary, Jamsetji Tata, and later Tata Steel. Both cities speak to a common predicament, however—the critical need for private investment in building the infrastructure for urban India.

In a widely cited report, the McKinsey Global Institute laid down the context for this contribution (Sankhe, et al., 2010). Urban India needs a staggering USD 1.2 trillion in investment to meet urban population growth by 2030 (ibid.: 20), when 40 per cent of Indians are projected to live in cities (ibid.: 15). This is the equivalent of a 'new Chicago' every year in new commercial and residential space (ibid.: 18). While state and local governments find themselves hobbled by all too real fiscal constraints, private capital is required to fill the investment gap, not only in basic services infrastructure, but also increasingly in building new urban nodes and townships. From 2001 to 2002, the central government provided a channel for these funding flows to enter the real estate sector by allowing 100 per cent foreign direct investment (FDI), for developing integrated townships, comprising residential and commercial spaces, including 'hotels, resorts, city and regional level urban infrastructure facilities such as roads and bridges, mass rapid transit systems'.

Gurgaon represented an early prototype for private urban development of this ambition and scale. Although the town started as an automobile manufacturing hub in the 1980s, private players such as Delhi Land and Finance (DLF) quickly spotted the new opportunities in the information technology (IT) and business process outsourcing (BPO) sectors. Leveraging the demand for office space on the outskirts of Delhi, private developers kick-started the development of a satellite city. General Electric was the first of the multinationals to move in, followed quickly by American

Express. Over the next quarter century, Gurgaon became the hub for multinational tech giants such as Motorola, Google, Dell, IBM and other Fortune 500 companies, and home to a burgeoning population of young IT and services professionals (Rajagopalan and Tabarrok, 2013).

This vibrancy, however, came at a cost. By 2013, Gurgaon had a plethora of shopping malls, golf courses and five-star hotels, but lacked citywide sewage, water and electricity systems (Rajagopalan and Tabarrok, 2013: 5). In other words, 'Gurgaon looks like Singapore in terms of private-sector development, but like other Indian cities in terms of public-sector development.'

In contrast, from its very genesis near the tribal hamlet of Sakchi in eastern Bihar, Jamshedpur was conceived as a masterplanned city, 'with wide streets', in the famous words of Jamsetji Tata, 'planted with shady trees, every other of quick variety', 'plenty of space for lawns and gardens', 'large areas for football, hockey and parks' and 'areas for Hindu temples, Mohammedan mosques and Christian churches' (quoted in Sinha and Singh, 2011: 265). Built around the economic locus of the Tata steel plant, Jamshedpur's foundations were laid by a series of landmark plans over the early decades of the 20th century. Moreover, for most of the first 100 years of its existence, Tata Steel provided Jamshedpur's resident-employees with high-quality basic services—water, sanitation, electricity, schools, medical and recreational facilities— free of charge. These early and concerted investments have yielded long-term dividends. The city has come to be recognised for its enviable quality-of-life indicators, and is one of the few cities in India to have received the ISO 14001 (EMS) certification for civic and municipal services (Sridhar and Verma, 2013).

Less prominent than Gurgaon, Jamshedpur has nonetheless proved to be a highly influential precursor to a lineage of greenfield 'steel towns' such as Bhilai, Bokaro, Durgapur and Rourkela (Sivaramakrishnan, 2009). Indeed, as the late K. C. Sivaramakrishnan underlined, in the new millennium, this broader company-town model, both private sector and public sector, provided an important template for the governance of the SEZs.

It is worth asking, then: What are the constitutive elements of the company-town model? What is the logic that animates it?

THE LOGIC OF THE COMPANY TOWN

To understand why the company town has emerged as such a durable template for private urban development in India, it is useful to return to the Gurgaon model.

Economists would read Gurgaon's maladies as a classic case of market failure, resulting from private provision of public goods and the failure to internalise the externalities associated with such private provision. To consider one example, private sewage lines in Gurgaon end up in tanks because there is no comprehensive sewage system. This sewage must then be periodically dumped, often into water sources and commons (Rajagopalan and Tabarrok, 2015). The result is the pollution of these groundwater sources over the long term, disproportionately affecting slum and low-income populations. In this way, Gurgaon's sanitation crisis reflects the well-known limitations of private provision of public goods.

Coming from a libertarian perspective, however, economists Rajagopalan and Tabarrok make a provocative proposal: Why not allow private developers to purchase and develop areas large enough to constitute a city of their own? The opportunity to internalise costs and earn rents would then provide adequate incentive for such a proprietor to plan for, and supply, high-quality civic infrastructure for water, sewage and power.

The broader principle that animates this conceptualisation of the 'proprietary city' also explains Jamshedpur's success in this view. As Rajagopalan and Tabarrok put it in a *New York Times* op-ed: 'Jamshedpur works because Tata owned enough land so that it had the right incentives to plan and invest in citywide infrastructure' (2015).

COMPANY TOWN AND PROPRIETARY CITY

While the notion of the proprietary city suggests a valuable lens to examine the Jamshedpur case, it is equally important to consider its history in light of the longer lineage of company towns round the world.

The earliest archetypes of company towns emerged in fact in industrialising Britain, in places such as New Lanark, built in 1816, to the Cadbury town Bournville, built in 1879 (Porteous, 1970). They were an urban innovation, particularly suited to the expanding American frontier, and came to be widely adapted in the

United States, starting with centres such as Pullman, near Chicago, a major centre of rail car production, or Hershey, Pennsylvania, and Scotia, California (Snider, 2014). All of these, like Jamshedpur, Bokaro and Rourkela in 20th century India, were towns built by employers to house employee populations.

Yet, the sheer growth in the number of company towns across the United States, United Kingdom, Latin America, Asia and Africa complicated all attempts at definition: at one point, there were 3,000 company towns in the United States alone (Schumpeter, 2011).

A broad definition, focusing on a single owner rather than the single employer, came closer to the Rajagopalan and Tabarrok conceptualisation of the proprietary city:

> The company town, a settlement completely owned, built and operated by an individual or corporate entrepreneur, is essentially a temporary pioneering device, especially suited to conditions obtaining in nations undergoing rapid economic development (Porteous, 1970: 127).

In pulling together the elements that make up the company town, a close linkage with employment and a unified, often private, pattern of ownership would seem to be fundamental. Porteous added another (ibid.). In the company town, the 'entrepreneur' remained the dominant political actor, and the official status remained 'unincorporated', i.e., without formal government. Indeed, as Sivaramakrishnan (2009) noted, India's company towns, such as Bokaro and Rourkela, similarly relied on informal arrangements that vested immense power in company officials in matters of urban governance.[1]

Another dimension common to company towns worldwide was spatial planning or at least a uniform architectural sensibility. Yet the scope of planning in these myriad company towns sometimes failed to be comprehensive, and in cases where the planning failed to account for future growth, shanty towns inevitably arose (Porteous, 1970).

Other connections can be seen between the company town and the 'company estate' (ibid.: 128). The latter associated with primary-sector activities, whether the tea estate or rubber plantation, has an equally storied lineage in India. At the other end of the spectrum, the Indian company town also bears an undeniable resemblance to the Cantonment, where the defence services is the benevolent employer, as well as to a wide range of public-sector townships and colonies. Indeed, in his landmark 1977 study of new towns in India, Sivaramakrishnan counted a myriad of public-sector townships, whether in metropolitan areas close to Bangalore and Chennai, or remote sites like Bokaro (1978).

POLICY FRAMEWORK FOR PROPRIETARY CITIES?

Deconstructed, the company town/proprietary city model comprises several discrete but related elements that bear close kinship to an emerging policy architecture for greenfield and private urban development in India in the new millennium.

Sood calls this policy framework 'corporate urbanism'. If the company town is a historical category, and the proprietary city its conceptual reification, 'corporate urbanism' can be said to embody the policy realisation of this ideal (2015).

The defining characteristic of such corporate urbanism is the transfer of key municipal functions to 'private governments', at the local level (ibid.: 1; Glasze, 2005). These powers and functions include the provision of basic services and infrastructures, social and physical, decision making and planning powers, as well as tax collection and disbursal powers. The legal scaffolding derives largely from the 'industrial township' exception in the 74th Constitutional Amendment, which allows for certain urban areas to remain exempt from the requirement of elected municipal government under the Amendment (Sivaramakrishnan, 2009). The adoption of the industrial township exception, combining differential services provision with non-representative forms of governance, represents a clear echo of India's company towns.[2]

Special Economic Zones, Special Investment Regions, or the integrated industrial townships proposed along the Delhi–Mumbai Industrial Corridor provide glimpses of this corporate urbanism (Sood, 2015). Policy apparatuses, not only at the central (Table 1) but also at the state level, have widely adopted features of corporate urbanism, with or without the invocation of the 'industrial township' clause. Interestingly, at both the state and central level, these policy and legislative initiatives have largely been led by ministries and departments of industry and commerce rather than those of urban development (Sood, 2015; Sivaramakrishnan, 2009).

Table 1: Facilitating Corporate Urbanism—Central Policies

Policy	Size
SEZ Act 2005 ♦ ♦ And Rules (SEZ Rules incorporating amendments up to July, 2010)*"	Various, 10—5,000 hectares depending on category; up to 50 per cent 'non-processing zone'
National Manufacturing Policy (NIMZ) ♠ & 2011	Minimum 5,000 hectares

Source: Extracted from Sood (2015).

Thus, vital to the policy momentum is a focus on infrastructure development as an instrument of economic growth and a locus of investment flows. Corporate urbanism can thus be seen to lie at the intersection of urban development and economic growth strategies.

Most intriguing, however, is the way that the policy model addresses or departs from both some of the dilemmas posed by the company-town model and the orthodoxies of the proprietary city. On the one hand, the focus in policy architecture remains on the developer usually, though not always, distinct from the primary employer. Although single-employer SEZs are not uncommon, a more diverse mix of employers and industries augurs a sturdier economic basis; historically, reliance on a single employer, in the face of changing fortunes in an era of globalisation, has undone many a company town. Perhaps the most important considerations around these sites of corporate urbanism revolve around their expanse. Size can be a key index of inclusivity. Excepting high-rise developments, the larger the size and scope of a city in this mode, the larger and more diverse is the population it may be able to accommodate. Even Rajagopalan and Tabarrok's vision of the proprietary city requires a property size large enough to ensure a degree of self-sufficiency.

The policy framework for corporate urbanism shows a mixed record on this front. As Table 1 shows, only the largest SEZs in Gujarat meet this criterion. Moreover, not all SEZs include a residential component. However, newer policy-promoted nodes, e.g., along the DMIC, are far more ambitious in their attempt to integrate a wide variety of land uses.

COMPANY TOWN AND SHADOW SETTLEMENT

The company town/proprietary city is no mere relic of India's pre-Independence and post-Independence past. Instead, it may come to shape a vast swathe of India's urban future. The question emerges: What can we learn from the history of India's company towns that can provide us pointers to an emergent mode of corporate urbanism?

It is important here to widen the perspective from the specificity of Jamshedpur to the broader lineage of the company town in India. As a vibrant million-plus agglomeration, Jamshedpur has come to be seen as the proprietary city par excellence. It is, however, only the first in a line of steel towns—Bokaro, in contemporary Jharkhand; Chhattisgarh's Bhilai; and Rourkela in Odisha—which display unmistakable parallels with the patterns and pathologies of growth and governance seen in Jamshedpur.

Much of the literature on India's steel towns has derived from ethnographic studies and has tended to foreground issues of labour relations and ethnic identities. Even though much of this scholarship has lacked an explicit spatial focus, it offers intriguing insights about the inclusions and exclusions built into the masterplanning and urban governance processes around India's 'old new towns'.

WHO BELONGS IN THE PLAN?

One resounding theme to emerge from studies of India's company towns is that the plan generates exclusions (Kennedy and Sood, 2016). Although comprehensive masterplanning was the sine qua non of India's company towns, planned housing and infrastructure rarely sufficed for the mass of unskilled and semi-skilled workers employed at these sites. The growing industrial workforce and populations of these towns further exacerbated gaps between need and provision.

These processes, although common to many company towns, were most starkly documented in Jamshedpur. Starting from about 4,000 in the early 1900s, by the 1920s, TISCO's workforce was just over 30,000 (Simeon, 1995). The population of Jamshedpur town in the 1921 Census was about 57,000. From the beginning, the city was plagued by housing shortages. Early commentators reported that TISCO-provided housing could house no more than a seventh of the population. Bahl (1995, 116) notes that in the late 1920s, TISCO's approximately 5,500 *pucca* houses and bungalows housed 10,000 of their skilled and semi-skilled employees, but the unskilled workforce was left to fend for itself.[3] Not being eligible for housing loan advances, these workers built *kutcha* huts that often housed upto eight persons in cramped conditions (ibid.).

Disparities in quality and access to housing were thus an integral, even if unintended, feature of the company town plan. These disparities were also reflected in the provision of services in Jamshedpur's early years. The 'skeletal' sewage system served the bungalows and pucca houses, while bustees lacked both proper sewage networks and water supply (ibid.). Bahl argues further that the entire machinery of the town, from retail to schooling, was geared towards the higher skilled workers (ibid.).

A second set of concerns arises from the close link between access to secure employment and access to high-quality housing in the company town. Unskilled and non-permanent employees always remained outside the ambit of housing provision in the company town, but changing labour regimes in the 1990s meant that the category of the permanent employee was itself a shrinking one. Sanchez echoes these concerns in the Jamshedpur case (2012a, 2012b). Through the course of the 20th century, Jamshedpur had come to be seen as an epitome of 'corporate paternalism', with high wages and secure employment, accompanied by access to company housing and welfare schemes. However, the decades since liberalisation saw increasing casualisation of the workforce, with access to company housing and healthcare becoming equally precarious. Thus, in key ways, the right to the city in the company town came to be mediated by the increasingly elusive promise of 'formal' and 'permanent' employment.

As Dupont argues in the case of post-Independence Delhi, workplace hierarchies were reproduced in housing arrangements in Jamshedpur (2004). Residential neighbourhoods were segregated by employee rank and earning levels (Bahl, 1995).

Scholarship on steel towns such as Rourkela and Bhilai shows how these patterns of class segregation also mirrored patterns of ethnic segregation. Parry and Strumpell argue that patterns of ethnic conflict were woven into the very fabric of industrial relations in

Bhilai and Rourkela, Nehru's famous 'temples to India's industrial modernity' (2008: 47). In Rourkela, even as early as 1959, a state government commission found that Oriyas were well-represented among Class 4 employees, but woefully under-represented among Class 1 and 2 employees (less than 12 per cent of the workforce in this category). In Bhilai, the percentage of Chhattisgarhis among the regular workforce was even lower.

The effects of such socio-spatial segregation played out in many ways in Rourkela (ibid.: 47). Oriyas and other ethnicities lived in the township, where their children could attend high-quality township schools. The Adivasis lived in the resettlement colonies, where schools were run by the state government and were of poorer quality.

Thus, the spilling over of patterns of economic segregation and exclusion into ethnic division would appear to have been a durable feature of the Indian company-town experience. Findings from census data suggest that these disparities find a clear spatial correlate in differences between the core company town and the shadow towns that have grown up around them.

BACK TO THE FUTURE OF THE PROPRIETARY CITY

Over the course of decades, these histories have left an unmistakable imprint on these company towns and their surrounds. The clearest symptom of these disparities can be seen in the fast growing, but poorly provisioned, shadow urban settlements that have emerged around the core company towns. Of the steel towns that have still evolved into urban agglomerations without urban local bodies are Bokaro Steel City's Chas, Rourkela Industrial Township's namesake Municipal Corporation Area, and Jamshedpur Notified Area Committee (NAC)'s Mango, Jugsalai and Adityapur.

Interestingly, recent work analysing Census 2011 data shows that some of these shadow towns have far outstripped the core company town in terms of population density, growth, and in some cases, even population (Sood, 2016). For example, Rourkela Municipal Corporation houses nearly 1.5 times the population of the Industrial Township at five times the density. Although Jamshedpur NAC continues to be the largest urban centre within the million-plus urban agglomeration, Mango, Jugsalai and Adityapur have seen far higher rates of growth as compared to Jamshedpur NAC.

Census data from 2011 and preceding decades reveal how patterns of differentiation in the provision of physical and social infrastructure persist over time. Despite their fast growth, shadow settlements continue to lag behind in key services. Thus, in 2011, for example, Rourkela Industrial Township had fewer allopathic hospitals than the Municipal Corporation, but nearly four times the number of hospital beds and doctors. The case of Bokaro was far starker. With three times the population of Chas, Bokaro Steel City had eight allopathic hospitals to one in Chas. It had 40 times the number of beds and doctors.

Similarly, Jamshedpur NAC showed the most remarkable disparities vis-à-vis the shadow towns, with primary, middle and secondary schools being disproportionately concentrated in the core company town compared to its neighbours.

Even in glimpses, empirical data provides remarkable testimony to the durability of the exclusions built into the company-town model. These exclusions continue to be mirrored in the unequal provisioning of social and physical infrastructures in emergent shadow settlements.

CONCLUSION

The renewal of policy interest in private forms of urban development is unfolding against the backdrop of growing urban population and the unforgiving fiscal capacity constraints faced by governments at all levels in India. This policy agenda has coincided with a growing commitment to the development of greenfield urban nodes as loci of global capital flows and as engines of economic growth. The burgeoning SEZs, SIRs and integrated industrial townships of the new millennium represent concrete embodiments of a 'corporate urbanism' model, which transfers the powers and functions of urban local bodies, both planning and governance, to 'private governments'.

Against the undeniable failures of the Gurgaon model of urban development, the company town/proprietary city template embodied by Jamshedpur has come to influence the imaginations of commentators and policymakers alike. Although Rajagopalan and Tabarrok provide the clearest articulation and defence of this paradigm of urban development, Indian policymakers from the beginning of this millennium have put into practice many of the aspects of the model (2014).

Nonetheless, the history of company towns in India offers a rich case study of the ramifications of privatised models of planning and governance. Exclusions are built into the masterplanning process itself. Even starting with the intent to house migrant and non-migrant workers, India's private and public sector steel towns in fact accommodated only a fraction of their entire workforce. The result of this originating disparity has left a clear spatial trail on the surrounding region, fostering fast growing but poorly provisioned shadow settlements. Policymakers would do well to learn from the growth trajectories of these company towns in order to best plan for success in India's emerging urban nodes.

◆

NOTES

1. In India, some company towns, such as Bhilai, have over time gained municipal governments under the 74th Constitutional Amendment Act.

2. See Sivaramakrishnan (2009). Urban centres such as Jamshedpur and Bokaro have relied on other specialised governance instruments, such as the 'notified area committee'.

3. Simeon (1995: 15) quotes management sources that state that in 1938, 8,150 housing units had been built by employees. The same sources claim that by 1938, company-constructed and employee-constructed (11,000 units) housing accommodated nearly 70 per cent of the workforce.

REFERENCES

Bahl, V., 1995. *The Making of the Indian Working Class: A Case of the Tata Iron and Steel Company, 1880–1946.* New Delhi: Sage Publications Pvt. Ltd.

Dupont, V. 2004. 'Socio-spatial Differentiation and Residential Segregation in Delhi: A Question of Scale', *Geoforum*, 35 (2), pp. 157–75.

Glasze, G., 2005. 'Some reflections on the Economic and Political Organisation of Private Neighbourhoods', *Housing Studies*, 20 (2), pp. 221–33.

Kennedy, L. and A. Sood. 2016. 'Greenfield Development as Tabula Rasa', *Economic & Political Weekly*, 51 (17), p. 41.

Kling, B. B. 1998.'Paternalism in Indian Labour: The Tata Iron and Steel Company of Jamshedpur', *International Labour and Working-Class History*, 53, pp. 69–87.

Parry, J. and C. Strumpell. 2008. 'On the Desecration of Nehru's "Temples": Bhilai and Rourkela Compared', *Economic & Political Weekly*, 43 (19), pp. 47–57.

Polanki, Pallavi. 2012. 'The Great Gurgaon Experiment: Has it Failed?', *Firstpost.com*, 24 April.

Porteous, J. D. 1970. 'The Nature of the Company Town', *Transactions of the Institute of British Geographers*, 51, pp. 127–42.

Rajagopalan, S. and A. Tabarrok. 2013. 'Lessons from Gurgaon, India's Private City', Department of Economics Working Paper Nos. 14–32, George Mason University. Republished in David Emanuel Andersson and Stefano Moroni (eds.) (2014), *Cities and Private Planning: Property Rights, Entrepreneurship and Transaction Costs.* UK: Edward Elgar Publishing, p. 199.

———. 2015. 'Designing Private Cities, Open to All', *New York Times*, 18 March.

Sankhe, S., I. Vittal, R. Dobbs, A. Mohan and A. Gulati. 2010. *India's Urban Awakening: Building Inclusive Cities and Sustaining Economic Growth.* Mumbai: McKinsey Global Institute, McKinsey & Company.

Sanchez, A. 2012a. 'Deadwood and Paternalism: Rationalising Casual Labour in an Indian Company Town', *Journal of the Royal Anthropological Institute*, 18 (4), pp. 808–27.

———. 2012b. 'Questioning Success: Dispossession and the Criminal Entrepreneur in Urban India', *Critique of Anthropology*, 32 (4), pp. 435–57.

Schumpeter. 2011. 'Company Towns: The Universal Provider', *The Economist*, 19 January.

Simeon, D. 1995. *The Politics of Labour Under Late Colonialism: Workers, Unions, and the State in Chota Nagpur, 1928–1939.* Delhi: Manohar Publishers.

Sinha, A. and J. Singh. 2011. 'Jamshedpur: Planning an Ideal Steel City in India', *Journal of Planning History*, 10, p. 263.

Sivaramakrishnan, K. C. 1978. *New Towns in India: A Report on a Study of Selected New Towns in Eastern Region.* Calcutta: Indian Institute of Management.

———. 2009.'Special Economic Zones: Issues of Urban Growth and Management', in *Special Economic Zones: Promise, Performance and Pending Issues.* New Delhi: Centre for Policy Research Occasional Paper.

Snider, Bruce D., 2014. 'In Good Company: Company Towns across the U.S.', *Preservation,* 1 July.

Sood, A. 2015. 'Industrial Townships and the Policy Facilitation of Corporate Urbanisation in India', *Urban Studies,* 52 (8).

———. 2016.'Slum in the Landscape of Gating: Industrial Policy and Urban Development in India.' Paper presented at International Seminar on 'Sustainable and Inclusive Urban Development in India: Learning from International Experiences and Devising Future Strategies.' August. New Delhi.

Sridhar, K. S. and S. Verma. 2013. 'A Way out of Urban Chaos', *The Hindu*, 4 October.

THE LOGISTICAL CITY*

RANABIR
SAMADDAR

While concluding our work on the new town in Rajarhat near Kolkata, we had brought in the concept of the logistical city (Dey, et al., 2013). In this brief essay, I want to carry this forward and discuss the transformation of the city into a logistical entity.

Three pillars of this transformation are: infrastructure, rent and migrant labour. Infrastructure makes the city a network of logistical practices. Rent becomes a main source of urban wealth. Transit labour makes the infrastructural and rental transformation of the city possible.

One of the main dimensions of the contemporary turn towards neo-liberal urbanisation in developing countries is that it compels the city to be a logistical hub, which requires a certain mode of infrastructural reordering and expansion of the city. The crucial thing to note is that in the process of transforming into a logistical hub, the city also becomes a site of extraction. It thereby becomes a rental site. Such a city survives on the extraction of physical capacity, air, waste, soil, water and other conceivable resources. At the same time, investment in land becomes an important outlet of capital. The postcolonial milieu of this double transformation makes more acute the contradictions between the urban policy regime and neo-liberal urbanity as a whole. These contradictions revolve around two crucial issues: (i) the relation between labour and urban space in this transformation, and (ii) the transformation of the city into a rental outlet, based on localised concentrations of migrant labour, a complex of place-based services to support the logistical economy and a maddening rush for extraction. The migrant stands at the centre of these relations.

◆◆◆

Let me first briefly turn to the issue of the city as an extractive site on its way to becoming a logistical city. The significance of extraction is that it represents the infrastructural self of the city in an almost natural way, so much so that we often forget that while infrastructure calls for extraction (say, iron ore or land), extraction also presupposes a particular form of urban infrastructural set up.

Therefore, I want to begin with the most fundamental of the extractive activity in the urban economy, viz., waste disposal or reprocessing, and the urban infrastructure ordered around it. In recent times, the logistics of waste has attained political significance, whether in the form of managing population segments or reprocessing the elements of waste back into the production process, such as reprocessing e-waste. Waste has acquired a contradictory character. At one level, waste, with its chief function being the engagement of migrant labour for reprocessing, will appear as a marginal element in the urban economy. Yet, at another level, waste reprocessing as an industry occupies a central role in the contemporary logic of capital accumulation. The logistics of waste collection, clearance, vending, reprocessing and disposal are issues pertaining to the circulation of commodity, transportation, and organising and institutionalising the sites of reprocessing and venues of sale of commodities (from cots, furniture, paper, battery, transistor sets, shoes, flower pots, dress, clothing, books, scrap metals, to human hair, mother's milk, the human womb, and all that surrounds us in our daily lives). The logistical organisation of waste reprocessing, while occupying the margin of neo-liberal modernity in this way symbolises a complex and, ironically, a central place in the city of our time.

What, then, is waste? What is reprocessing? The answers in short will be: Waste is that product which will not enter into the value chain any more. Reprocessing is that logistical dynamic which brings the so-called non-productive back into the production chain. Waste reprocessing is the eternal deferral of the end of the production chain.

This logistical organisation, of course, has a profound territorial aspect. What does it mean when we say that certain areas in the city are polluted, or some people live near or even inside a dump or in a cement or iron pipe, or that certain areas in the city are known for cheap second-hand goods (perhaps old mobiles, DVD players, computers, printers and hi-fi stereos), or certain areas must be free from industrial and chemical effluents, and such a site of pollution must be shifted somewhere else? What does it mean to say that the city produces waste, which must be managed, if the city has to live and reproduce itself? What is the implication, in other words, of waste on space and management of the circulation of a commodity called waste? Against the background of neo-liberal restructuring of the city, these questions reflect on the links between urban policy, governance, forms of labour, migration and urban rent. If we look at Kolkata, at one level we can simply say that the problem reflects the relationship between ecological space, economic space and political space, but at another, perhaps deeper, level, the problem tells of the way capital operates by first colonising a space and then making the unproductive a productive element of economy. These sites of extraction, thus, are not wastelands of capital as the late economist Kalyan Sanyal (2007) described them, but marks of a circulation economy that a city has come to represent. Recycling, simply put, is valorising. It is, if you like, the urban image of a centuries-old process of extracting minerals.

Chandni Chowk, at the heart of Kolkata, is a site of reprocessing of several forms of waste. To quote one observer,

> Rows of sweatshops, thin benches outside these shops, on the side of the streets, and thousands of workers disassembling, and re-assembling, old electronic devices and household appliances of every sort mark the place. A newspaper remarked of the activity, 'What is trash in the West is cash east of the Hooghly'.[1]

Narrow shops, narrow lanes, busy labour and exchange of cash will tell you of the circulation of commodities coming from China or Korea (television sets, refrigerators or mobile phones), which now get their second life.

But Chandni Chowk is not the only such place in Kolkata. There is Bagri Market, Chor Bazar, and then scores of places where newspapers and several other discarded goods are being brought, sifted, categorised, reprocessed, repackaged and sold. These are also places of transferring goods from wholesale to retail sale. Likewise, new flesh-reprocessing areas have cropped up, places of trading in flesh and human organs. In the areas adjoining Kolkata port, the city has other earmarked places for trading in, and circulation of, various types of commodities, including care and service as commodity. Delhi has service villages, as does Kolkata in the new town of Rajarhat. Care centres supplying caregivers (ayahs) too have their logistical emplacement in the city. These places tell us of the city as a grid of movements and services—a logistical grid. They also tell us of certain kinds of supply chains. These supply chains are mostly subaltern in nature. Thus, trafficking of flesh and goods, for which Kolkata, like Mumbai and all other port cities, has been long infamous, requires its logistical set up involving reconnaissance, knowledge of routes, supply depots, consumption chains, exchange points and an involvement with the legal surface of the activity (including stations of policing and surveillance, and posts of excise and customs inspection).

◆◆◆

Yet we must not think that the metamorphosis of the city into a logistical site takes place only along para-legal and illegal lines. Or that this metamorphosis is taking place only in big cities like Kolkata or Delhi or Mumbai. In some sense, this is equally evident in what may be called 'borderland cities' like Siliguri or Imphal where modes of spatial control are issues of fierce contention. The formal infrastructural expansion of the city is the official way in which the city as a logistical entity announces its arrival. An enormous amount of energy is spent on passing appropriate laws, formulating policies, setting up boards and committees, imagining a city as a region like the national capital region or the greater Kolkata vision of KMDA (Kolkata Metropolitan Development Authority, *Vision 2020*), etc.

Consider this select list of enactments and policies, really a severely selected list, towards this urban restructuring to a logistical entity, whose raison d'être will be to facilitate transportation, communication, and the circulation of men (and now women also), money, credit, information and goods: Delhi Master Plan; Standard

Operating Procedures (SOP) for Child Protection by Indian Railways; Calcutta 300: Plan for Metropolitan Development; Manual Scavengers and Construction of Dry Latrine (Prohibition) Act; Building and Other Construction Workers Welfare Act (1996); *Samajik Mukti* Card for Building and Other Construction Workers; Unorganised Sector Social Security Act; Maharashtra Slum Areas Act, Second Amendment; Maharashtra Private Security Guards (Registration of Employment and Welfare) Act; Jawaharlal Nehru National Urban Renewal Mission; Mumbai Urban Transport Project; Mumbai Urban Infrastructure Project; Revised Development Plan of Greater Bombay; Smart Cities Mission; New Towns (in contrast to ghost towns) policy; National Policy for Hawkers; and several others.

This vast range of policies, measures, acts and plans backed by money, and to be implemented mostly in the mode of private–public partnership (PPP), necessitates one thing which is constant (besides raw material like cement, steel, glass, electronics material, and financial and credit infrastructure)—and that is migrant labour, or what I have called here transit labour. By transit labour I mean labour is in transit form: labour engaged in creating places of transit like roads, ports, flyovers, tunnels, ATM kiosks; transit towns like Cyberabad in Hyderabad; warehouses, truck terminals, IT networks, including cables and poles; and labour that is engaged in transitory activities—in short, labour engaged in the circulation economy.

The phenomenon of transit labour becomes comprehensible when we keep in mind the conjunction of infrastructure, logistics and labour at which the Indian economy stands today. Hundreds of projects involving construction of the special economic zones (SEZs), power plants, airports, railway corridors, highways, bridges, new towns, new buildings and houses, flyovers, IT parks, data centres and other residential and commercial projects, need not only steel, cement, aluminium, fibre glass, among other materials, but also labour, particularly in the construction and mining sectors.

The construction industry is one of India's largest employers. Thousands of construction workers build new apartments and offices while living in squalor in roadside tents along the new buildings that come up in due course. They are like the informal miners of the country: migrants from the decimated agricultural sector, escaping poverty and disease at home, only to be sucked into a labour market which is characterised by exploitative labour practices, hazardous work conditions and environment, and almost complete social exclusion with almost no, or little, labour security, and their income varying in response to various sorts of fluctuations (seasonal or otherwise) in the demand for labour. Migrant workers move from one construction site to another, labour camp to labour camp. At times the entire family moves, at times the male members only. According to one report, on an average, one labourer dies in the city of Bangalore every day.[2] In all these sites, as in West Bengal, a local contact in the village supplies workers to the contractor. Both extract cuts from the wages paid to the labourers. There is no direct transaction between the builder and the labourers, and this system of sub-contracting frees the actual employers of all responsibilities towards the labour.

In Mumbai, consider the Bandra–Worli bridge that links Bandra and the western suburbs of Mumbai with Worli and downtown Mumbai; or the Thakur Village, a new residential township, which stands apart from other planned localities in Mumbai due to its spectacular skyline, with mostly upper-middle class citizens living there; or the Bandra–Kurla Commercial Complex under construction, which is to be the first of a series of what is called growth centres; the National Stock Exchange building at the Bandra–Kurla Complex; and ICICI Bank headquarters. In Bangalore, consider the Brigade Metropolis, an integrated enclave located on Whitefield Road; the flyover to connect the city centre of Bangalore with the Electronic City, an industrial park which houses more than 100 industries, with around 60,000 employees; or in Delhi, thousands of labourers building the Airport City, the national highway leading to Gurgaon—these are all parables of the current phenomenon of transit labour, because these places symbolise the conjunction of infrastructure, logistics and labour. Add to that the construction of several fast corridors, smart cities and SEZs in various parts of the country, and we get a fair idea of the conjunction earlier mentioned.

But we have to be mindful: these facts do not tell us of a story of seamless hyper-urbanisation, although the impact of urbanisation in terms of resource transfer and perceivable increase in employment opportunities (particularly in the unorganised sectors) is far greater than what the official figures suggest. They tell us of a deep-seated contradiction between the two images of the city—as an engine of economic growth through infrastructural expansion, and as a site of breakdown of an integral entity called the city. With spaces carved out to suit logistical practices, Indian cities, after the outbreak of neo-liberal reforms in the 1990s, are beginning to appear as sites of continuous fragmentation and gentrification, as well as ruralisation.

Yet readers will notice that I am trying to avoid the old imageries like gentrification or political society, because these are only sociological appearances beneath which a deeper structural transformation is taking place, viz., the city, in order to survive, must become a logistical hub. Never before had the city been so deeply caught in the logic of global supply chains.

In such a situation, the city becomes a rental outlet. Along with interest, rent becomes perhaps the most crucial component of urban wealth.

The logistical expansion of the city on the one hand gives rise to Third World mega-urbanisation, but on the other, it resurrects the rent factor from oblivion in a capitalist economy. Through rental earning, the bourgeois economy makes up the loss it incurs in industrial investment. Rent and interest become the new images of profit; indeed they are at times intertwined. Yet the return of capital to rent does not signify a Hegelian onward journey of some original form—an unfolding. It is important to ask: What does the revival of the rent question mean for postcolonial accumulation? Is this a recent phenomenon? Perhaps—but urban wealth always had something to do with rental income. Significantly, Thomas Picketty, in his investigation of capital in the 21st century, discussed many of the 'original' factors (such as rent, income, public debt, inheritance) in the production of wealth. He said,

> ... every reader knew full well that it took a capital on the order of 1 million francs to produce an annual rent of 50,000 francs..., no matter whether the investment was in government bonds or land.... For nineteenth century novelists and their readers, the equivalence between capital and annual rent was obvious, and there was no difficulty in moving from one measuring scale to the other, as if the two were perfectly synonymous (2014: 207).

As we know, landed property presupposes some persons (in India it includes the state, the *eminent domain*) enjoying the monopoly of disposing of particular portions of earth as exclusive spheres of their private will to the exclusion of all others. Once this is given, it is a matter of developing the economic value of this monopoly, i.e., valorising it on the basis of capitalist production. At least two things should draw our attention here: This extraction of ground rent is not pre-capitalist, but a phenomenon intrinsic to capitalism and bourgeois rule as a whole; and second, the economic value of the monopoly is nothing if not developed through its valorisation on the basis of the capitalist mode. But something more happens. The postcolonial bourgeoisie, in search of extra profit, becomes a hound. The mad rush for land by Indian capitalists is governed by this search for surplus profit, no matter the social cost. Thus, on this consideration, they may like to invest in, say, a town in Telengana or Andhra Pradesh instead of, say, West Bengal or Haryana. In other words, the neo-liberal urban economy facilitates accumulation on the basis of the bourgeoisie's surplus profit. Surplus profit transforms into ground rent. Landed property is here merely the cause for transferring a portion of the commodity-price from one person to another, from the capitalist to the landlord. Think of Gurgaon near Delhi, or other growing settlements on the outskirts of Delhi (and thus the significance of the National Capital Region), or Navi Mumbai, or the land deals on the eastern fringes of Kolkata, including Rajarhat.

What happens to the rent of buildings, of mines, and the price of land? What happens to the rent of bridges, highways, houses, steel and glass buildings, shopping malls, gigantic showrooms, multiplexes, airport cities, studios, cables, poles, transmission towers, dish antennas, ATM kiosks, data centres like Belapur in Mumbai, and other creations of developers and financiers? What happens to the interface of rent and interest (with interest rate becoming crucial to developers)? Again, they show that the question here relates to 'excess'—excess of what we may call average profit, excess of the surplus-value characteristic of a particular sphere of production; in other words, not the net product, but the excess of the net product in this sector over the net product of other branches of industry. In other words, the boundaries of postcolonial accumulation, though made by the fundamental dynamics of capital, are influenced to a great extent by the illusions that the same process of accumulation creates. We have indicated already what informal labour means in the context of the neo-liberal transformation of the city into a rental outlet, such as a forcible increase in surplus labour time (through unregulated long working hours, increasingly dense physical labour, the relative absence of labour laws and labour security, labour deregulation, discrimination on the basis of caste and gender, etc.). It produces not only surplus value, but also surplus profit, in as much as we have seen that at times, without much increase in constant capital, surplus profit is created through the dynamics of rent and interest.

The city will now survive on the basis of rental income, the way this income will be distributed among public institutions, private individuals, banks and other lending agencies, and the extent to which part of this will be spent on retaining and reinforcing the public character of the city. But the phrase 'public character of the city' may be misleading, because this will mean in turn a particular form of the so-called public character, only that form which will facilitate the kind of accumulation indicated in the preceding paragraphs. The labour that makes such a transformation possible will be there in city life, but invisibly. Labour is the vanishing mediator in this neo-liberal metamorphosis.

The neo-liberal city encapsulates the central social contradiction of modern global capitalism, viz., increased return from global connectedness accompanied by hyper-commodification and financialisation of land and new forms of social marginalisation, most notably the increasing informality and precarious nature of labour and life. Migrant labour represents this contradiction. The infrastructural transformation (including financial and informational infrastructure) of the city we have spoken of is not possible without migrant labour, and yet infrastructural transformation requires migrant labour to be invisible, dispensable, but ready at hand.

◆◆◆

One has to ask: With neo-liberal capitalism revolving around logistical expansion, does the neo-liberal city symbolise infrastructural power (and some say 'infrastructural sovereignty'), and how much can the city be a 'state'? Even with all the Weberian attributes of a modern bureaucracy, can professional government agencies control the movement of the migrants and settle the population of a city? At the same time, can these professional government agencies, faced with all the republican demands of citizenship, free themselves, at least partially, from dependence on the fiscal resources generated from the capacity of the state to extract revenues from the private sector, which turns the city into a site of rental and other forms of extraction? More important, what is the nature of capital that sticks like a parasite on the logistical city?

Partly, the outcome will depend on the social struggles around the resources of the city, including, and primarily around, land. The fight for space will be relentless, occasionally put in check by governmental interventions. This will be the bloody nature of the 'right to city'. And the central question in this will be around the place of the migrant labour. We shall have to ask: What is the transformation in the nature of urban labour that can be now described only by the term, *transit labour*, in which all the features of migrant labour in a neo-liberal milieu are congealed? As indicated in the Rajarhat book mentioned at the outset, the political question of claims over the city—*the city as territory*—will also reflect on the hidden processes of the shift of the modern city as a site of industrial production to a site of logistics-based economy, which requires, besides localised concentrations of human capital, place-based services to support logistical operations. In such situations, general politics will crystallise to a great extent around the city.

This *urban turn* is now dominant in postcolonial thinking, exactly like 40 years ago when the rural defined the postcolonial. It suggests: (i) infrastructure reorganises the city in a way that not only fragments work and reproduces old social conditions, but calls for the permanent presence of the migrant as the impossible but necessary factor in this process; (ii) this reorganisation of the city is also a reorganisation of space that depends on rent economy; (iii) yet, the reorganised city (always in the process of reorganisation) in terms of urban governance has a permanent problem posed by the anomalous figure of the migrant, the migrant labourer, who cannot be dispensed with and who cannot be settled; and (iv) consequent to all these, the city is not a harmonious entity brimming with the energy of the citizens, but an extremely contentious place marked by groups of people fighting for resources, space, rights, claims and justice. I think that urban politics in Kolkata or Delhi symbolises these salient features of our time.

This, of course, challenges the hypothesis of the 'bypass model' of urbanisation made famous by postcolonial theorists. The urban recycling, as one observer puts it, facilitates a continuous juxtaposition of displacement and accumulation of human and other resources as part of the urbanisation process. It is a process where tenancy makes little sense, because struggles over time, territory, family structures and occupational patterns increasingly take place in and around dwelling/work areas. If we go back to the earlier point of waste, is it not a fact that the act of aggregation and segregation of waste is at the heart of the informal urban economy, which in turn moulds the relationship between the contingencies of occupation and social reproduction of urban space? This is true of not only Kolkata but also Mumbai, where, for instance, garment manufacturing units in a place like Dharavi once again demonstrate the interrelated dynamics of work, workplace and shelter that on the one hand enable the urban economy to extract maximum labour from a migrant worker, but on the other hand keep the worker homeless and in a precarious condition.

Recall the classic study by Arjan De Hann (1997) on the migrant jute workers in Kolkata[3] and contrast it with an exhaustive report on Kolkata slums,[4] and we will understand the transformation of the migrant question. The scale and form of migration have changed. Informalisation of work is linked to the availability of migrant labour—whether in the scrap metal industry, or waste-processing zones, including processing of e-waste, or the care and entertainment industry that has expanded enormously, or the rental economy that has grown exponentially, requiring all kinds of new services to be performed by migrant labour. Yet what is important to remember is that migrant labour, with construction labour as the classic case, never settles. Rather, it unsettles the city. Roving bands of labour moving from one construction site to another remind us of the late 19th century phenomenon of destitute labour. At the same time, they indicate that the neo-liberal city is based on a combination of the most virtual and primitive forms of accumulation. In this paradoxical combination, migrant labour becomes *transit labour*.

More than a decade ago, Partha Chatterjee threw at us the by now famous question, 'Are Our Cities becoming Bourgeois at Last?'

I believe the observations put forward in this brief essay indicate the answer. Our cities are not becoming bourgeois at last (or, as Chatterjee put it, 'alas' in place of 'at last') in the sense of becoming integrated entities. The city as the ultimate republican entity, which will incorporate all its inhabitants on the basis of political equality notwithstanding other differences, will never materialise. The bourgeois dream of a city as the maximum republic conjoining industrial production, consumption, culture and politics of citizenship has been always a displaced site of a reality of competing claims, class conflicts and contentious politics. It is this reality that the city in its logistical form exacerbates. There will be no bourgeois city, but a logistical city.

◆

*I have drawn on a growing body of work by colleagues in Calcutta Research Group and Western Sydney University.[5,6] My acknowledgements go to them.

NOTES

1. Giorgio Grappi, 'Kolkata as Extraction Site', https://www.academia.edu/8938818/Kolkata_as_Extraction_Site - (accessed on 1 October 2016).

2. See http://msrelli.com/migrant-workers-in-india/ (accessed on 12 October 2015).

3. Based on the data of the 1960–80s, 'Unsettled Settlers: Migrant Workers and Industrial Capitalism in Calcutta', *Modern Asian Studies*, 31 (4), 1997, pp. 919–49.

4. See 'Urban Slum Reports: The Case of Kolkata', 2003, http://www.ucl.ac.uk/dpu-projects/Global_Report/pdfs/Kolkata.pdf - (accessed on 1 October 2016).

5. http://transitlabour.asia/home/

6. http://logisticalworlds.org

REFERENCES

Dey, Ishita, Ranabir Samaddar and Suhit K. Sen. 2013. *Beyond Kolkata: Rajarhat and the Dystopia of Urban Imagination*. New Delhi: Routledge.

Sanyal, Kalyan. 2007. *Rethinking Capitalist Development: Primitive Accumulation, Governmentality, and Postcolonial Capitalism*. New Delhi: Routledge.

Piketty, Thomas. 2014. *Capital in the Twenty-First Century*. Cambridge, MA: Harvard University Press.

◆◆

CITIES AND SMARTNESS

PRASAD
SHETTY
RUPALI
GUPTE

WHAT HAPPENED TO E-GOVERNANCE?

While attending an annual JNNURM (Jawaharlal Nehru National Urban Renewal Mission) meeting in Delhi, a town planner from Dadra Nagar Haveli Union Territory had heard that in Pune, architects submit soft copies of building plans to the Municipal Corporation, instead of hard copies, for obtaining approvals for building construction. The Pune Municipal Corporation had a computer programme that could scrutinise the plans in minutes, identify problems, and also provide a scrutiny report. Moreover, since a computer was doing the scrutiny, human subjectivity, and hence any corruption related to it, was out of the question. The planner was very impressed and as soon as he returned to his town, he got in touch with the concerned engineer from Pune who had initiated and implemented the computer-based approval process. The engineer told the planner that under JNNURM, it was necessary to implement the computer-based building approval system called 'AutoDCR' to accomplish one of the reform components. Although the planner was aware of e-governance reform under JNNURM, he did not know the specifics that were required. After hearing about AutoDCR, he felt that this was something that had to be done. He immediately contacted the company that had created AutoDCR for the Pune Municipal Corporation and invited them to make a presentation to the Dadra Nagar Haveli Administration.

The Government of India started JNNURM in December 2005. Under this scheme, national and state governments gave large amounts of funds to city governments to improve their infrastructure. However, to get these funds, city governments had to undertake a large number of reforms in management, administration, governance, policy, service delivery, etc. 'E-Governance' was the first reform in the long list of reforms to be undertaken. For the implementation of e-governance reform, several steps were needed. These included undertaking an assessment of the existing condition of automation in cities, preparing an e-governance plan, re-engineering municipal processes towards adopting e-governance, and managing 12 services using e-systems. These included the management of property tax, financial accounting, user charges, birth and death registrations, citizen's grievances, personnel administration, procurements, project monitoring, building plan approval, health programmes, licenses, and solid waste.

A software company, based in Pune, had approached the Pune Municipal Corporation with an idea for developing software to manage building plan approvals. The idea was to develop software that could read computer drawings. For this, the drawings had to be made in a certain manner. The company had discovered that most architects made their drawings using a drawing programme called AutoCAD. It negotiated with the creators of AutoCAD and developed a plug-in to AutoCAD called PreDCR, incorporating all development control regulations and building byelaws of Pune. Architects had to download PreDCR from the company's website and recreate their drawings according to specified formats and then submit this drawing to the Municipal Corporation. The drawing was then opened in AutoDCR, which reviewed the drawing as per the regulations and produced a scrutiny report.

AutoDCR was an immediate success. It was seen as a programme that reduced scrutiny time and corruption. It became extremely popular and many cities got their own PreDCRs made in accordance with their development control regulations. The company's business not only increased, but its sustenance was also ensured as the PreDCR had to be changed every time there was an amendment to the development control regulations—and the amendments took place every now and then. The creators of AutoCAD were also happy as the architects were required to submit drawings made in their software if they wanted quick and bribe-free approval. In many ways, the city and the architects became linked to the specific software companies. The planner from Dadra Nagar Haveli had PreDCR developed for his town and had AutoDCR installed in his department.

While some tech-savvy commissioners and engineers from big cities plunged into implementing 'e-governance', most others struggled with understanding the scope of work involved and various jargons that were floating around. For some smaller cities, the implementation of e-governance did not mean anything more than buying a few computers. Municipal officers looked at e-governance as another project, which involved procurement of hardware and software. As all procurement in municipalities was done through a tendering process, municipal officers of most cities started looking for consultants who could prepare 'e-governance tenders'. While every software company tried to be a consultant, regular engineering consultants got a few software professionals to update themselves for the e-governance programme. Most consultants saw it as a software development project. Tenders were floated and companies were appointed to undertake the different parts of e-governance reforms. Software firms started developing a variety of software for different municipalities—software for accounting, property tax calculation, registration of birth and deaths, issuing licenses, tracking solid waste trucks, keeping health records, etc. One city developed a programme for making an inventory of all slum-dwellers; another city developed a project monitoring system, where information on project progress was transmitted to municipal engineers via SMS; and yet another city developed an online water-management system. Many cities started making geographic information systems to put together information on property and improve property tax collection. However, most of these efforts remained incomplete as it was impossible to map complicated property claims in cities. Cities started spending a large amount of funds on new software. While some of these were useful, most of them became white elephants sitting in some municipal computer and not being used—they were either too complicated, or not updated, or simply involved cumbersome operations. Money was spent in abundance since there was no District Schedule of Rates available for software, as it was available for civil engineering works. Many software companies charged cities heavily for maintaining the software systems and managing data.

Several smaller municipalities were unable to do anything as they could not afford either consultants or software companies. E-governance was evolving as a sector in awkward ways.

Taking stock of this situation, in May 2008, the national government announced special grants for implementation of e-governance in cities under JNNURM, and prepared guidelines for implementation. The grants were announced as a part of the National Mission Mode Programme (NMMP) for e-governance. To obtain the special e-governance grants, each municipality had to prepare a detailed project report (DPRs) for implementation of e-governance in the city and submit it to the national government for approval through the state government. This process was similar to the one for obtaining grants for other infrastructure projects, and cities were experts in quickly appointing consultants for preparing DPRs. In Maharashtra, eight cities submitted e-governance DPRs to the state government within four months of the announcement of special grants. The next problem was the evaluation of the DPRs. These were not like the usual water supply and sewerage DPRs, which the state engineers could quickly crunch. Each of these DPRs was prepared by different consultants, who were preparing such DPRs for the first time and, moreover, nobody in the state government had any idea about the format for an e-governance DPR. There was no capacity inherent in the state government to evaluate DPRs that discussed computer architecture and software. However, in the competitive environment of JNNURM, there was always pressure to forward the DPRs to the national government as soon as possible. Since everyone was new, the officers at the state level quickly forwarded four of the eight DPRs to the national government without spending much time on them. On the remaining four, some queries were raised and returned to the municipalities for clarification. The situation was not very different at the national level. There was no chance that the engineers from the Public Works Department or teachers from planning schools would be able to scrutinise the e-governance DPRs. After looking round, the government appointed a Hyderabad-based public–private partnership company specialising in smart governance for the purpose of evaluating the e-governance DPRs. The company reviewed the DPRs and recommended all four DPRs of Maharashtra to the Government of India for approval.

After the first phase of approving e-governance DPRs, nobody was sure about the approaches that were used by different consultants or the success of any specific approach against another. They were all in various experimental stages. The Hyderabad company recommended putting together a toolkit for the preparation of e-governance DPRs so that there could be some basis for evaluating them. The Government of India agreed and asked the company to prepare such a toolkit. The company roped in an international development consultant for the purpose, and the toolkit was prepared. In June 2009, the toolkit was circulated across the country. The toolkit focused on making the e-governance reform workable in cities—it insisted on aspects such as outcome planning, capacity building, monitoring and evaluation, which were beyond software creation. In August 2009, the Ministry of Urban Development organised a workshop for all the state-level and city-level officers in charge of e-governance. The purpose was to explain the nitty-gritty of the new toolkit. The Department of Technology (DIT) was also invited to the workshop. After listening to the company and the consultant's presentation, the DIT officers raised two issues. The first was regarding the problem of different approaches and software used in various cities. The people from DIT observed that such a situation would not allow the creation of coherent, useful data at the state level. The second problem was the absence of state-level infrastructure and the state's role in e-governance. Subsequently, in September 2009, another meeting was held between officers of the Ministry of Urban Development and Department of Technology and it was decided that state governments need to set up state-level infrastructure and employ a common approach across the state with common software. This would not only be cheaper to procure, but would also produce data in similar formats which could be then compiled together. The only problem was that many municipalities had already spent large amounts of funds in setting up some form of e-governance system. It was then decided that large municipal corporations would be allowed to have a stand-alone system, as many of them had already spent crores of rupees to put such systems in place. The e-governance reform has had a complex working out in cities, where the ambition of technological advancements has sat awkwardly with existing capacities.

In two distinct ways, the e-governance of JNNURM is clearly the predecessor of the current Smart Cities Programme of the Government of India. First, both, the smart cities programme and the e-governance reform, seek to improve efficiency in service delivery through software-driven technological solutions. And, second, both of them are centrally initiated programmes, where cities are lured through availability of finances. For the past 20 years, various national governments have initiated programmes where funds are directly allocated to cities to improve infrastructure, and cities have been oriented towards aggressively getting such funds. The Smart Cities Programme could be seen as one of the other such programmes, such as the Mega Cities Scheme, JNNURM, the Rajiv Awaz Yojana, the Integrated Housing and Slum Development Programme, the Urban Infrastructure Scheme for Small and Medium Towns, the Atal Mission for Rejuvenation and Urban Transformation, etc. Although they were conceived as quick-impact infrastructure development programmes by the national government, they have simply been programmes to access large funds for the city governments. Hence, in many ways, the smart cities programme has been one of the many programmes through which cities expect funds from the national government. It was perhaps important to have a detailed review of the e-governance reform before embarking on the smart cities programme.

BUT AREN'T CITIES SMART ALREADY?

A street in Irla, a suburban neighbourhood of Mumbai, had, over the years, become one of the most popular destinations for retail shoppers. The street began as a quiet residential neighbourhood, comprising low-income state housing board apartments and slums. Slowly, the ground stories of the housing board typologies were transformed into shops. The intensity of shopping grew as more and more ground floor apartments became shops, and as new extensions to these shops emerged. Many of these extensions were further rented out to other smaller traders. Banking on the footfall on this street, other street vendors selling small wares set up shop. The street became one of the liveliest shopping streets in the suburbs. Many specialised shops came up in the area. One of them was called 'Alfa', which was able to source large amounts of imported goods including electronics, food items, accessories, toys, etc. Alfa became a Mecca for middle-class shoppers with a taste for 'foreign goods'. Soon the shop diversified: luggage, mobile phones, household wares, electronics, garments, and even a foreign exchange centre. Alfa gave the best rates in the market and accepted almost all currencies. The shop felt the need to expand. The owner kept buying shops on the street, naming them Alfa 1, Alfa 2, 3, 4 and 5. The street was often nicknamed the 'Alfa Street'. As the street became saturated, its tentacles moved into the large slum behind. There was a high demand from shopkeepers for warehouses and living space for their labour. While the houses in the slum closer to the street sold their spaces for showrooms and display-type shops, the ones behind got rented for housing of labour and goods. The change of Irla Street had been gradual and textured. This slowness affected many people as they found ways to deal/engage with it. People were not thrown out, but new people came in. They were accommodated generously, as well as awkwardly.

In 2004, a mall came up on the street, trying to piggyback on the footfall already created by the other enterprises. The smaller traders were afraid that their businesses would be taken over by a big mall. However, the story of the mall unfolded in a very different way. No big retail business came into this mall. Even the bigger spaces were subdivided into small shops. The mall was taken over completely by small traders. The prices of goods in these shops were obviously more than those of the other enterprises of the street. So people would go to this mall not to buy goods, but to take an air-conditioned break. Others came to use the toilets. The mall became a large air-conditioned public toilet and a recreational space. With very little business in the shops, many shopkeepers decided to dispose of their properties. Rents remained low and the owners of the mall found it difficult to maintain the space. Their first step was to shut down the air-conditioning. With that, the number of people visiting the mall further reduced. The shopkeepers installed their own small air-conditioning units. Their compressors were kept outside the shops, spewing heat into the common spaces of the mall. So the lobbies and corridors became extremely uncomfortable places. Some shoppers, looking for discounted deals, still came to the mall, bearing the brunt of the heat-spewing atriums, dodging quickly into the air-conditioned shops. However, many of the shops in the mall remained closed. The owners of the mall were desperately trying to keep the mall alive. Slowly, the mall disintegrated into the street, blurring the boundaries between the inside and the outside, the formal and the informal. Irla street 'settled' slowly over time. When 'the mall'—an alien type—came up, it had to work its way out on the street.

'Settling' is a process through which people come to terms with each other's lives and their landscapes. It is not a process in which contradictions get resolved; instead, through settling, contradictions are able to coexist. It is a set of elaborate mechanics, which keeps the city in a perpetual state of becoming. However, the city never settles completely. These spaces, practices and objects get layered further, or change, or disappear. The logic of this transformation is often incremental, sporadic and based on parameters that are beyond the detection of empirical methods. This is an emotional intelligence that is built into the making of cities. Historically, cities have been made through this form of settling.

On Lamington Road, an electronic cluster in Mumbai, a bright sign on the pavement says 'laptop repairs', with an arrow pointing towards a chawl. As one enters, one finds the staircase block with a courtyard at the corner. Below the staircase block is located a laptop repair shop belonging to Purshottam, who uses fake Chinese models of branded items. He claims that the China-made battery is a much better deal and runs for the same time as the original. He opened the shop four years ago and pays a rent of ₹ 700 to the landlord. After his twelfth grade, he would help around in a few shops along Lamington Road. He did not have enough money to open a big shop. His mother was suffering from arthritis and he had to spend a lot of his earnings on her. He decided to open a shop in the same building where he lived, to take care of his mother. The only way he could do this was because the landlord rented him the space below the staircase. He is indebted to the Internet and thinks it is the greatest invention of mankind, constantly updating his knowledge through it. He learnt the basic working of a laptop from dismantling his old second-hand laptop, which he had bought after saving for months on end. He earns approximately ₹ 30,000 rupees per month by servicing laptops. He is proud that everyone in Lamington Road knows him as 'the guy under the staircase'. In most parts of the inner city of Mumbai, spaces get doubled or tripled like Purshottam's staircase shop. The street edges, particularly, corrode to accommodate shop entrances, extensions to shops, shops on walls that are one foot inside and a foot outside the building, the vendors on the sidewalks, the vendors on the carriage way, etc. There is usually a complex relationship between all of these. It appears that along the edge of the street, things diffuse into each other. It is difficult to identify where one shop ends and where another one begins. The street edge has a very high 'transactional capacity'. Transactional Capacity is that capacity of a space/practice/object that allows flows of bodies, commodities, ideas and money through it: the higher the flow, the higher the transactional capacity.

In Behrampada, a slum in Bandra East, a community has put together a large settlement on a marshy land. The settlement rises up to four floors at places. One such cross section houses a shop on the ground floor that rents out large vessels for making biryani during festivals; an embroidery unit on the first; a hostel for migrant workers on the second; a library on the third; and a mosque on the fourth floor. Cities provide large numbers of such transactional capacities per unit space.

However, one also sees that as the degree of formality of cities increases, transactional spaces become inversely proportional and the number of resources consumed becomes directly proportional. In Kalbadevi, in the inner-city market areas, porters can be hired to transport goods from shops. They are all members of a porters' association. They carry around large baskets to transport goods. In the afternoons, one often finds many porters taking a nap inside these large baskets. The baskets are transactional objects that transcend their utility as porting devices and become spaces of rest on the street. Similarly, hand-carts used to transport goods come together, forming communities of leisure spaces in the market. The staircase shop, the street, the complex section of a slum, the basket, are all spaces, objects and practices with high transactional capacities. The city produces these during its process of settling. These spaces/objects/practices help cities settle and contribute significantly towards their smartness.

Swami Electronics on Lamington Road makes customised LED signboards, as well as lights and props for TV shows. The shop is located at the entrance of a building in front of the staircase block and occupies an area of 1.5m². About 60 years ago the shop was purchased by Manoj's father, who was a tailor. Manoj then took over the shop 24 years ago and started selling lights. In 1981, the film *Yaarana* had just been released. Manoj loved the film. Its dance sequences, the lights, costumes and Amitabh Bachchan, all fascinated him. He would watch the movie multiple times in the course of the year and was awestruck by the light-suit worn by Amitabh Bachchan. Manoj made a light-suit of his own, with his father's help, and would wear it in the evenings. Thus started his fascination with lights. This suit made him famous in the neighbourhood and he decided to start a light shop. Over the years, his shop evolved into an LED signboard shop. Many of his components are obtained from Delhi or imported from China. Manoj often visits China to see what new products are being manufactured with LED lights and tries to make the same here. He has made the indicators at Ratnagiri railway station. These lights are priced between ₹ 500–50,000. He has also got a few offers from MTV to do the lighting for some of their shows.

Just ahead of Manoj's shop is Parasmani Electronics: sellers of remote control devices for air conditioners, televisions, DVD players, and of Universal remotes. Located along the boundary wall of Agbotwala compound, it is lined with shelves on all three sides, displaying remote control devices of all kinds. A large billboard outside the shop advertises its wares. Here, Jignesh—self-taught— makes, repairs and programmes the devices. Most of his material is obtained from Delhi or imported from China. There is a small acrylic donation box on the table right by the entrance. Jignesh collects money every year for a *gowshala* (cow shelter) in Gujarat. This gowshala has about 800–900 sick cows. Eight years ago, when he visited his village, he decided to go to the gowshala nearby. The plight of the sick cows really saddened him and he realised that they needed more money to provide better facilities. Being a member of the Jain community, it is part of his religion to take care of animals. Since then, he has been putting ₹10 every day in the box. His customers willingly donate to the cause. At the end of the year, he makes his yearly visit to his village and personally goes to the gowshala to hand over the money. Sometimes he also spends a day or two there, helping with the activities.

In the lane behind Jignesh's shop is Nicki Auto Garage, a vintage car workshop. One wall of Imperial Cinema is a part of this garage. The garage was opened in 1975. Behram Engineer owns this workshop. His son now runs it and manages its day-to-day affairs. The workshop has 10 permanent repairmen, while he hires four or five more people on a monthly basis. The office at the corner has one cabin, which is occupied by Engineer, where he entertains customers, and the one outside is for his son and two other people who maintain the accounts. Since the garage has been in existence for years, he has a regular clientele who are vintage car enthusiasts. Because of his steady clientele, he picks his clients, and not the other way round. He has had a few bad experiences with people with 'new money', as he calls it. All his advertising happens through word of mouth and through Justdial. He gets clients from South Bombay, Bandra, Andheri, Thane, etc. Since the diamond trade business shifted to BKC, most of his customers have moved there. Moreover, there are not many shops that specialise in vintage car repair and re-sale in the city. Most of their material is procured online. Engineer loves vintage cars and his love for cars has been passed on to his son. Since childhood, his son would saunter around the garage, playing with the cars. He loved to dismantle his toy cars and would often end up rendering them useless. On entering the cabin, one finds a sofa that resembles the front part of a car, coupled with a set of working headlights designed by his son. He is enthralled by vehicles of all sorts, and in the cabin hangs a picture of a fighter jet.

People in the city have preoccupations of different kinds—getting an electronic shirt made, collecting money for dying cows, designing strange furniture, collecting strange objects, behaving like spies, writing stories, achieving mundane targets, dismantling machines, opposing new ideas, trying to walk across five countries, counting every tree, tracking obscure data, etc. These 'trips' are practices that go beyond the acts of routine. These practices are not useful to produce grand conceptualisations of cities and are often discarded as stray individual preoccupations. While some of these obsessions are related to earning and occupations, others are simply 'useless'. Everyone seems to have a trip. Trips seem to provide individuals with their energy. Such energies cumulatively produce a city.

The idea of 'smartness' in cities seem to be hijacked by the discussions around 'Smart Cities', and are limited to either the celebration or criticism of software driven technological projects. But cities are not projects, nor are they a math problem that can be solved with a formula. They are formally complex, experientially intense, with logics that are incoherent. They fold spaces, practices and relationships together to create an enormous, perpetually transforming morph. This morph is characterised by unclear geographies, absurd lives, unstable forms and the coexistence of sharp contradictions within it. Smartness of cities is a function of its complexity. Through the ideas of 'Settling', 'Transactional Capacities' and 'Trips', we attempt to talk of a very different smartness that makes cities. Settling, transactional capacities and trips are the emotional quotients through which cities are made. They bring about smartness in cities. This is the smartness of the everyday—an inherent smartness that has grown from within the city and a smartness that makes the city.

The discussions around 'smart cities' have gained currency in India ever since the new government promised to make 100 new smart cities. It appears that the government soon realised that it is not possible for it to make even one new city, as the promise was toned down towards making existing cities 'smarter'. The critiques of smart cities broadly articulate three problems: first, that it is a ploy of software companies to accquire projects; second, that there are low internal capacities within municipalities to handle advanced technological developments; and, third, that spending money on such software driven projects is a misplaced priority when the condition of basic services in cities is extremely poor. However, the contention here is that cities are not docile and dormant absorbers of policy—they will fold into them any new policy, programme or project to create unexpected things. Irrespective of the arrogance of the government, the smart cities programme today appears to be the most loosely structured programme, where cities have been themselves asked to articulate what smartness means to them. Like the e-governance reforms, it appears that the 'Smart City Programme' will have to work its way through the strange realities and inherent smartness of cities.

◆

PUBLIC SPACES AND PLACES:
Gendered Intersectionalities in Indian Cities

SARASWATI
RAJU
TANUSREE
PAUL

INTRODUCTION

C ities and the built environment provide the artefactual settings where gendered meanings are developed and represented as well as reproduced. The built environment not only evokes experiences and behavioural responses, but also reproduces and structures institutional norms and social relations. The city has been perceived primarily as a male place in which women and other underprivileged social groups and minorities have survived in its interstices in their own particular way. Massey (1994) suggests that the spatial and social organisation of a city is constructed through an articulation of 'public' and 'private', and through the characterisation of urban experience in the figure of the (male) *flâneur*. For women, however, the public spaces are 'transit ways to other regions, not loci of interest in themselves' (Gardner, 1990: 315).

Women can access public spaces 'legitimately' only when they can manufacture a sense of purpose for being there and adhere to 'appropriate' behaviour (Paul, 2011; Ranade, 2007). According to Gardner (1990), such regulations imply informal social control of women, leading to their subordination within public spaces without explicitly excluding them from having access to the latter.

While the 'modern' city privileges a male city culture in general, the contemporary postmodern city, with its cluster of commercial and consumption spaces such as shopping malls, Western-style coffee shops, cinema houses, etc., not only facilitates women's participation in public spaces, but also reconstitutes gender roles/relations (Massey, 1994). Central to these constructs is the publicly imagined figure of the 'new Indian woman' who most often belongs to the middle class.

It is within this framework that we question the extent to which the altered/evolved urbanscape in India offers enhanced opportunities of engagement to middle-class women, and whether the increased visibility of women in the urban public spaces of India marks a blurring of the public–private spatial binaries, or a reconstitution of the same. This discussion is organised into four sections: (i) an introduction to gender and urban space, (ii) a theoretical discourse on spaces and places that would help situate the subsequent case studies in perspective, (iii) a discussion around the blurring of gendered spaces in the context of Indian cities, and (iv) the conclusion.

SPACE, PLACE AND GENDER

The notions of space and place come across as commonsensical and need no specific definition, and yet these are difficult concepts to expand and contemplate. Although they bear the imprint of disciplinary orientations, eluding a neat formulation within as well as across disciplines, at the risk of simplification it may be mentioned that for long, spaces and places were seen as distinct categories in their own right: space conventionally more as an absolute, static, fixed and bounded block—a thing in itself, an independent and 'individuate phenomena', whereas place is the lived experience at multiple levels (Raju, 2011: 4). Over the years, however, spaces and places are not conceptualised as disconnected binaries or separate domains, particularly by feminist geographers. To them, the two are intertwined: space provides the physical locale through which meanings and subjective positioning, with implications for lived experiences, are expressed. Different cultures invest gendered meanings into spaces and places, articulated through various means and mediums, where sex-differentiated practices are negotiated. Such gendered spaces thus emerge as settings that are used strategically to inform identity, and produce and reproduce asymmetrical gender relations of power and authority. For example, most activity spaces are replete with meanings, connoting a hierarchical order of power in which women are associated with the inside, private and home vis-à-vis the outside, public and market.

GENDERED PUBLIC SPACES IN INDIA: CONFINED OR FLUID?

At this juncture it needs to be emphasised that these binaries may have greater relevance in the West, but they are neither simple, sexually segregated geographical locations nor are they mutually exclusive; they are overlapping, interchangeable and often interlocking in the Indian context. The complexities of Indian society in terms of the caste–class–gender milieu necessitates the conceptualisation of spatial binaries through a different lens. As pointed out by Butalia (2012: 3), 'inequalities of gender and class, indeed of location and caste, are built into...[the] very concepts of public and private, and therefore they cannot be taken at face value'. According to Raju (2011), one of the unique features of most Asian countries is the fluidity of binaries. In India, for example, it is very common to witness public lanes (even in busy city neighbourhoods) in the morning turning into semi-private spaces in the afternoons, where women sit and indulge in numerous household chores.

Abraham (2010), in her study of Bikaner in Rajasthan, notes that understanding the street as public and the home as private places them in opposition to each other, and prevents an understanding of the continuities between the two. The *patas* or platforms in town *chowks* are used by men for chatting, eating and even sleeping. On the other hand, the front room, or the *donkhé*, has large windows that open onto the street so that a person sitting at the window is visible and can engage people in conversation. This room is considered to be a threshold within the home where visitors are entertained; the rest of the house is inaccessible to them. This room, essentially, is associated with men. A married woman, if sitting at the window, makes sure that her head is properly covered, otherwise she could well be on the street in the *mohalla* even though she is physically within. If the pata (for those houses that have one) is one kind of threshold, the donkhé or front room(s) is another.

In an altogether different context, Butalia (2012) cites the example of honour killing—a ghastly practice largely prevailing in north Indian villages whereby men and women marrying outside socially legitimised matrimonial norms are brutally murdered. Although this crime takes place within the families to which these couples belong, in reality, this practice is very much publicly accepted and sometimes even publicly celebrated. According to Butalia, such practices add new dimensions to the public spaces where the private is implicated in a very strange manner. Tenhunen (2006), in a case study of Kolkata, shows how the absence of men during the day leads to a redefining of the spatial boundaries, whereby the 'inside' or the private domain extends to the immediate neighbourhood. The latter thus becomes the locale of 'collective domesticity', whereby women engage in the pursuit of home-based wage work as well as private tasks such as bathing, lighting coal stoves, washing dishes, etc. They can move about freely within this swathe of 'public' space, but never venture out in those 'real' public spaces where men gather and indulge in leisurely chats, or *addas*, as known locally.

Intriguing ramifications exist with respect to public transport in India. Tara (2011), in her study of the Delhi metro, shows how private spaces are produced within the public transport of Delhi. Accordingly, the dedicated ladies' compartment provides women with a sense of security, claim and control over public space. It becomes a space that endows women with symbolic capital to help recognise themselves as a group and to look upon men in this public space as the other. Such an identity lets them exercise power in situations when this 'other' group tries to impose upon them. Phadke et al. (2011) has somewhat similar observations to make on women commuting in Mumbai. She observes that although the introduction of the ladies' compartment appears to reiterate parochial patronage to some, in reality it actually enables women to access public transport and thus ensures their access to public spaces. Her study indicates that although extremely crowded, 'because all the densely packed bodies are female, and are assumed to be heterosexual, this is not considered threatening' (ibid.: 74).

'NEW INDIAN WOMEN'

It would not be out of place to comment on the emergence of the so-called 'new Indian women' in this context. They are construed as those who are 'practised in the ways of the West, and at the same time retain their Indian values' (Munshi, 2001: 90); those who can successfully achieve 'the balance between (deep) tradition and (surface) modernity'. Thus, the new woman marks the locus of contestation between the Western and the Indian, tradition and modernity. It is at the intersection of such a construct that the 'new' women ceaselessly try to strike the delicate balance between

Indian home life and global professional life. These women often work in white-collar service sectors, particularly in information and communication technology, organised retail, financial intermediation, etc. For these professional women, work and personal life may conflict but are carefully reconciled because for them, professional careers must be circumscribed by their families. As pointed out by Radhakrishnan

> where previously, Indianness and Westernness were opposed to one another, a discourse of global Indianness makes the two compatible....The adherence to 'Indianness' is tied to commitment to the family and this has to be reiterated by perfectly balancing work and family life, more so by asserting it (2009: 9).

The question that we pose, then, is: With enhanced mobility and 'acceptability' within male spaces, to what extent has such increased spatial access been able to redefine the traditional interactive pattern with spaces? Several studies have shown how the emergence of new generation sectors has provided women with emancipatory spaces in the public sphere of urban India. Call centres are cases to consider. They provide educated young people decent employment with reasonable emoluments. However, this should not be misconstrued as indicative of women's empowerment, since the 'physical space and the nightscapes traversed by female call centre employees are relatively fixed and confined because their movement is based on a strict home-to-work journey and the spaces they occupy are closely monitored' (Patel, 2006: 10). The organised retail sectors also provide employment to young people with limited human resources—those belonging to the lower-middle classes—enabling them to construct different kinds of identities by being associated with First World working conditions. These women have been able to acquire sufficient symbolic as well as economic capital by dint of working in these modern, relatively more egalitarian sectors such that they symbolise the new social regime in India.

Notwithstanding these positive intercepts being made by Indian women in the male public realm, scholars have also shown how the spatial boundaries of new urban spaces in India are actually being reconstituted and redrawn in a manner that does not challenge traditional gender roles and gender relations.

As the number of women engaged in technical education, such as engineering, increases and their participation in professional sectors escalates, it may be expected that traditional gender roles will disappear, providing women with a level playing field to participate in public life. However, empirical evidence suggests otherwise. Patel and Parmentier (2005) observe that technological advancement can adapt to the existing social structure. The persistence of such gendered spaces, even as the women engage with public life, neither enhances their socio-economic and political status, nor provides opportunities for equal participation in the information economy. Even in these 'modern' sectors, women are not seen as equal, contributing participants in the realm of technological development because the existing social structure continues to define 'women' in terms of their reproductive and care roles, paid work being seen as of secondary importance. The data collected by IIT–Mumbai from 1992 to 2002 also indicate that the participation of Indian women fails to deconstruct the traditional gender roles which place women on the periphery of an employing organisation (ibid.).

According to Radhakrishnan (2009), while women IT professionals work in global workplaces and embrace the consumption pattern of global middle classes, the 'sacred' construction of the Indian family forms the fulcrum of their cultural legitimacy in public spaces. It is presumed that despite working in technologically driven modern sectors, they would prioritise their families over their careers. It is through such adherence to family values that these women consciously exhibit balance and restraint, and embody the so-called freedom, distinguishing themselves both from the 'dissolute' West as well as from other Indian women of previous generations and of different class positions. Dutta and Hussain (2010), in a study of women workers in the information and technology sector of Kolkata, observe that contrary to claims that the IT sector would provide less exploitative avenues of employment for women and would enable them in strengthening their bargaining position at home, the organisational process in this sector is shaped by social context.

Paul (2013), in a study of women workers in the IT, BPO and organised retail sectors, observes that even the new generation sectors are infused with engendered meanings. On the one hand, the women's positioning within private spaces, their familial responsibilities and constraints influence their career decisions and, on the other hand, their performance appraisals by the employing organisations often tend to be governed by the conception that careers are second choices for women. This lack of freedom of mobility, not only across city spaces during 'odd' hours, but also the inability to relocate if required, has been reported by more than half the women working in the new generation sectors as a major obstacle which hinges on the care and reproductive roles they are expected to perform within private spaces. All these factors, cumulatively, place women in a secondary position, even in these new generation sectors. Women are followers rather than leaders, having jobs rather than careers. Thus, it is evident that the public vs. private sphere binaries get replicated within the paid labour force itself.

Not solely that. The so-called feminine traits of being creative, persevering, compliant and cool-headed are also routinely used to assign women-specific jobs within these sectors. Thus, women are mostly employed in 'soft options' like human resource management, client handling, software testing, etc. This clearly indicates that the constructs of the inside and the outside, the private and the public overlap through the manner in which women engage with urban public spaces.

A joint study by Associated Chambers of Commerce & Industry of India (ASSOCHAM) and National Commission of Women (NCW)—comprising 272 participants, including 216 women doing night shifts, at least for the last six months, 56 employers supervising women therein and various key personalities from diverse backgrounds such as women's organisations, universities, the police, law-enforcing personnel, hospitals, industrialists, etc.—observes that about one-third of the employees felt insecure while working the night shift. The respondents felt that equal opportunities could be celebrated, only if the gender discrimination act is implemented in society and women feel comfortable. Women can acquire respect in society provided night shift jobs do not crush their moral and ethical values. The opinions of all key informants ventilate their anxieties over the safety of women working night shifts and emphasise the need to scale up security measures to 'protect' them. It would not be incorrect to argue here that such anxieties clandestinely allude to the fact that paid work by women in the night-time city is indeed undesirable.

Hence 'appropriate' vigilance measures need to be adopted to protect them. As Patel observes, 'women's physical mobility and access to urban areas are regulated by a timescape that limits their presence during the evening and night, particularly if they are going out alone' (2010: 48).

Historically, all rules and legislations in India pertaining to women's employment—the Indian Factories Act, 1911; the Bombay Maternity Benefit Act—resulted in limiting the scope of women's participation in the labour force in the name of protecting women and, consequently, legitimised the social construct of the nightscape as a male domain through legal sanctions (ibid.). Article 66 (c) of the Indian Factories Act (1948) prohibited the employment of women in factory premises beyond 6 pm to 7 am. This act was finally amended in 2005 in response to the need of the hour necessitated by globalisation, whereby employment of women was allowed between 7 pm and 6 am. According to Patel, instead of re-envisioning women as individuals who have an inherent right to work whenever they see fit, this law focussed on the ability of industry to employ women at night while also ensuring that provisions for their protection would remain in place (ibid.). Allowing women to move about in ways that are considered inherent rights for men reflect that women remain tethered to a patriarchal framework that dictates what a woman can, and cannot, do. The 'dignity and honour' rule inadvertently marked women as outsiders and spatialised the factory as a site where undignified and dishonourable behaviour is a norm from which women must be protected' (ibid.: 50). The National Association of Software and Services Companies (NASSCOM) has pledged to organise a series of events and activities to educate, engage and empower its workforce, including self-defence and attitudinal training for handling a crisis-like situation. Authorities reiterated that it is the fundamental right of every woman to work, and it is the responsibility of the entire ecosystem to ensure that there is a conducive environment for the same.[1] The security measures adopted by various BPO companies include GPRS tracking devices in vehicles, security guards escorting the women to their homes, strict and thorough background checks of drivers and security guards who accompany women employees at night, strict monitoring of the women's pathways till their arrival at home, self-defence, etc.[2]

While these attempts mark sincere intentions on the part of employers to oversee the security of their women employees and facilitate their work participation, nevertheless, it cannot be denied that these efforts also reify patriarchal regimes of surveillance and morality–mobility encodings. Through these strategies, notions of women and respectability are constructed as a way to control and confine women, with respectability used as a mechanism operating between identity and space and producing gendered subjectivity, spatial knowledge and, ultimately, gendered space. Certainly, the night-shift employment of women marks the locus of the blurring of public–private spaces.

Such ambivalence in the public and the private is clearly apparent in spaces of consumption as well. Many scholars (Paul, 2011; Phadke, 2005; Ranade, 2007) have pointed out that in the Indian context, women are expected to use public spaces in purposeful ways and not for pleasure-seeking. However, there are complex nuances in this regard, especially when interfaced with class specificities. The newly emerging consumption spaces in terms of shopping malls, departmental stores, coffee shops, etc., have widened the vistas for women's engagement with public spaces for leisure. However, these spaces, being stringently surveilled and monitored are, in essence, semi-public in nature. Phadke posits these as 'new private spaces' for both lower as well as middle- and upper-middle-class women. While the former enter as salesgirls, the latter enter these spaces as privileged consumers. Nonetheless, all of them are exposed to global practices of consumption and

> ...much of the consumption and purchase that takes place is either part of the apparatus of disciplining female bodies or an effort towards the embellishment of the private realm underlining women's private location. In these contexts, one also notices that women play out various scripts of femininity, often evocative of the 'docile disciplined bodies' suggested by Michel Foucault' (2005: 48).

Discotheques and pubs are some of the other spaces which embody intriguing ambivalence. According to Phadke, women are not only actively desired within these spaces as often groups of women or single women are allowed to enter but not men on their own;

they are also provided with security by musclemen against overt harassment (ibid.). Phadke thus concludes that

> [t]hese spaces, then, approximate in some strange but real way new 'private' spaces (for those women who can afford to buy them) where women are safe in a similar tenuous and ambiguous way that they are within their homes, that is, safe from the unwanted attentions of outside men (ibid.: 48).

Paul (2013), in her study on new consumption spaces in Kolkata, notes that these spaces are strewn with gendered connotations. Most often, departmental stores or shopping malls are portrayed as 'safe' and pleasurable spaces where women can enjoy their 'freedom' as astute consumers without compromising their respectability as purposeless users of public spheres. Although these spaces enable women to combine their daily chores of grocery and other shopping for the family with leisure, it must be admitted that these are stringently monitored and surveilled spaces which, essentially, institutionalise the public gaze on women.

CONCLUSION

The blurring of public and private spaces in Indian cities is in the enactment of everyday lives as there exists considerable ambiguity as to what comes under the purview of the 'public' and the 'private'. At another level, the behavioural norms that women have to adapt to in public spaces are circumscribed by stereotypical constructs of appropriateness and honour. This overlapping makes us question the supposedly 'gender neutral' nature of public spaces.

◆

NOTES

1. *The Times of India.* 27 January 2013.
2. *The Times of India.* 25 December 2012.

REFERENCES

Abraham, Janaki. 2010. 'Veiling and the Production of Gender and Space in a Town in North India: A Critique of the Public/Private Dichotomy', *Indian Journal of Gender Studies,* 17 (2), pp. 191–222.

Butalia, Urvashi. 2012. 'The Fear that Stalks: Gender-Based Violence in Public Spaces', in Sara Pilot and Lora Prabhu (eds.), *The Fear that Stalks*. New Delhi: Zubaan, pp. 1–12.

Dutta, Mousumi and Zakir Husain. 2010. 'Satisficing and Structured Individuation: A Study of Women Workers in Calcutta's IT sector', http://mpra.ub.uni-muenchen.de/20899/MPRA Paper No. 20899, posted 23 February 2010 (accessed 20 March 2012).

Gardner, C. B. 1990. 'Safe Conduct: Women, Crime and Self in Public Places', *Social Problems*, 37, pp. 311–28.

Massey, Doreen. 1994. *Space, Place and Gender.* Minneapolis, MN: University of Minnesota Press.

Munshi, Shoma. 2001. 'Introduction', in Shoma Munshi (ed.), *Images of the 'Modern Woman' in Asia: Global Media, Local Meanings*. Surrey: Curzon Press, p. 116.

Patel, Reena and Mary Jane C. Parmentier. 2005. 'The Persistence of Traditional Gender Roles in the Information Technology Sector: A Study of Female Engineers in India', *Information Technologies and International Development*, 2 (3), pp. 29–46.

Patel, Reena. 2010. *Working the Night Shift: Women in India's Call Center Industry*. Stanford, California: Stanford University Press.

———. 2006. 'Working the Night Shift: Gender and the Global Economy', *ACME: An International E-Journal for Critical Geographies*, 5 (1), pp. 9–27.

Paul, Tanusree. 2011. 'Public Spaces and Everyday Lives: Gendered Encounters in the Metro City of Kolkata', in Saraswati Raju and Kuntala Lahiri-Dutt (eds.), *Doing Gender, Doing Geography: Emerging Research in India*. New Delhi: Routledge.

———. 2013. 'Gender and Reconfigured Urban Spaces: A Case Study of Kolkata.' Unpublished PhD Thesis. New Delhi: Jawaharlal Nehru University.

Phadke, Shilpa. 2005. 'You can be Lonely in a Crowd: The Production of Safety in Mumbai', *Indian Journal of Gender Studies*, 12 (1), 41–62.

Phadke, Shilpa, Shilpa Ranade and Sameera Khan. 2011. *Why Loiter? Women and Risk on Mumbai Streets*. New Delhi: Penguin Books India.

Radhakrishnan, Smitha. 2009. 'Professional Women, Good Families: Respectable Femininity and the Cultural Politics of a "New" India', *Qualitative Sociology*, 32, pp. 195–212.

Raju, Saraswati. 2011. Introduction: 'Conceptualizing Gender, Space and Place', in Saraswati Raju (ed.), *Gendered Geographies: Space and Place in South Asia*. New Delhi: Oxford University Press, pp. 1–30.

Ranade, Shilpa. 2007. 'The Way She Moves: Mapping the Everyday Production of Gendered-Space', *Economic and Political Weekly*, 42 (17), pp. 1519–26.

Tara, Shelly. 2011. 'Private Space in Public Transport: Locating Gender in the Delhi Metro', *Economic and Political Weekly*, XLVI (51), pp. 71–74.

Tenhunen, S. 2006. 'Transforming Boundaries: Women's Work and Domesticity', in Lina Fruzzetti and Sirpa Tenhunen (eds.), *Culture, Power and Agency*. Kolkata: STREE.

READING THE CITY THROUGH ART

CHRISTIANE
BROSIUS

Particularly since the new millennium, India's metropoles have undergone rapid change in the manner in which they organise and manage populations, traffic, nature, housing and work. Often, the transformation is so dramatic that it is difficult even for long-time residents of these cities to recognise familiar environments, to continue habitual practices and nurture well-oiled networks. Construction and demolition work impact the everyday—visual, built and soundscapes—in residential neighbourhoods, on streets or stretches of formerly barren land. While the many daily newcomers witness the speed and growth of the city, unaware of the layers of metamorphosed urban landscapes, residents living in the cities over generations or decades seem to quickly forget the colonial bungalows and gardens, shrines and small shops, or long stretches of 'wilderness'. Hardly any place remains uncontested, used or occupied by humans and animals, and nature seems to survive merely in protected and gated contexts. The urban imaginary of cities like Bengaluru, Mumbai, Kolkata or Delhi is often emphasised in commercial media or personal gossip and seems to be torn between an apocalyptic 'megacity' narrative sparked with thorns of informality, poverty and lethargic stagnation, poor infrastructure, and planning and population density. The 'world-class city', on the other hand, is associated with confident progress, seemingly endless fountains of surplus wealth and globalised aesthetics.

How do people navigate a fluid city like Delhi? How do they engage with the city as an assemblage of sites of residency, leisure, work and transit?[1] And why should we consider art production as an interesting optic to view urban space, change and diversity, here, in the instance of Delhi? Often, art is understood as an elite or 'Western' product, or as folk and rural—and somehow not belonging to the Zeitgeist of a booming city. Moreover, art has been examined as a form of political activism of a particular organisation or protest movement, as a means of education and mobilisation. More recently, particularly with respect to urban planning and policies, public art practice has come to be discussed as both a vehicle for democratisation, social cohesion and community engagement, and, simultaneously, as flagging future gentrification, and thus, further social exclusion (Lees and Melhuish, 2015: 242–60).

Without wanting to push it towards either of these 'directions', I propose that art helps us explore urbanisation processes 'between' the mega and the world-class city, the apocalyptic and the euphoric narrative. It may contribute some more, and needs fine tuning to remove those processes from the developmental and modernist optic critiqued by scholars like Jennifer Robinson or Ananya Roy. Art practice offers challenging and highly interesting insights into the in-between spaces of a city, and often engages with the generation of temporary, alternative views of, and insights into, the 'world-class city' (Brosius, 2010). The world-class city is marked by a strong normative drive to reach globally indexed benchmarks of development, by the aspiration to catch up with other world-class cities and move from the status of 'third world' to 'first world city'. Based on Asher Ghertner's (2015) 'future-oriented technology' or 'project', the notion of Delhi as a world-class city scans, classifies and maps it in ways different from the 'ordinary' city. It is this vernacular or the everyday that art projects highlight and engage with—also, but not always, as a critique of global city aesthetics and politics that demolish and displace, disrupt and gloss over. So if the world-class city trains a particular way of seeing and puts in place a form of power and knowledge that produces a particular aesthetic, it is the art projects, I would argue, that 'look' back and 'work against' this grain, slowing down or altering the high speed and linear direction of 'global cities' narratives. This approach is also followed by Jordan and Lindner when exploring 'some of the ways in which visual culture responds to, intervenes in, decelerates and critiques global conditions of urban speed and mobility' (2016: 2). Interruption through art in our case would open up a space for ambiguity and exploration.

ART WORLDS: BUILT AND NATURAL ENVIRONMENTS

Along with the construction and demolition boom in New Delhi, particularly since the 2000s, we can see the growing interest of urban artists in the fabric of their city, with its precarious ecology and gendered as well as class-based politics of access, with the speed and quality of its transformation. This interest is not coincidental, even though the background of the artists, their biographies and aspirations may differ greatly. It seems as if the artists, more than other cultural practitioners are, at this moment, spearheading a move towards excavating and contemplating forgotten or marginalised layers of Delhi's histories, becoming environmental activists and stock-takers of what could be defined as natural, cultural, social and historical resources of, and in, the city, many of which are either lacking or face extinction. Other artists directly address issues of habitat, such as land grabbing, social inequality and exclusion. Their attention is often facilitated by a research-based aspiration to pierce through the glamorous surface of the city, dig deeper into layers that reveal natural microcosms, repositories and alternative habitations.

Almost ethnographically, the artist-activist-archivist collects and assembles diverse data, as if the city were a laboratory. There is careful study—sometimes from a distance, sometimes in intimate closeness—of the farming of marigold flower beds, the lifeworlds of farmers and resettled rickshaw pullers, the habitats of homeless industrial workers or nomadic *sadhvis*. This is, for instance, the case with Atul Bhalla's work (1964) that is deeply entwined with environmental issues and water resources in the city: 'Questioning distribution, regulation, commodisation and pollution of water, Bhalla has, over the years, explored its physical, historical, spiritual and political significance in relation to the population of New Delhi' (2014: 123). Another artist whose work often consists of layer upon layer of materials that reveal different qualities of the city, and largely the river Yamuna, is Sheba Chhachhi (1958). Her poetic and skilful research-based and participatory works weave together spatial and temporal facets and thus reveal connectivities that for her represent an eco-philosophy of, and for, a city and life therein. The third artist is Gigi Scaria (1978). His fascination with the city of Delhi brings to light social structures and hierarchies of built and imagined environs of urban living. Like Bhalla and Chhachhi, Scaria creates think spaces that enable a critical distance, yet an emphatic intimacy, with the ways in which 'world class' canon can be challenged by 'everyday world' narratives and strategies.

This article explores three artists, their work and public art events that have surfaced since the early 2000s. It thus addresses a small temporal window of art production related to the reflection of the city and how artworks experiment with new ways of exhibiting in urban space. This certainly does not suggest that art interventions are new to India: especially informed through activist and protest movements in the late 1980s, art has been crucial in the form of street theatre and performances or with respect to a critical positioning vis-à-vis communalism, gender violence and the labour movement (Achar and Pannikar, 2012). This article considers the role of waterscapes—here, the river Yamuna—and brings in aspects of urban planning and habitation.

TAKE A WALK ON THE WILD SIDE (OF THE RIVER): ATUL BHALLA

One morning in January 2012, I accompany Atul Bhalla to the Yamuna, to one of the sites of his work on the river. I have been wanting to go for quite some time. We drive past the Chandrawal water treatment plant, a piece of industrial heritage along the NH1 bypass (also named Dr. K. B. Hedgewar Marg, after one of the founding fathers of radical Hindu nationalism). Atul mentions that artist-activist Vivan Sundaram and he thought that this building ought to be a protected site, maybe even turned into a gallery or museum space (quite like other industrial heritage sites, such as Tate Modern in London). He also explains that we are headed to a biodiversity park, which is less than five years old, and that there are plans to relocate the zoo from Sundar Nagar there. No, not because this will be better for the animals, as I spin off, thinking about the dilapidated animal environs, but because then one of the prime properties can be opened up for real estate development. We pass by Kudsia ghat in the north of the city, where people immerse the ashes of the dead. (…) Then we drive up to Wazirabad, passing by the Yamuna biodiversity park. To the left, says Atul, there were fields just until a few years ago. Now, all has been 'willed' (not sold) to people who then started constructing houses on the fields. There is no electricity, no sewage, yet, only drains. This, says Bhalla, will grow further, unless and until the grounds are protected. Suddenly we leave all this behind and I can't believe my eyes: we see no more electric poles, no more houses, hardly any cars. Water buffalo, the pump houses Atul has been taking pictures of earlier, every 200 or so metres, all inhabited by one caretaker who is paid ₹2,500 to switch the water on and off at particular times. This is where many Gujjars live, an ethnic pastoralist community of both Muslim or Hindu affiliation. We reach the river. Sand, water, plots of agricultural land, birds and boats, as far as the eye can see. And we are just a few kilometres away from the city centre of Delhi (field notes by the author, 2012).

Atul Bhalla began coming here in 1998, more regularly since 2000, and has, ever since, documented its change. Walking is a central element in Bhalla's work and a way to explore often geographically close but infrastructurally remote areas of the city. His works emerge at the interstices of culture and nature, humans and their natural environment in the city. Moreover, walking is a particular way of experiencing the city; it allows for access to sites with no roads, enables other views of the city and other encounters with buildings, people, animals and plants. Bhalla collects photographs of everyday sites related to access to water, such as pump houses and water taps or manhole covers, mapping the underground networks of water distributed to households across the city. Several works about the Yamuna exist, such as the *Yamuna Walk*. This diary-like photographic account, covering 22 km that Bhalla walked over four days within Delhi's boundaries in 2007, shows a face of the city and the river that is unknown to the majority of Delhites (Noorani, 2012). The series of over 150 images depicts the harvesting of marigold fields, water pipes, landscapes of fields, sewage and garbage, cattle and huts. A xeroxed selection was exhibited at the Select City Walk mall in Saket, an expanding, upcoming part of south Delhi. The intention was to bring the beautiful and forgotten river onto the radar of Delhi's affluent middle class, which often considers 'wild' nature as 'wasteland' and available for urban development, or as garbage dumps. The intervention was part of 'The Hunt', an initiative curated under the auspices of KHOJ International Artists' Association, to challenge people's perception of public art and the city.

Another key work by Bhalla is *Chabeel*, an installation of an enlarged walk-in water vessel placed next to Kashmere Gate (a Mughal monument under 'protection' by the Archaeological Survey

Atul Bhalla, 2008
Still from the work *Chabeel*, installation at 48°C Public Art Ecology,
New Delhi (Kashmere Gate)
Sand, cement, water, ceramic tiles, stickers, recyclable paper,
plywood, video projection; dimensions variable

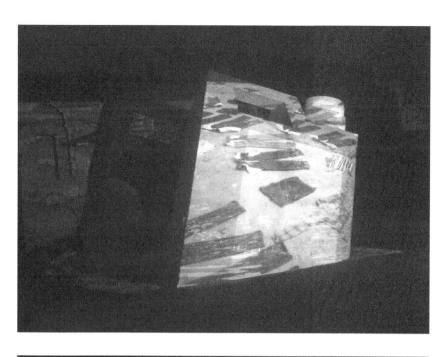

of India, located near one of the city's largest metro stations and normally closed to public). The vessel, alluding to the pilgrims' habit to return from their travels with sacred water, also serves as a kiosk, and is based on the northwest Indian ritual of handing out free drinking water to the public, which is considered to be a means of earning personal merit. To Bhalla, it represents a rare quality of civic responsibility and care, the revitalisation of which he would like to see. Moreover, aimed at remembering the forgotten and shifted ways of the Yamuna—and in that sense showing parallels to Sheba Chhachhi's *Water Diviner* (mentioned later)—Bhalla pursues the idea of multilayered histories and narratives. He retrieved one such connected history from old maps of pre-1956 Delhi and discovered that the Yamuna once ran next to Kashmere Gate. Moreover, Bhalla connected his performative installation to the Yamuna with signboards in the metro station and stickers in Hindi and English that asked, 'Have you ever seen the Yamuna? Have you ever touched the Yamuna?' He thereby suggested that the river has been dramatically cut off from the city's everyday life, since for many 'city-zens' it has become a restricted area or a polluted 'nuisance' to be avoided (Sharan, 2014).

One might argue that in Bhalla's work the Yamuna functions as an 'in-between' place, which, though precious and fertile to some (e.g., as provider of agricultural production, as ritual cremation ground, as site of ritual immersion), to others is a polluted space and a burden; indeed, this is demonstrated by the fact that leisure use of its embankment is 'restricted'. In Bhalla's view, the river is 'shunned' by the middle classes and the elite, and is thus not a public but rather a marginalised and discriminated space. The highly mediated cleaning efforts by environmental groups or spiritual communities (e.g., *Meri Dilli Meri Yamuna* [My Delhi, My Yamuna]—a large river-cleansing agitation coordinated by the religious–spiritual Art of Living Foundation) since 2010 reveal a growing desire to recover and include the river as a cleansed, reclaimed and potentially rejuvenating (middle-class) leisure space, thereby triggering a reinterpretation of accessibility to, and ownership of, natural resources. Although stressing the importance of recovering the river and water's multiple meanings for a more complex understanding of nature's relevance for urban recreation, civic responsibility and participation, *Chabeel* was also one of the few artworks at the public art festival, *48°C Public Art Ecology* (2008), that dealt with religious practice in 'secular' cities. The presence of religion in contemporary global art in India is closely tied up with notions of modernism and rationality and the tensions caused by a 'political doctrine of secularism' that impacts contemporary art production (Zitzewitz, 2014: 5). Thus, the inclusion of religious themes in the secular field of gallery art is often accompanied by contestations, or avoided.

OF WATER BODIES AND LOVE STORIES: SHEBA CHHACHHI

The increasing interest of artists in the city and its fabric coalesces with experiments of developing and displaying the artworks in, and for, public consumption. Reflections on urban change thus also translate into a new landscape of 'in-between spaces' (Brosius and Schilbach, 2016: 1–6) as laboratory for both art and life in the city. One of the most remarkable artists combining these two perspectives in her work is Sheba Chhachhi. Like Atul Bhalla, she has been part of some of the pioneering public art interventions in Delhi in the past decade. For instance, Chhachhi's interactive video sculpture, *Bhogi/Rogi* (consumption/disease), was associated with the KHOJ curating project at the same mall that also had previously exhibited Bhalla's *Yamuna Walk*. Placed in the entrance hall, the walk-in space dealt with knowledge of food and body relations.

The city is often described in terms of decadence, destruction, exploitation and social inequality, a seemingly faceless place with little humanity. Even though she critically and intellectually engages with environmental politics, civil and women's rights, and the dramatic pollution of the Yamuna, there is something intrinsically mythical and poetic about Chhachhi's work, her visual, spatial and verbal language that itself forms a body of work. Yet, no taste of romanticisation emerges from the many scenes that deal with an eco-philosophy of water bodies, mythologies, places and people. Likewise, despite the concern with ecological damage and toxicity in many of her works, there is, in all the concern for climate change and social inequality, no trace of cynicism nor anger—instead, a tender retrieval of dignity amidst harsh lifeworlds. Chhachhi's camera has accompanied, and represented, courageous women as they claim spaces and rights; women's empowerment and civil rights surface in individual life portraits, but also in collective acts of urban protest and demonstrations. They span decades of being part of the

Sheba Chhachhi, 2005
Jamuna 3, from *The Jamuna Series* (triptych)
Moving Image Lightbox, 40 x 20 x 40 inches, Digital Print on Duratrans, 2 layers

feminist movement, environmental activism, and artist/performance groups such as SAHMAT or the KHOJ artist network. Chhachhi is a pioneering contemporary artist when it comes to experiments with site-specific interventions in the city, with public art formats of kinds, deeply rooted, but not only deriving from, leftist street theatre and feminist protests. I focus on two works by Chhachhi, *The Water Diviner* (2008) and *The Yamuna Series* (2005). In her book *ArcSiltDive*, the artist articulates an impressive elaboration of how her deeply immersive installation at the Old Delhi Public Library's basement developed:

> It was while walking through the sites of the '48 Degrees' project in the northern and central parts of the city, absorbing details of their layered history, that I realised how much of what we stand on, gaze at, was once water. From the dried-up lake of Roshanara Bagh to the teeming thoroughfare outside Old Delhi railway station, today's dry, dusty, polluted and fraught urbanscape shimmers and dissolves into waterways and water-bodies of less than a few hundred years ago (Chhachhi, in Sangari, 2016: 29).

The work fills a large room in the basement of the library with piles of books in which, like waves, lightboxes of miniature paintings seem to float, depicting the Yamuna and scenes from Krishna mythology, as well as montaged shots of Delhi today. Resembling a pathway, another lightbox on the ground shows a detail from a pre-colonial map, connecting a bust of a lion's head (reminiscent of the fountain in the former colonial swimming pool) and a screen showing an elephant diving and dissolving time and again in the sea. This work resonates as 'affective reservoir for people to respond to the city's environment',[2] present in Chhachhi's description:

> A wide range of materials—scientific, historical, mythological—coalesce in this underground cavern. A map of Shahjahanabad, circa 1830, showing waterways and gardens; stories of the river-goddess Yamuna replete with transgressive desire; medieval miniature paintings recording the lives that flourished along her banks, reports on the… disappearance of the dolphins… (Chhachhi, in Sangari, 2016: 29).

The public art work, along with its placement in the Public Library, is also an attempt to nurture belonging and a vocabulary to think differently and across people's relations to the river in past and present.

A work made for gallery space is *The Yamuna Series*, a triptych of moving lightboxes that engage a female gaze onto the changing city and the environment, with several layers of visual representation and some in slow motion. *Yamuna 1*, for instance, shows metal taps as if they emerge from the background photographs of a river made of sewage and white foam:

> ... the empty taps come out of my years in the basti, of watching these incredible fights at the water queue, the youngest girl of the house joining the queue at four in the morning ... (personal conversation with Chhachhi, June 2016)

The second image takes on the perspective of an old woman as she gazes, sitting, across a landfill that is covered by a grid of colonial Delhi, and the third one presents a younger woman, demonstratively holding up a paper to the viewer as she moves across a picture of the river's embankment:

> While one (woman, CB) witnesses the erasure of the last areas of wilderness by uncontrolled urbanisation, another holds identity papers aloft, fragile protection against impending displacement. ... The politics of urban planning have reduced the waters of the River Yamuna to narrow drains, her floodplains to potential real estate... a painful reminder of the present condition of the river in Indian cities (Chhachhi, in Sangari, 2016: 38).

With her work, Chhachhi also criticises the grabbing of the floodplains for potential real estate development. Especially, but not only, in *The Yamuna Series* (2005), the artist is concerned with displacement at large, and marginalised (female) groups—such as ascetics—in particular: 'The river bank is where the marginals of the city find a place, this has been true for hundreds of years', the river and its embankment are on the one hand associated with ritual, from simple worship to funeral rites. But they are, says Chhachhi,

Gigi Scaria, 2013
Installation view of *City Unclaimed, with the Fountain of Purification*
Mixed media including epoxy, digital print, motor system, paint, plastic, polyurethane, and water
Courtesy: Artist. Commissioned by the Smart Museum of Art

also liminal places hosting travellers, mendicants, new migrants, runaway women, the homeless: 'So, for example, if you are a sadhu, have spent some years living by the river and have then built yourself a hut and a shrine on the embankment, nobody will ask you to leave, it's a public space.' In conversation, she tells the story of Poonam Giri, a woman sadhu living on the banks of the Yamuna beyond the cremation grounds at Nigambodh Ghat. Rescued from drowning in the river by an *uddasin*, she took on robes and acquired the ironical, but much wanted, government issued ID, proving that she was a bonafide sadhu. When the Delhi development authorities (DDA) pushed out hundreds of thousands of people settled on the embankment, most famously the people from Yamuna Pushta in 2004 as part of a clean-up project, she almost lost her hut next to a small Shiv temple. Poonam Giri took refuge in a Hanuman temple in town and went to court, asserting her right to live on the embankment and maintain the temple. We see her holding the precious ID as she moves, unmoored, across the river and the ghats. The third work from *The Yamuna Series* shows a woman looking at the urban grid moving across landfill sites on the edge of the river: 'This witnessing of urban change, from a women's perspective, is a critical part of this whole period of my work, coinciding with and informing my engagement with the river Yamuna,' says Chhachhi (personal conversation, June 2016).

MINIATURE WORLDS, MODEL CITIES: GIGI SCARIA

Gigi Scaria's work reflects socio-economic inequalities that are connected to the hungry tide of urban development and real estate (Khandelwal, 2015). His miniature worlds, maps and sculptures play with the scale and perception of urban growth, and carry a self-reflexive element in that they engage with how we 'pattern' our notions of our position in the city that constantly changes, produces the new, superimposes or destroys 'the old' (*Panic City*, 2006), how it creates new views and assemblages each day (*Amusement Park*, 2009).

Scaria's work is entrenched with reflections on urban imaginaries and experiences, with great emphasis on the fluidity of urban codes within a regime of attempted order, such as the Master Plan, with themes of migration and displacement. *Panic City* is the video of montaged patches of buildings in Delhi that, as the camera eye flies over them, move up and down asymmetrically to the interrupted tunes of Western classical music, clumsily dancing along. In fact, says Scaria, the shots were taken at a time when the whole area was under threat of demolition for the sake of 'beautification', which, then, gives a different layer of meaning to the title and the movement of houses jumping up and down, in disharmony with the invisible omnipotent 'conductor'. In *City Unclaimed* (2013, Chicago University), he argues that it is migrants and socially underprivileged people who make up the city, and that he intends to bring them as well as their precarious temporality to the fore, pointing at the taboos of 'world class' citizenry.

Scaria started to engage with the city by means of map-making (*Keep Delhi Clean*, 2007, part of the series, *Absence of an Architect*) when the clearing process began in preparation for the Commonwealth Games. Here, aesthetics, spectacle and surveillance are enmeshed. Moreover, Delhi's Master Plan is like a labyrinth of walls; no one knows the city as a whole, and the master plan could be a place where you lose yourself as a *chiffre* of bureaucracy. Remarkable are Scaria's large-sized models—bulldozers, or wheels from amusement parks, both made up of apartment blocks, or the Trojan horse made of apartment blocks (*Someone Left a Horse on the Shore*, 2007)—which play with the marvel and surprise but also the surreality and absurdity of promises related to the 'innocent' world-class city. Scaria writes in his artist statement:

> The layers of social structures and hierarchies one encounters in a single day in Delhi leaves thought for the understanding of a much larger and wider notion called 'India'. The urban and the rural, class and caste, religion and practice, and the endless list of eccentric and idiosyncratic exchanges of different social groups somehow create its own mystery in any urban space in India.[3]

MAKING THE CITY PUBLIC THROUGH ART

Scaria's *Fountain of Purification* was first exhibited at *Yamuna Elbe*, a public art event in 2011, situated on the river bank next to the Old Yamuna Bridge. Like a utopian wonder of modernity and progress, the 24ft high, multistorey apartment tower shoots seemingly endless amounts of water out of the top. The absurd wonder behind this fountain is that the Yamuna's highly contaminated water is, through its transfer, converted into public drinking water (only that there is no public, so the water seems to be wasted).

The three artists discussed here assembled in one public show curated by artist and activist, Ravi Agarwal, which dealt with the role of the river in urban development of Hamburg, Germany, and Delhi.[4] The project was part of a seminar at the Goethe Institut, Delhi (2010), and Agarwal had carefully chosen the site that had been cleared for urban development, ahead of the Commonwealth Games, 2010, unsettling tens of thousands of people. The artworks next to the so-called DDA Golden Jubilee Park 'attempted to unlock this binary of polluted–clean river by bringing in ideas from contemporary culture, global economics, changing ideas of nature and urbanization' (Agarwal and Krause, 2013: Preface). The exhibition also included Chhachhi's work, *Black Waters Will Burn* (2011), a large installation dealing with complex repositories of texts and ritual worship of the Yamuna as goddess and the notion of the river as an urban ecosystem,[5] and Atul Bhalla's network of small local wells (*kuin*) and lit-up, gigantic plastic bottles.

Yamuna Elbe followed from an earlier public art festival mentioned, *48°C Public Art Ecology* (2008). It deserves to be noted here because it was one of the strongest and largest art interventions in Delhi, referring to the highest-ever temperature measured in the city, and the 'heat' of construction and demolition caused by 'world class' development. This festival was a fascinating example of collaborative work between artists, curators, environmental activists, the Goethe Institut, architects and urban designers. The aim was to explore the way in which art in public could engage with the challenges of urbanisation today—to connect broader concepts to local contexts. The site-specific works, exhibited at eight particular locations, were made by more than 20 national and international artists, and accessible through the new metro transport system. The aim of the event, co-sponsored by the German Society for International Cooperation (GIZ), was to stimulate a lively dialogue between artists and urban sites around the issue of the environment, climate change, the scarcity of water, clean air and green in the city.[6] But it was also a passionate experiment with new forms of art and publics in the city, uncovering Delhi in ways other media would probably not have succeeded.

CONCLUSION

Cultural productions like art are a good lens on the ways in which people make and engage with spatial and changing environments and imaginaries. Cities have become challenging arenas for the study of shifting everyday life, but also art worlds and productions. For instance, public art poses interesting questions about new sites and topographies of social spatialisation, with respect to the role of cultural heritage, natural resources and social diversity. In this context, cultural practice must not be seen as a 'luxury surplus', but as something that engages with the fabric of everyday worlds and marginalised groups. Art initiatives thus help in making 'other' cultural maps and narratives of habitation, reading the city differently, revealing unexpected resources and narratives, and building new cross-community connections. The works by Bhalla, Chhachhi and Scaria stand in for a larger web of artists and art practices that help us understand artworks as place-making strategies, as excavation tools and the production of (alternative) knowledge.

◆

NOTES

1. Owing to limitations of space, other important artists and their works on the city of Delhi could not be included—for example, the works of Vivan Sundaram, Asim Waqif, Inder Salim and Vibha Galhotra. Artists such as Archana Hande, Hema Upadhyay, Navjot Altaf, to mention only a few, who work on and in cities like Mumbai, could also not be considered for this article on Delhi. See Kapur (2013).

2. From a comment by Shuddhabrata Sengupta, in a discussion following Chhachhi's presentation of her work at a Seminar, Goethe Institut. Sengupta proposes that in Delhi there is no affective belonging to a space like the Yamuna because most Delhiites are migrants or children of migrants, and have not yet developed such a relationship. Session II: The River and the City—Separate/Connected; URL: http://yamuna-elbe.org/proceedings/ (accessed 6 November 2016).

3. Statement, Signature Art Prize 2014, Singapore Art Museum (URL: https://www.singaporeartmuseum.sg/downloads/apbf/india/Gigi_Scaria.pdf (accessed 1 November 2016).

4. http://yamuna-elbe.org/

5. http://www.yamuna-elbe.de/index.php?title=Sheba_Chhachhi (accessed 6 November 2016).

6. viwww.48c.org

REFERENCES

Achar, Deepta and Shivaji Pannikar (eds.). 2012. *Articulating Resistance: Art and Activism*. Delhi: Tulika.

Agarwal, Ravi and Till Krause (eds.). 2013. *Yamuna Manifesto*. Delhi: Archana Press.

Bhalla, Atul. 2014. *Atul Bhalla: You Always Step into the Same River*. Delhi: Vadhera Art Gallery.

Brosius, Christiane. 2010. *India's Middle Class: New Forms of Urban Leisure, Consumption and Prosperity*. Delhi: Routledge (paperback edition with added Introduction: 2014).

Brosius, Christiane and Tina Schilbach. 2016. '"Mind the Gap": Thinking About In-between Spaces in Delhi and Shanghai', *City, Culture & Society*, 30.

Jordan, Shirley and Christoph Lindner. 2016. *Cities Interrupted: Visual Culture and Urban Space*. UK: Bloomsbury.

Kapur, Geeta. 2013. 'Delhi', in Antawan Byrd (ed.), *Art Cities of the Future*, pp. 89–92. UK: Phaidon.

Khandelwal, Payal. 2015. 'Gigi Scaria: Lost in the City', *The Open Magazine*. http://www.openthemagazine.com/article/art-culture/gigi-scaria-lost-in-the-city

Lees, Loretta and Clare Melhuish. 2015.'Arts-led Regeneration in the UK: The Rhetoric and the Evidence on Urban Social Inclusion', *European Urban and Regional Studies*, 22 (3).

Noorani, Maliha. 2012. '22 km: A Journey into the Present', in *Yamuna Walk*. Photographs by Atul Bhalla. New York; Sepia Eye, Seattle: University of Washington Press.

Sangari, Kumkum (ed.). 2016. *ArcSiltDive: The Works of Sheba Chhachhi*. Delhi: Tulika.

Sharan, Awadhendra. 2014. *In the City, Out of Place: Nuisance, Pollution and Urban Dwelling in Modern Delhi, c. 1850: 2000*. India: Oxford University Press.

Zitzewitz, Karin. 2014. *The Art of Secularism: The Cultural Politics of Modernist Art in Contemporary India*. London: Hurst & Co Publishers; Delhi: Oxford University Press.

❖❖

IV
URBAN POLICY, PLANNING AND GOVERNANCE

INDIA'S 'URBAN' AND THE POLICY DISCONNECT

AJAY K.
MEHRA

... On the other hand, obviously the urban situation in India is
one of deep crisis, and calls for measures analogous to those used
when a house is on fire, or there is a citywide epidemic. *The need
to act becomes an overriding imperative.* And this action must be
taken on the basis of a prima facie cause, derived from the existing
facts, past experience and human insight [italics as in the original]
(GOI, 1998: Vol. I: p. 2).

INTRODUCTION[1]

The Narendra Modi-led Bharatiya Janata Party (BJP)-majority
National Democratic Alliance (NDA) government gave a big push
to urban policy soon after it came to power in 2014, with its own
signature schemes parallel to those launched by its predecessor,
the United Progressive Alliance (UPA), in its decade-long rule. The
fanciest of them all is the creation of 100 smart cities across the
country; the scheme that was inaugurated on 25 June 2016 by the
prime minister seeks to vault India's 'urban' into the future. India is
already on the urbanisation expressway: from a slow urbanisation
rate of 11.4 percent in 1901 (when British India included Pakistan
and Bangladesh, and the cities of Lahore, Karachi, Rawalpindi,
Peshawar and Dhaka that went to the respective countries in 1947)
India's rate more than doubled a century later to 28.53 per cent
in 2001. The 2011 census reported the rate of urbanisation at
31.16 per cent.

In 1951, the first census in independent India four years after
partition reported a phenomenal 41.38 per cent decadal growth in
the urban population, obviously spurred by the pressure of refugees

crossing the borders from East and West Pakistan. As we assess the prospects a century later, a UN analysis indicates that '...China, India and Nigeria are projected to account for 37 per cent of the increase of nearly 2.5 billion people in the urban population by 2050'. Their significant projection is that, between 2014 and 2050, urban areas in India are expected to grow by 404 million people. India's contribution to the urban population in these three-and-a-half decades is projected to be the largest.[2]

Clearly, this would work in two ways. On the one hand, there would be a larger concentration of people in the existing urban centres, increasing population density, and, on the other, new cities might also arise. Thus, while qualitatively smart cities would add a new paradigmatic change to India's urbanscape, there would be a need to seriously imbue the existing cities with a qualitative upgrade of, even provision for, basic amenities and the latest infrastructure, and enhance their productive capacity to become engines of growth that would be sustainable. Since India has several ageing cities, a combination of conservation, renewal and planning for new neighbourhoods is important. Also, with India's extreme weather conditions, the design has to comply with harsh summers and winters, and an extremely wet monsoon that virtually floods the streets. Indeed, the emerging scenario begs the question as to what was, is, and would be, India's 'urban'—a question that encompasses retrospection, reality and the prospects of India's Urbanisation.

DEFINING 'URBAN'

The use of the term 'urban' in this analysis requires definition. Derived from the Latin *urbānus* [*urb*-(stem of *urbs*) city+-*ānus*], it is defined as 'of, relating to, or constituting a city or town, living in city or town'. The word also refers to music emerging from, and developing in, densely populated areas of large cities, especially those populated by people of African or Caribbean origin, perhaps with a derogatory meaning. In the early 17th century, it meant 'of, or pertaining to a city or city life'; it was rarely used till the mid-20th century when the United States began using the word to denote the urban sprawl, suggesting the concentration or expansion of African–American settlements, and was reduced to a euphemism for slum clearance. It has since become an accepted expression for composite city life—good and bad. Here, 'urban' is used with this broad sweep which conveys shades of the phenomenon that we love and hate simultaneously.

RETROSPECT

Cities in India, as also 'urban', are as much a part of the process of evolution and growth globally as they are ingrained in civilisational history. The processes underlined by urban historians and sociologists such as Robert McC. Adams (1966), Gordon Childe (1964), Noel P. Gist and Sylvia Fleiss Fava (1964), and Arnold Toynbee (1934) point out that cities across the world emerged with the sedentariness of humanity, mostly along rivers or in river valleys that made an agricultural revolution possible by producing an agricultural surplus. This surplus was collected (even extracted), secured, concentrated and distributed in an organised fashion by a formalised leadership, and by a well-developed power structure to build alternative settlement and habitation centres with non-agricultural pursuits. The availability of foodgrains was essential to feed the population engaged in alternative economic activities being fostered in cities. As built space has been involved in the competition for possession along with power politics from time immemorial and cities represent power, pomp and politics in each of their dimensions, class in structure and habitation would naturally have been reflected in early cities (Pahl, 1965).

The mention of grand cities, such as Ayodhya, Mathura, Hastinapur, Indraprastha and Dwarka, in Indian classics clearly indicates that drawing upon their present, the writers of India's prehistory imagined grand urban form and structure as essential to empires. The Indus Valley civilisation, one of four prehistoric urban civilisations along with the Sumerian, Egyptian (Nile Valley) and Mayan, was predominantly urban, although villages continued to prosper. In some places the villagers seem to have been dispossessed and the Indus settlements were built over the village sites. In any case, some kind of centralised state, and certainly fairly extensive town planning with the use of burnt brick, weights and measures, the domestication of animals, various crops—cotton, sesame, peas, barley—as well as the presence of a merchant class that engaged in extensive trading in the Indus Valley, shows the emergence of 'urban' early in the history of the subcontinent.

If prehistoric and ancient India witnessed growth and expansion, and the imagination to develop cities, medieval and colonial periods also witnessed new urban forms with the patronage of contemporary empires. Obviously, this added layers to India's urban experience. However, historically, cities have been habitats and spaces with a deeply ingrained exclusionary bias. The 'urban' in design, and as an economic magnet, has pushed out and neglected the margins and those who inhabit marginal spaces due to its inalienable consanguinity to regimes and political power. This changed marginally in the modern era. While the consonance of political and economic power allows urban spaces exclusionary designs and policies, democratic politics and governance bring in a balance that minimises exclusion through inclusionary policies.

APPRAISING INDIA'S URBAN

While India's urban would need an appraisal in the context of the requirements of the 21st century, layers of existing urban forms, persisting deficits in urban development since independence, weak civic engagement in shaping and governing cities, and emerging needs must be factored in.

The colonial preoccupation with economic and political priorities added a new layer, a new trend and a new morphology (of the West) to Indian urbanisation. The characteristic feature of the layers and form that were contributed by the colonial masters was the creation of exclusionary civil lines (meant mainly for British officers, Europeans and the local collaborating gentry) with facilities of piped water, drainage systems, neatly planned residential areas, metalled roads, exclusive shopping colonnades, and so on. Their multiple needs either created new urban forms or redesigned the existing ones. The characteristic features of colonial urban development reflect these needs: administrative control (sub-divisional, district, commissioner-level and provincial capital urban centres); commercial (including industrial) and port towns; cantonments for stationing the military while setting them apart from the local population; railway colonies; and entertainment, vacation and recuperation needs that led to a new urban form that still persists in India and other British colonies—hill stations.[3] It is not to be wondered at that Lord Rippon's Local Self-Government initiative in 1882 had an urban bias, and it introduced municipal government in several cities and towns across the country.

India's independence and its partition created the challenge of resettling millions of refugees and since most of them preferred to stay in cities, resettlement was largely an urban challenge. Rehabilitation colonies and sub-towns were set up in Delhi, Bombay (now Mumbai), Ahmedabad, Uttar Pradesh, Haryana, Punjab and Calcutta. The Union Government constituted an Environmental Hygiene Committee in June 1948, which estimated that in addition to the one million houses needed for the resettlement of refugees, the shortage in urban housing in the country was 1.84 million (Dwivedi, 2007: 41). Clearly, for a decade after independence, the focus of urban planning in India was to create temporary shelters for the refugees, which developed over the years into permanent residential neighbourhoods.

The beginning of planned economic development in India, with the setting up of the Planning Commission in March 1950, also naturally gave priority to housing. The First Five Year Plan (1951–56) focused on housing, and the speedy spatial and occupational rehabilitation of the refugees. The Union Government simultaneously established a Ministry of Works and Housing for the purpose. The Second Five Year Plan, with its focus on industrialisation, led to the creation of several industrial cities from 1956 onwards. The steel cities of Rourkela, Durgapur, Bhilai and Bokaro; refinery towns of Barauni, Noonmati, Haldia and Ankleshwar; fertiliser towns of Sindri, Mittrapur, Naya Nangal and Namrup; port towns of Kandla and Paradeep; and, aluminium towns of Korba and Ratnagiri are some examples of new urban centres. Although these industrial cities were largely planned, they became the new magnets that brought rural migrants in search of work. The emergence of slums naturally followed. Programmes for slum development and resettlement, coated with the socialist rhetoric that was then part of national planning, followed and took into consideration the resettlement of slum residents with minimum dislocation, entailing re-housing at the existing sites of slums, and enabling employment and the provision of only 'minimum standards of environmental hygiene and essential civic amenities' so as to 'keep rents within the paying capacity of the slum dwellers' (Batra, 2009: 6).

The Third Five Year Plan recognised the importance of cities and towns in balanced regional development and recommended a regional approach to urban planning, factoring in urban land regulation and a check on urban land prices. Planned urban development presupposes a master plan and it was recommended for big cities. However, the preparation of master plans was considered the responsibility of state and local governments. Further, keeping in view perspective planning for cities, it was recommended that as far as possible new industries be established away from large and congested cities, and the municipal administration be strengthened (Bhagat, 2014: 4). The first three Plans thus had a three-pronged approach to urban development: provisions for housing, slum clearance and rehabilitation. Most of the states introduced master plans to achieve each of the three objectives. As a result, expensive low-density urban settlements emerged that did not factor in rural migrants arriving in the cities. Obviously, the strategies of urban development produced skewed results.

The Fourth, Fifth and Sixth Five Year Plans marked the second phase of India's urban planning. This phase witnessed policy shifts such as slum clearance, and the upgrade and improvement of environmental conditions in slums through better drainage, sewerage and sanitation. This was combined with the earlier policy of a 'balanced regional development'. The development of small and medium towns was adopted as a strategy to contain the further growth of large, over-crowded and metropolitan cities. Housing for the urban poor became a priority in order to make land available for the provision of services, which necessitated controlling land prices. The Sixth Five Year Plan (1978–83) recommended the Integrated Development of Small and Medium Towns (IDSMT) aimed at promoting the growth and development of medium-sized towns with a population of less than 100,000, providing them with infrastructure and basic services along with improvements in the economic and physical infrastructure of cities with populations of up to 500,000. The strategy was to establish them as engines of economic growth, which would shift the 'pull factor' away from the metropolises and relocate them at such urban settlements that could take the pressure. However, despite covering 1,854 towns, slackness in implementation and the unavailability of land as well as the states' inability (or reluctance) to match their share virtually aborted the scheme (GOI, Vol. III, 2008: 397).

The Seventh (1985–90) to the Eleventh (2007–12) Five Year Plans, covering a period of 27 years, mark the third phase in India's urbanisation. The period coincided with the Indian economy beginning to open up with Rajiv Gandhi as prime minister. Following a two-year period of political uncertainty, the P. V. Narasimha Rao government provided political stability and opened up the economy. There was a policy shift in the urban sector as well, and private participation and the participatory approach in urban development brought greater focus on city planning, strengthening the link between urban growth and economic development, and employment generation. The Seventh Plan pitched for a radical transformation of housing policies, leaving this to the private sector. In the process, the government began to reduce its role in resource mobilisation for housing, for subsidised housing for the poor, and the acquisition and development of land (ibid.: Ch. 11).

The first National Housing Policy (NHP) announced in 1988 was aimed at reducing homelessness and improving the conditions of the inadequately housed. The provision of minimum levels of basic services to all conceived the role of the government as a provider for the poorest and vulnerable sections, and as a facilitator for other income groups and the private sector by the removal of constraints, and the increased supply of land and services (GOI, 2008: Vol. III). A National Housing Bank (1988), under the aegis of the Reserve Bank of India, was set up even as a scheme for the Urban Basic Services for the Poor was launched. Also, the first-ever National Commission on Urbanisation (NCU, 1988, chaired by Charles Correa) was set up to link urbanisation and economic development. It identified 329 towns as GEMs (Generator of Economic Momentum) that were further subdivided into NPCs (National Priority Centres) and SPCs (State Priority Centres). Besides GEMs and NPCs, the Commission also identified 49 SPURs (Spatial Priority Urban Regions). The future growth in urbanisation was expected to take place along these nodes and corridors. The detailed recommendations included were mostly on land, housing, water and sanitation, transport, urban poverty, urban form and urban governance (GOI, 1988). However, political uncertainty ever since 1989 reduced the *NCU Report* to an academic document.

Liberalisation in India in 1991 impacted urban policy in the Eighth Plan (1992–97), which recognised economic development as key to urban growth and emphasised public–private partnerships in urban development. The Mega City Scheme, introduced in 1993–94, covering Mumbai, Calcutta, Chennai, Bangalore and Hyderabad, sought to build urban infrastructure in collaboration with the Planning Commission and the Ministry of Urban Development. The 74th Constitutional Amendment Act brought statutory support to urban local bodies. The focus during this period was on moving to a market-based financing regime from state transfers and subsidy-based urban infrastructure (Batra, 2009).

The focus on centrally sponsored schemes increased from 2004. The Union Government launched the Jawaharlal Nehru National Urban Renewal Mission (JNNURM) in December 2005 to focus attention on integrated development—basic services to the urban poor, including housing, water supply, sanitation, road network, urban transport, the development of downtown/inner city, etc.—in 63 select mission cities by merging it with earlier programmes—Mega City, IDSMT, National Slum Development Programme and Valmiki Ambedkar Awas Yojna (Bhagat, 2014: 5). The non-mission cities and towns were covered under the Urban Infrastructure Development Scheme for Small and Medium Towns (UIDSSMT) and Integrated Housing and Slum Development Programme (IHSDP). The Ministry of Housing and Urban Poverty Alleviation (MoHUPA) was the nodal agency for basic services for the urban poor and IHSDP programmes, which catered for housing and basic amenities for the urban poor, especially slum-dwellers. These schemes also catered for other basic services such as sanitation, water supply, sewerage, solid waste disposal, etc. On the other hand, the Ministry of Urban Development (MoUD) supervised Urban Infrastructure and Governance, and UIDSSMT schemes under JNNURM.

The midterm evaluation of the Eleventh Plan acknowledged that urban development and renewal under JNNURM required around ₹3–4 trillion, whereas JNNURM allocated only ₹660 billion for a seven-year period (2005–12).[4] The Twelfth Five Year Plan (2012–17) sought to consolidate JNNURM with investments in Urban Infrastructure and Governance, Rajiv Awas Yojana, slum rehabilitation and capacity building. It noted barriers in implementing the programme; notably, the failure to mainstream urban planning, incomplete reforms and the slow progress in project implementation, the delay in securing land for projects and obtaining approval from various regulatory authorities, and the exclusion of the peri-urban areas outside city limits from the planning process. Several cities had yet to start urban planning and making the process participatory.

MAKING INDIA'S 'URBAN' SMART

Even as India is attempting to rapidly advance into the international league of smart cities with high-technology hubs, her stuttering 'urban' journey ever since independence to merely build and maintain her towns and cities with the minimum basic infrastructure and public services is proceeding at a snail's pace. Ignoring the 'local' since independence, populism in launching multiple top-down programmes has left local bodies emaciated and unable to perform even their basic functions. In addition, the disregard for local and specific needs of urban centres of different sizes and capacities, the pressure of the push factor from rural areas with adverse economies and demography, and the absence of continual planning efficaciously implemented have combined to keep the Indian urban in a perpetual mess. Equally, it has been argued that the focus after independence on the country's 80 per cent rural neglected the urban base, and by the time the need for their maintenance and rejuvenation was realised, the task had become multi-sectoral and gigantic (Mehra, 1991).

The National Democratic Alliance (NDA) government's well-intentioned plans to place Indian urbanisation on a global pedestal with the smart cities initiative has been positioned ahead of other schemes on the Urban Development Ministry's website. However, schemes such as AMRUT (Atal Mission for Rejuvenation and Urban Transformation), planned for augmenting and building urban infrastructure, appears to follow the earlier model of a signature scheme to politically highlight the party and its leaders. For, the scheme's mission states steps that should be normally and routinely undertaken by the government. In fact, many of the measures belong to the realm of local bodies and the state government.

That the earlier scheme, Capacity Building for Urban Local Bodies, continues on its agenda gives the impression that the thrust of urban rejuvenation is based on paternalistic, if not patronage, support of the upper echelons of government. Indeed, state governments and all the political parties are guilty of this intentional neglect and indifference. Whether or not the older ongoing schemes, such as JNNURM, CBULB, and the like, succeed, the more recent ones, such as AMRUT, HRIDAY (Heritage City Development and Augmentation Yojna) and the Swachh Bharat Scheme (another basic scheme of local government), are likely to burden the Union Government with the responsibilities of both state and local governments, and could cause implementation disarray, some of which could be politically motivated.

Cities as habitats are products of human technological advancement; the more advanced a civilisation, the more innovative it becomes in design and day-to-day operation. Hence, I would argue, the 'urban' in any form, anywhere, civilisationally, is a smart concept for human habitation. The current wave of conceiving and making cities smart, ever since the early 1990s, begins with situating information technology, combined with infrastructure, architecture and everyday objects with our own local and administrative bodies to address social, economic and environmental problems. Obviously, the beginnings are from those parts of the world that have used each bit of their civilisational and technical advances to make their 'urban' smarter, where even quotidian living is based, and dependent, on smart technology. Since smart cities are presently part of the Western and advanced-tech world, we must factor in our own environment where they would exist with the normal 'urban' that is far from smart. Even in the West, critical questions are being asked: 'What if the smart cities of the future are buggy and brittle? What are we getting ourselves into?'[5]

While we must look at this opportunity to advance the 'urban' in India with enthusiastic optimism, we must also discard the elements of political opportunism and grandstanding from the programme and the vision. The country as much needs to keep pace with international developments as make her habitats and quotidian living safe, stress-free, and complete with basic requirements and infrastructure.

◆

NOTES

1. Research help of Jeetendra Kumar, Assistant Professor, Shaheed Bhagat Singh Evening College, University of Delhi, is gratefully acknowledged.

2. *World Urbanization Prospects: The 2014 Revision*, Department of Economic and Social Affairs, New York: United Nations, 2014; Highlights https://esa.un.org/unpd/wup/Publications/Files/WUP2014-Highlights.pdf (accessed on 27 June 2016).

3. For an empirical and critical account of colonial urban development, see King (1976).

4. http://planningcommission.nic.in/plans/mta/11th_mta/chapterwise/chap18_urban.pdf (accessed on 19 October 2016).

5. Townsend (2013) cites an example: 'Bugs in the smart city will be more insidious, living inside lots of critical, interconnected systems. Sometimes there may be no way to anticipate the interdependencies. Who could have foreseen the massive traffic jam caused on US Interstate 80 when a bug in the system used to manage juror pools by Placer County, California, erroneously summoned twelve hundred people to report for duty on the same day in 2012?'

REFERENCES

Adams, Robert McC. 1966. *The Evolution of Urban Society*. London: Weidenfeld and Nicolson.

Batra, Lalit. 2009. 'A Review of Urbanization and Urban Policy in Post-independent India.' *Working Paper Series*. New Delhi: Centre for the Study of Law and Governance, JNU, April, CSLG/wp/12.

Bhagat, R. B. 2014. 'Urban Policies and Programmes in India: Retrospect and Prospect', *Yojana*, September.

Childe, Gordon. 1964. *What Happened in History*. Harmondsworth, England: Penguin.

Dwivedi, R. M. 2007. *Urban Development and Housing in India*. New Delhi: New Century.

Gist, Noel P. and Sylvia Fleiss Fava. 1964. *Urban Society*. New York: Thomas Y. Cromwell Company.

Government of India (GOI). 1998. *National Commission on Urbanisation. Vols. I & II*. New Delhi: Ministry of Urban Development.

Government of India (GOI). Planning Commission of India. 2008. *Eleventh Five Year Plan, Vol III*. New Delhi: Oxford University Press.

King, Anthony D. 1976. *Colonial Urban Development: Culture, Social Power and Environment*. London: Routledge & Kegan Paul Ltd.

Mehra, Ajay K. 1991. *The Politics of Urban Redevelopment: A Study of Old Delhi*. New Delhi: Sage Publications.

Pahl, R. E. 1965. *Whose City*? Harmondsworth, England: Penguin.

Townsend, Anthony. 2013. 'What if Smart Cities of the Future are Chock Full of Bugs' (https://placesjournal.org/article/smart-cities/ (accessed on 20 October 2016).

Toynbee, Arnold. 1934. *A Study of History, Vol. II*, London: Oxford University Press.

CHANGING TRAJECTORIES OF URBAN LOCAL GOVERNANCE

AMITA BHIDE

Governance is an arena of the performativity of the state. By extension, local governance may be understood to be associated with the performativity of the local state. The governance of a 'place' embeds several other institutions of the state and brings to the fore key debates associated with state–society relations. These are associated with the degree of democratisation, the extent of decentralisation, the capacity of the state to regulate, implement and enforce its will/intent, the way in which civil society and public sector interface and define the role of government, socio-economic divisions and inequality in society, and so on. It also represents a conjuncture of place and time, and contexts that bring in changing notions of good governance. This article tracks the changing ideas of urban local governance in India from the colonial years to the contemporary. This gives some insight into why the current state of urban local governance is one of such disarray and confusion, and why Indian cities seem to be exceptions to a global trend of decentralised and participatory local governance closely aligned with the objective of attracting international capital.

CONCEPTUALISING LOCAL GOVERNANCE

Local governance is conceptualised from two distinct, but interlinked, perspectives. One of these is linked to the act and processes of government, i.e., the substantive or the technocratic aspect. The other looks at governance from the point of view of deepening democracy.

For a long time, governance was synonymous with 'what governments do'. In recent years, it has been understood as multi-stakeholder arrangements through which a society copes with external challenges, decisions are taken, executed; resources are allocated and norms for the same are developed, and forms of preventing conflict and promoting collaboration are developed (Mohan, 2005).

Stoker (1998) proposed a set of five interlinked propositions to identify the varied aspects of governance. The key dimension of these propositions is that governance involves institutions and actors in government, but also stretches beyond government in establishing and utilising autonomous networks, and using tools that do not necessarily evolve from sovereign power. These propositions reiterate the change in processes that earlier relied on authority to ideas of partnership, collaboration and networking. This change has a particular resonance at local levels because of the peculiar character of globalisation that has tended to reify particular places which emerge as sites that can attract international capital. Local governance, then, is seen as the 'frontier' at which global capital interfaces with particular place attributes. The local state, thus, carries the responsibility of economic development and enabling global capital to access requisite infrastructure, labour, services and culture. The efficiency of the local state, its ability to coordinate across institutions and deliver, its management of internal conflicts and the development of an orientation to external capital assumes critical importance. In several countries around the world, this has ushered in a range of changes in intergovernmental roles and relationships, and city governments have been considerably empowered to rise to these challenges.

The other view of governance attempts to move away from the nation-state focus in discussions of democracy and moves towards ideas of the deepening of democracy through decentralisation, direct participation, rethinking representation, collective action and voice. These ideas are especially important in contexts where, in spite of the establishment of representative institutions, the basic rights of associations are challenged by vertical dependencies, social exclusions and the failure of public legality (Heller, et al., 2007). Local government is particularly important from this perspective as it represents a government that is closest to the people, and where substantive services are delivered and, therefore, matter the most.

Consequently, this view stresses on local governance as a political issue, with implications for democracy and its conduct. The operationalisation of participatory democracy in cities is complex as there are issues linked to the large population size, the density and complexity of cities, and the fact that cities cannot be reduced to a series of proximate neighbourhoods as they involve interconnected webs of activity. Yet, since the 1980s, there have been several attempts globally to decentralise, devolve and thereby strengthen local governance, with a few attempts to add themselves on to the democratisation agenda. Such moves have helped to institutionalise ideas of direct participation at the local level in several cities, e.g., participatory planning, budgeting, and strengthening of the mayoral office and the institution of forums involving people at various levels of governance.

This discussion makes it evident that urban local governance has emerged as a site of dynamic changes from varied, and even contradictory, perspectives in the last couple of decades. In India, too, urban governance has seen several changes; the discourse has been significantly influenced by global processes and yet, the trajectory of these changes is quite distinct from those in several cities in the world and the Global South. These distinctive features have to do with the way the Indian state was founded in the colonial period, its legacy, the evolving ideas and contours of democracy superimposed on the same, and the unfolding institutional design and interplay of politics and bureaucracy in contemporary times in response to globalisation.

THE COLONIAL LEGACY

Aijaz (2007) traces the trajectory of urban local governance in India through colonial history and the evolution of municipal institutions since the 1870s. As a series of reforms advocating the elective principle, the principles of decentralisation were suggested by Mayo (1870), Ripon (1882) and the Royal Decentralisation Commission (1907); very few of these were put into practice. Thus, other than a few cities like Bombay and Calcutta, and a few towns in the Northwestern and Central provinces, the administration of cities and towns remained firmly in the hands of the district administration. There was resistance to both a transfer of functions to lower levels of institutions and to the involvement of citizen representation.

Even in cities like Bombay, where the Municipal Corporation emerged as a strong entity with significant powers and the presence of elected representatives in the Standing Committee, there were several issues linked to the municipality–citizen relationship. For one, the electorate of the Corporation was confined to rate payers—i.e., property owners of long-standing—with no place for those living on rent, or other occupants. They were, thus, non-citizens who were expendable to a city which sought their labour but denied them any rights. This meant that those considered fit to participate in the governance of the city, or the city 'elders', were the city's socio-economic and educational elite.

It was only when the Government of India Act was enacted in 1935, following the Montague–Chelmsford reforms, that the responsibility of local government was transferred from the district government to a department controlled by a popular minister at the provincial level. The electoral franchise of local bodies was then gradually widened and elected officials were made heads of local committees. This represented the first induction of non-officials at the highest level. Simultaneously, as Aijaz remarks, there were no moves that prescribed the day-to-day management of affairs and fiscal responsibility of these institutions (ibid.). Municipalities were seen to become inefficient and corrupt with the induction of these non-officials and several cases of supersession followed.

The colonial legacy of cities is, thus, divided along lines of citizenship and governance, and of institutions that were structured to pay minimal attention to the non-tax payers, and whose performance rested upon directions from the bureaucracy. The insertion of 'democracy' in this framework was confined to elections.

POSTCOLONIALITY

Independence failed to bring any change within this framework other than the extension of adult franchise. The Constitution of India recognised the need for local democracy in villages, but urban local governments received cursory attention. They were seen to be 'ultra vires', i.e., creations of the superior institution, which was the state government. As a consequence, state governments could determine the functions, powers and finances, and the sheer existence of municipal institutions. The formation and institution of local governments was not systematic and arbitrary. Therefore, industrial townships, notified area committees and planned townships had no locally elected bodies. The elections to urban local governments became a matter of political choice and expediency. Representational structures differed and supersession was a fairly entrenched phenomenon. In cities like Chennai, the corporation was suspended for over 13 years. It is this legacy that perpetuates terminology like 'urban local bodies' (ULBs), which connotes bodies without agency or substance of their own.

An increasing number of informal settlements, housing and industry beyond the law emerged as the other big challenge in the postcolonial period. The municipal institutions had very few powers, resources and capacities to deal with these issues. The state governments formed separate institutions, such as Slum Boards, to deal with such issues, thereby leaving local governments to deal with the maintenance of infrastructure laid down by state institutions. The structuring of municipal institutions in accordance with municipal law regards many of these poorer citizens as 'encroachers', 'nuisance creators', and provides for only penal actions. On the other hand, such settlements were now being conditionally tolerated, even improved, by state institutions. This resulted in a confusing, uncertain situation of governance, where penal action coexists with tolerance, service provisions exist without norms and entitlements, and institutions are expected to maintain infrastructure and deliver services without financial contribution. To complicate matters, several of the lower rungs of municipal bureaucracy themselves lived in such settlements and, thus, were embedded in their everyday concerns. This creates a porous bureaucracy which sustains informality and those dependent on it, but is characterised by several contradictions.

The Slum Boards were only one of the many state institutions created in the postcolonial period. Increasing numbers of parastatals, such as sewerage and water supply boards, development authorities and planning directorates, were created from the 1970s onwards as cities began to grow bigger and problems of urban management began to be seen as significant. These institutions, largely agencies of state governments, were manned by experts and bureaucrats with very little political representation. With the creation of these institutions, larger cities were subjected to multiple jurisdictions. Resources and expertise were vested in these state agencies.

Over a period of time, these institutions took on the task of capital investment in cities, while urban local bodies were reduced to maintenance functions. Overlapping domains and the uncertain fixation of responsibility and accountability have meant that, on the one hand, the disempowerment of urban local governments runs deep, while, on the other, a culture of politicised institutions, poor service standards, opacity and non-accountability also thrives, resulting in apathy and alienation towards local governments. Unsurprisingly, the voting levels for urban local government elections are lowest in the country.

Postcolonial developments have therefore added to the levels of distress in urban local governance. The disempowerment of local municipal institutions, the distortion of democratisation to politicisation, and the overlap of institutional jurisdictions and domains has generated a situation where the capacity to take cognisance of, and deal with, growing urban challenges has become highly constrained, fragmented and unsynchronised.

REFORMING URBAN GOVERNANCE: THE 74TH CONSTITUTIONAL AMENDMENT AND BEYOND

The 74th Constitutional Amendment (CAA) is widely hailed as a 'fresh lease of life' to failing ULBs. By according a place to these bodies as the third stratum of government with distinct functions as outlined in the 12th Schedule[1] of the Constitution and claims to resources via the state finance commissions, the 74th CAA ensured that municipal bodies were now etched into the body politic of India (Sivaramkrishnan, 2006). The overall framework of changes envisaged were:

(i) creating a systematised framework for the establishment of local government at various scales;

(ii) giving a constitutional mandate for urban local governments through functions, specific resources and regular elections;

(iii) broadening representation by providing for reservation of one-third seats for women, and proportional representation for scheduled castes and tribes;

(iv) introducing the notion of citizen participation through ward committees.

The framework of decentralisation introduced by the 74th CAA has been considered widely acceptable and necessary, although its implementation in practice remains selective, especially in terms of transfer of functions, powers and finances. Other than isolated experiments like Kerala, where 33 per cent of state budgets were transferred to the local governments and operationalised through a People's Plan (Heller, et al., 2007), the 74th CAA has meant very real strengthening of both local governments and participation. Urban development schemes that have followed the 74th CAA have converted the same into conditionalities or reforms that state governments would be compelled to undertake prior to availing of any scheme funds. This was done by the Urban Reforms Incentive Fund (URIF) and the Jawaharlal Nehru National Urban Renewal Mission (JNNURM), which followed. The JNNURM added a few more reforms to the basket, which included:

(i) Reforms in the mapping of properties, revisions in the property tax system, encouragement to public-private partnerships, and the introduction of user charges to improve the finances of urban local bodies.

(ii) Community participation law, which seeks decentralisation at an electoral booth level as an attempt to deepen democracy.

(iii) Public disclosure law, which seeks voluntary disclosure of financial and performance data by urban local bodies.

(iv) Statutory spending on the urban poor to the tune of 20 per cent of the overall budget, and the reservation of land for the urban poor.

The overall packaging of all these items as 'reforms' is interesting as it gives the impression that each of these has received legitimacy through due process and all that remains is implementation. On the other hand, other than the transfer of funds, finances and functionaries, which is a continuation of changes introduced by the 74th CAA, all the earlier mentioned changes, including the proposed legislations for community participation and public disclosure are new, and have never been publicly debated. The origin of these ideas, the reason for their introduction to the central government agenda and the mode of their introduction, which further negated public debate, is highly questionable. An assumption which underlies these processes is that (i) the central government is pro-decentralisation, and (ii) the real obstacles to decentralisation are state governments and the low capacity of urban local bodies. The approach to reforms as stick to the carrot of funds is a strategy chosen to work around the reluctance of state governments to decentralise power.

If we classify the reforms into three categories based on their overall thrust, such as those directed at decentralisation, efficiency directed and those directed at participation, it is observed that the trajectory of how they have played out is different. The initiatives aimed at decentralisation are, in actuality, producing a more complex structure of intergovernmental relationships and governance outcomes (Bhide, 2014). The transfer of functions and functionaries is more notional than actual. The transferred functions are being executed at the local level by multiple institutions, or by functionaries who are part of a state cadre, or under directions of parastatals at the state government level. The emerging structure of governance appears to be more centralised than ever. Municipalisation has become even more entrenched in parts of the country where it was non-existent. It is a structure where local governments will perhaps be key service providers, but under directives of several other institutions.

Performance-linked reforms include those targeted at restructuring human resource provision (seen as bottom heavy), local revenues and financial management (strengthening the property tax base and rates, double-entry accounting systems and user fees), and the improvement of housing and infrastructure. The emergent human resource paradigm is one in which the top-level management at the local level is being strengthened, while the bottom is being hollowed. There are some initiatives to create independent sources of income for local governments, but these sources themselves are mired in reforms that go against the grain of local politics. Meanwhile, local governments struggle to bear the increased burdens of infrastructure created under JNNURM's reform-led agenda and the cost of new functionaries placed by state governments with them, while local politics resists them. Service provision and infrastructure have seen some improvements, though largely uneven and unequal across various parts of the cities.

The attempts towards deepening democracy at the local level through ward committees are clearly subverted by political and bureaucratic interests holding onto different domain powers. New reforms in this direction, such as community participation law and public disclosure law, have not seen light in a majority of cities. On the other hand, several state governments (Maharashtra, Bihar) have passed laws to extend the reservation for women in electoral seats at the municipal level to 50 per cent. While seeming inclusionary, these provisions, on the other hand, have sought to bypass women active in politics and instead served to perpetuate the culture of family sycophancy. The provisions for the reservation of budgets and land for the poor also remain an act of tokenism. This is because local governments have few independent financial resources and land of their own. Thus, these resolutions have been passed in most states but have seen very little implementation. Representation has, therefore, been strengthened, but inclusion and participation have remained distant dreams.

CURRENT STATE OF URBAN LOCAL GOVERNANCE

Multiple, competing and contrasting ideas and forces seem to govern the state of urban local governance today. The idea of decentralisation has not found too many advocates at the state level, where changes are critical. The tussle between bureaucratic and political interests, which is not fully resolved, reflects in a divided institutional landscape that leaves municipal bodies bereft of critical capacities and resources, while functions have been devolved to them notionally. Reforms have added to the financial burdens of municipal institutions, done little to equip them with independent and reliable sources of revenue, and produced a bureaucracy that is thin on delivery and unaccountable to local publics.

Municipal institutions are highly politicised, responding to local and short-term interests. They are used as pawns in politics that take cognisance of their weaknesses and use them to perpetuate a politics of informality. This use of politics is institutionally irresponsible and, hence, is vulnerable to containment by higher institutions and authorities, thereby further weakening the municipalities. In this context, decisions taken by higher authorities are also vulnerable to weak enforcement and even being turned on their head, as higher institutions have no delivery mechanisms in urban areas and have to depend on the municipal interface. Such dynamics produce a zero-sum game in which institutions are not aligned to each other and politics disenfranchises the very institutions that elect it to power.

The embedding of such a conflicted institutional landscape into a deeply unequal and divided urban society enhances these conflicts and results in directionless governance. Indian cities are, thus, neither able to move towards global competitiveness nor towards democratisation, let alone the convergence of these two goals. Chattaraj (2012), in studying why Mumbai was not able to realise its goal of being a world-class city despite an ostensible elite and political determination at the highest level, comments that such a transformation requires a sub-national state partner capable of developmental interventions, and that such a capacity, both technocratic and democratic, is lacking. Mumbai's case is not isolated. It is reflective of a more generic state of governance in Indian cities.

CONCLUSION

Instituting strong and decentralised governments at the local level, particularly in cities, in order to be economically competitive and attractive for capital, is a global trend. This narrative illustrates that the Indian trajectory is considerably more complex. On the one hand, the colonial legacy of divided cities and incomplete citizenship continues; on the other, new developmental challenges have further exacerbated a divide between state governments, which seek to centralise power, and highly politicised local governments whose service levels are largely poor. The attempts to reform have been characterised by internal contradictions and, therefore, all kinds of reforms, whether oriented at decentralisation, performance and efficiency, or those linked to the deepening of democracy, seem to be poorly implemented and with few positive outcomes. The state government's initiative is only seen in reforms linked to the expansion of representation for women. Distrust in local institutions and local politics seems to be at the heart of it. Initiatives to attract capital too are focused much more at the state level.

This raises two further questions. First, is this mistrust of local governments, which has existed since British times, deserved?

During British times, the indigenous people were seen as incapable of self-governance until they were 'civilised' enough to align themselves with the colonial government. The post-independence government saw local interests as narrow, provincial and non-inclusive, and thus tended to favour a higher level of government. In the contemporary period, in which cities are becoming significantly populous, can we afford to continue this mistrust?

The second question is whether the higher level of government, i.e., state government institutions, are able to step in and perform at a reasonable level. The answer to that is not clear. Further, these state-level institutions are not immune to the ills that pervade local governments. In fact, regional politics and parochialism have been often perpetuated by state-level politics using cities as the site. The neglect of local issues, an inability to address issues with sufficient urgency, non-accountability to citizens, and using local governments as a vehicle to develop electoral bases are outcomes of the presence of state-level institutions in local realms.

What can bring about a change in this scenario? Changes that were effected in different parts of the globe were a result of the change in the external environment, i.e., globalisation and the emerging importance of place. In the case of India, this trigger has not been critical, perhaps because the current phase of urbanisation concerns itself more with the internal restructuring of population rather than economic growth. In terms of internal triggers, the central government has not been successful as an initiator of reforms and decentralisation as seen from the experience of URIF or JNNURM. State governments are disinclined to do the same. As a consequence, a clear change in favour of local government seems to be impossible unless driven by local forces, such as citizen movements and local politics emerging as a strong force as in the case of Delhi. Neither is there a strong move towards overhauling institutional design and creating a more aligned and convergent institutional landscape. This will require an alignment of politics at the national, state and local levels. Until then, India should be reconciled to uneven, half-hearted attempts at reforming local governance in cities or making them attractive for international capital.

◆

NOTE

1. The 12th Schedule outlines 18 functions of local governments. These include urban and town planning; service distribution functions, like solid waste management; water supply and agendas for inclusion, like poverty alleviation and improvement of weaker sections.

REFERENCES

Aijaz, Rumi. 2007. 'Challenges for Urban Local Governments in India', Asia Research Centre Working Paper, 19. London: London School of Economics and Political Science.

Bhide, Amita. 2014. 'Directed Decentralization: Analysing the Experience of Decentralization via JNNURM in Maharashtra.' Paper presented at the International Seminar on Social Dynamics of the Urban at IIAS, Shimla, June 2014. Forthcoming as a chapter in a book by the same name.

Chattaraj, Shahana. 2012. 'Shanghai Dreams: Urban Restructuring in Globalising Mumbai'. Unpublished PhD Dissertation. USA: Princeton University.

Heller, Patrick, K. Harilal and Shubham Chaudhari. 2007. 'Building Local Democracy: Evaluating the Impact of Decentralization in Kerala, India', *World Development*, 35 (4), pp. 626–48.

Mohan, Sudha. 2005. *Urban Development and New Localism*. New Delhi: Rawat Publishers.

Sivaramkrishnan, K. C. (ed.). 2006. *People's Participation in Urban Governance*. New Delhi: Institute of Social Sciences and Concept Publications.

Stoker, Gerry. 1998. *Governance as Theory: Five Propositions*. UNESCO, 1998. UK: Blackwell Publishers.

◆◆

URBAN DEVELOPMENT, HOUSING AND 'SLUMS'

SWASTIK
HARISH

INTRODUCTION

The popular idea of the 'slum' is often made up of a bundle of perceptions that characterise such areas as overcrowded, unplanned, squalid and dilapidated. The areas are considered crime-prone or even crime-infested, and the people here are generally considered to be living in extreme, if not relative, poverty. Most official Indian definitions, such as from the census, and state level laws and regulations, rest largely on the physical characteristics of areas, such as state of repair and stability of structures, light and ventilation conditions, the availability of basic services, etc. (Census, 2011; Government of Karnataka, 1973; Government of Maharashtra, 2013).

The United Nations notes five basic characteristics that define a slum area—lack of access to water and sanitation, poor quality housing, overcrowding, and an insecure residential status (UN-HABITAT, n.d.). The last defining characteristic of the UN definition—insecure residential status—is an important addition over popular and official Indian definitions, and this distinction will be referred to later.

According to the UN, about a third of the urban population in developing countries lives in areas that can be described as slums (UN-HABITAT, 2012), and according to the Census of India, 2011, about 17 per cent of our urban population lives in slums (Registrar General, 2013a). A look at the distribution of the proportion of urban households living in slums across states (Figure 1), while calling out the usual suspects, such as more urbanised states, brings to attention the rather implausible outliers that emerge from definitional issues (Bhan and Jana, 2013). States like Bihar and Jharkhand report very few slums, while some states in the north-east report no slums at all. This clearly points to the inadequacy of the definition of 'slum' insofar as the census is concerned, implying that there may be an undercount of slums, and, as Bhan and Jana further state, that slums are not necessarily the only sites of poverty or lack housing and services (ibid.). They may, in fact, be symptomatic of a general challenge in the developmental pathway of our cities.

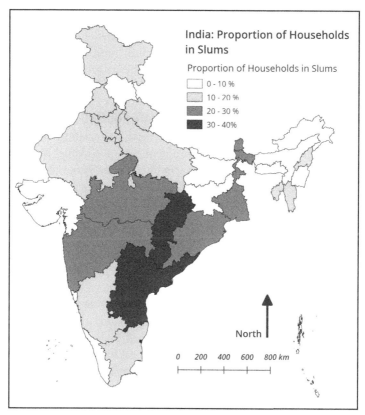

Figure 1: Distribution of proportion of households in slums: states of India
Source: Registrar General; Map: Author.

In other words, addressing slums and 'housing poverty' is a key element of urban development policies, programmes and strategies.

In resource and capacity-deficient contexts such as India's, it is imperative to think of urban development not only as a 'plan' or bundle of projects, but also as a paradigm of incremental growth and resolution—reflective of, and responding to, actual practices—to be realised by framing progressive legislation and regulations that are able to balance orderly *and* equitable development. These, typically, include procedures for land titling, land use reservations, development controls, and building bye-laws (Payne, 2005) that can enable a financial and institutional environment that encourages incremental growth as an equally effective and efficient process of urban development as compared to one that depends on the implementation of master plans and mega projects.

It is in this context of a paradigm of incremental growth that the question of 'slums' and housing for the income-poor will be addressed.

DIMENSIONS OF AFFORDABLE AND ADEQUATE HOUSING

Development policy in the country is now increasingly engaged with the question of urban development and 'affordable' housing. Starting from the Jawaharlal Nehru National Urban Renewal Mission (JNNURM), successive governments at the centre and the states have formulated and implemented policies and programmes aimed at accelerating equitable and efficient urban growth, and the provision of housing for income-poor groups. While urban development programmes have largely focused on the system-wide development of basic services and policy reform, housing programmes have aimed to streamline the delivery of 'affordable' housing.

Affordable housing is typically defined as housing that is available to the median income group of a particular region. Another definition of affordability is formed by benchmarking the house price to five times a household's annual income, i.e., if all the members of a household together earn, say, ₹5 lakh per annum, then the household can afford to buy a home that costs ₹25 lakh. This definition gives a clear methodology to policymakers to estimate the shortage and formulate programmes to address it. Official data show that in Karnataka, the annual income of up to 70 per cent of the urban population of the state may be ₹2 lakh or less (MoSPI, 2013), critically implying that affordability for the vast majority needs to be seen as a house price in the range of ₹10 lakh or less.

Considering that Karnataka is quite urbanised and is a middle-to-higher income state of the country, it is incumbent upon us to refer to this house price range as the upper end of affordable housing for the vast majority of households in Indian cities.

The Ministry of Housing and Urban Poverty Alleviation (MoHUPA), Government of India, estimated that urban India faces a shortage of just under 190 lakh housing units, of which more than 95 per cent was faced by households in the Economically Weaker Section (EWS) and Lower Income Groups (LIG) (MoHUPA, 2012). Significantly, it noted that homelessness was not a very common condition in Indian cities. Rather, it articulated the housing condition in our cities in this way—affordable housing that is inadequate, and adequate housing that is unaffordable—underlining the deeply paradoxical condition that there are crores of houses that are vacant, while vast populations live in slums or slum-like conditions (Registrar General, 2013b).

Disaggregating census data from 2011 over social groups reveals further structural issues in the housing condition in urban India. If we visualise three typical conditions that describe adequacy of housing (Figure 2)—*kutcha* or semi-*pucca* building, congestion and access to basic services—over socio-economic categories, patterns of housing inadequacy start becoming apparent. Households of Scheduled Caste and Scheduled Tribe categories face higher levels of inadequacy. Typically, female-headed households face higher levels of inadequacy than male-headed households, with

	Female-Headed Households				Male-Headed Households				TOTAL	Of the Total, in Slums
	Total	SC	ST	Others	Total	SC	ST	Others		
	26.7%	35.5%	42.4%	24.0%	20.5%	30.0%	35.6%	13.7%	21.2%	29.2%
Congested										
					5.7%	8.8%	8.1%	6.0%	5.7%	7.9%
Without Basic Services										
	20.8%	34.9%	44.0%	16.4%	18.7%	34.7%	40.4%	14.9%	19.0%	27.6%
Have Banking Facilities										
	62.0%	51.7%	53.7%	64.6%	68.6%	56.6%	59.6%	71.0%	67.8%	53.2%

Figure 2: Proportion of components of housing inadequacy: social groups in urban areas
Source: Registrar General; Visualisation: Author.

26.7 per cent not living in a pucca house and 20.8 per cent of them without basic services, while the same numbers for male households stands at 20.3 per cent and 18.7 per cent, respectively. Households in slums are far more likely to lack access to basic services, and live in a kutcha or semi-pucca house. The same pattern is visible in levels of access to banking services, with significant downward movement with increasing socio-economic vulnerability.

This condition then reinforces the ministry's restatement of the housing condition, and compels us to think of housing not merely as a house or unit, but a bundle of needs. The key question that emerges in such a scenario is: How can housing be made affordable *and* adequate?

A third concept to grasp in order to approach the question of housing is of *viability* (Deb, 2016), especially in the context of programmes to develop new affordable housing. Viability in the context of urban housing can be seen as the combination of access to development opportunities, such as employment, integration with the urban fabric and sufficient access to social infrastructure, like schools and health facilities. In slums that are often located in city centres or in areas that provide at minimum a set of options for gainful employment, these criteria are resolved to a certain extent.

Last, but not least, is the question of security of residence, which refers to the degree of the right to stay in a particular location. This could range from illegal squatting on land to full ownership rights, with a range of intermediate conditions such as no-eviction guarantees, occupation or use rights, and rental/lease. The conceptualisation of actions based on tenure range from Hernando de Soto's notion of unlocking land potential through the grant of titles to occupying households, to harsh, and often lethal, evictions of slums and squatter settlements without any rehabilitation.

Thus, it is the nexus between affordability, adequacy, viability and security of residence that forms the condition of housing.

THE 'SUPPLY' OF HOUSING

In order to address the housing condition in this context, it becomes key to understand the potential of different supply streams of housing. First of all, is the government able to sufficiently provide the required housing? The simple answer is, no. In an action research conducted by the Indian Institute for Human Settlements, which helped the Government of Karnataka formulate its affordable housing and slum development policies in 2016, it was found that in the last 10 years, the government was able to provide approximately 2 lakh housing units and 1.5 lakh house plots for economically weaker sections, as compared to a calculated current demand of more than 11 lakh units. This demand increases to about 20 lakh units if future projections of urbanisation are taken into account. Even the much celebrated Slum Rehabilitation Authority of Maharashtra has produced 1.27 lakh units for slum-dwellers in Mumbai from its inception till 2011 (Supreme Audit Institution of India, 2011). The number of households living in slums in Mumbai is estimated at 11 lakh in 2011. A back-of-the-envelope calculation on the financial resources required to build new housing for all slum households in Mumbai shows that this may be in the order of ₹1.1 lakh crore, based on an average house price of ₹10 lakh. The entire budget of housing programmes of the central government, such as NDA's Housing for All or UPA's Rajiv Awas Yojana, does not amount to this. Clearly, the government in itself does not have, or aim to commit, the resources necessary for supplying the new housing required.

The other supply stream that can be considered is from private developers. Private developers tend to supply premium and upper-income group housing segments far more than the affordable segment, as this largely suits their core profit motive. However, in the last decade or so, there has been an increase in the number of developers and projects that are aimed at the relatively lower income groups (Agarwal, et al., 2013). Yet this does not satisfy the sheer scale of demand, especially from the sub-₹10 lakh house price range. Few, if any, developers are looking to develop housing in this price range.

This leaves one last stream of housing production—people themselves. Considering that homelessness is not massive in urban India (2.5 households) (Registrar General, 2011), it can only be estimated that urban citizens have themselves provided the housing that they need. While a proportion of these will be auto-constructed, i.e., physically built by households themselves with inputs from relatives and friends, it can be surmised that many households leverage the existing building materials and labour market to develop their homes. Invariably, this form of development is incremental, i.e., households invest in their housing based on the creation of a small corpus, or the ability to raise funds from the local market from time to time. This manner of housing may or may not satisfy planning norms and regulations, but often is developed in areas that satisfy basic conditions of access to work and social infrastructure. In this form of housing development, slums are a key location. Slums, in their physical location and ability to absorb diverse financial capacities of income-poor households, address two of the four main concerns to a certain extent—of affordability and viability.

The core question, then, can be finally formed in the following manner: What strategies can help slums and other forms of inadequate housing become vibrant, secure, sustainable and efficient neighbourhoods?

APPROACHING URBAN HOUSING

At the outset, it has to be accepted that we cannot build enough new housing to satisfy the demand, considering the resources required. Again, a quick calculation will show that if we were to build 190 lakh new units at ₹10 lakh each, the total investment required would be in the range of 30 per cent of India's annual GDP. Even if we consider that this investment be phased over a period of 10 or 15 years, the provision would fall short of catering to future urban growth and housing requirements. While it can be said that development and building activity significantly boost employment and productivity, it should also be considered that building at this scale may lead to potentially severe environmental degradation. Lastly, it has to be accepted that there simply isn't that kind of appetite within development stakeholders to make these scales of investment on urban housing, considering the range of pressing developmental issues that compete for their attention.

This article does not make the argument that we should not build new housing. It merely points to the fact that the approach to addressing the urban housing condition needs to be forged in the context of the aspects stated so far. For example, governments at different levels have taken steps to encourage investment in affordable housing by private developers by offering incentives in the form of financial and non-financial benefits (Government of Karnataka, 2016a; Government of Maharashtra, 2007; Government of Rajasthan, 2012; MoHUPA, 2013). These initiatives are indeed laudable and will help lower the pressure on the housing market at the top end. Yet they are not enough to address the housing conditions at the very low income segments that constitute the majority of the demand.

The key argument here is that we need to utilise our resources, especially our limited public resources, in the most efficient way possible—by improving existing housing. Whether it is housing that is developed in contravention of planning norms, such as land use or physical layout planning, or it is slums, notified and non-notified, this article argues that there are legally viable and physically feasible methods to incrementally integrate them into the city. Key to the effort will be taking a holistic approach that addresses concerns of tenure, infrastructure, quality of housing, financial ability, and last but not least, maintenance of social and economic relations between, and within, settlements. Three approaches are elucidated in the following sections—upgrading, reconfiguration and redevelopment—that are not necessarily exclusive, i.e., a single or combination of the approaches may be suitable to a particular location. The key common factor to the approaches is that they address the question of improving housing in the same location, i.e., in situ, thereby maintaining critical social and economic relations that have likely evolved over significant periods of time.

SETTLEMENT UPGRADING AND RECONFIGURATION

Upgrading refers to the incremental development of some of the components of inadequacy in a settlement. Upgrading can address questions of tenure of residence, and physical and social infrastructure. Reconfiguration involves some interventions in, or changes to, the layout and buildings of the settlement along with upgrades in tenure and/or infrastructure, largely in order to enable these provisions in an unsuitable physical environment.

Upgrading tenure of residence is a wrought affair in most circumstances, and almost always so in the case of slums. About 57 per cent of slums in India are on public land, i.e., land that belongs to the central, state or city government, or any of their agencies (MoSPI, 2010). This means that the households in these slums would be dependent on public authorities to enable or increase their security of residence. Most public authorities, however, are not in favour of providing such slum-dwellers any security of residence since it may condone squatting behaviour (Jain, et al., 2016). Of the 40 per cent of slums that are on private land, it is not known how many slum-dwellers actually own the land or may be squatting on another private entity's land. This means that upgrading of tenure requires the concurrence of at least another party besides the government and slum-dwellers.

At the same time, there are enabling provisions within most state Acts on slums to provide forms of security of residence. The declaration of slums, i.e., the official recognition of a settlement as a slum, along with the provision of identity cards to slum-dwellers, leads to a condition wherein the state can intervene in the physical condition of the settlement in order to either improve them, or, if required, rebuild them (Government of Karnataka, 1973; Government of Maharashtra, 2013). However, the application of such provisions is sometimes lax due to definitional and procedural issues, or sometimes mired in political interests, considering interests in large populations in slums as socio-political support groups. In this context, it is interesting to note the provisions in the Karnataka Slum Areas Development Policy, 2016, which aims to streamline the process of declaration through clear definitions and institutional structures, and a time-bound structured process (Government of Karnataka, 2016b).

Another form of security of residence is the right to use land. Some state agencies rely on instruments, such as occupancy or possession certificates, which confer a right to the holder to occupy and use a public land asset. Typical slum upgrading projects come bundled with such rights with restrictions on inheritance, exchange and transfer. In the city-wide slum upgrading project in Ahmedabad called *Parivartan* (transformation) that aimed to connect the slums to the city's infrastructural network, the Ahmedabad Municipal Corporation included a 'no-eviction' clause to slum-dwellers that guaranteed that they would not be evicted from their locations if they signed up and invested in the programme (MoHUPA, n.d.). Scholars and institutions have noted the positive outcomes of the programme, finding that many households invested in toilets and maintenance mechanisms, and improved their quality of life, once trunk infrastructure was provided to them (WIEGO, 2010; WSP, 2007). It was further also found that there are perceived to be critical changes in the idea of legitimacy of these settlements, including increased willingness on the part of the slum-dwellers to pay property tax.

Elsewhere, I have proposed an advanced version of a similar regime—converting slums on Urban Local Body (ULB) land to rental housing (Harish, 2015). In this approach, the slum house is unbundled into the house asset and the land asset, and rightful ownership is applied to both—the local body owns the land, but the house unit is an investment made by the slum-dweller. This protocol consists of allowing such slum-dwellers to continue to live there under a no-eviction guarantee, in exchange for a nominal or subsidised rent for the utilisation of the land. If such a condition can be created, it can lead to significant developmental goals for the slum-dwellers as they gain security of residence, and significant revenue for the ULB. Such revenue can then be cycled back into infrastructure provision or its maintenance. Since the ULB would gain a clearer claim on their own land in such a scenario, its credit rating, as well as financial independence, could potentially grow as well. Considering that about 40 per cent of all slums in the country are on ULB land, such a model can make a massive positive impact on the quality of life of the slum-dwellers and the city in general.

The physical component of upgrading and reconfiguration consists of interventions in the settlement in order to provide basic services, such as water supply and sanitation (WSS) infrastructure, paved roads and pathways, street lighting, etc. Where required, community facilities, such as common areas, working areas, *anganwadis* and schools, primary health centres or sub-centres, etc., may also be provided. Figure 3 is a visualisation of typical physical interventions for settlement upgrading and reconfiguration. As can be seen, while upgrading with physical and social infrastructure can be the key step, there may be a requirement to intervene in the housing units and street pattern in order to enable the provision of water and sanitation pipelines and facilities, as well as the development of community facilities, and green or open spaces.

Institutionally, the most favourable arrangement for upgrading settlements would be a partnership between the government, especially the ULB, the slum- or settlement-dwellers, and potential

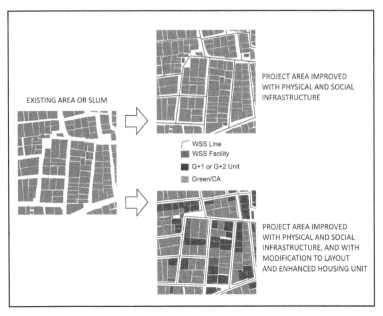

Figure 3: Physical components of settlement upgrading and reconfiguration
Source: Author.

private and non-governmental organisations (NGOs). While the NGO can play a key role in the mobilisation and articulation of the demand, the community of dwellers can form key interest groups that assist the state in making lists of dwellers, planning, the monitoring of implementation, and subsequent operation and maintenance of assets created. Private parties can contribute financially either directly or through Corporate Social Responsibility (CSR) channels, and a proportion of the investment can be borne by the local government, as well as the dwellers themselves. This arrangement has successful precedent in *Parivartan* (WIEGO, 2010; WSP, 2007).

SETTLEMENT REDEVELOPMENT
In situations where the physical attributes of a settlement are in no shape to be upgraded, a redevelopment scheme is an option to address housing inadequacy. Redevelopment involves a significant interruption in the lives of dwellers as well as a substantial resource investment. A decision to redevelop must be taken after a thorough

examination of the current physical situation of the settlement, keeping in mind the age of the settlement, the quality of housing, the status of tenure, and the effort required to provide basic services (Government of Karnataka, 2016b).

The key action in a redevelopment is the demolition of all or most of the structures of a settlement, and the development of new housing and infrastructure. A redevelopment plan can be imagined as a plotted layout with small houses or rooms with toilets. This kind of a plan is typically referred to as a 'site with shell and services' project. The key advantage of such a plan is that the settlement-dwellers are accommodated on individual parcels of land. This allows them to continue their socio-economic activities in a largely similar manner as before, while, at the same time, incrementally develop their house according to their specific requirements over time.

In situations where the density of an existing settlement is too high to accommodate all the households on individual plots, the option of multi-floor apartments can be considered. While such a redevelopment model has the advantage of rehabilitating settlement-dwellers in the same location and, therefore, potentially maintaining their socio-economic relations, there are usually concerns regarding adapting lifestyles to apartment living. These concerns typically take the form of challenges in accessing upper floors, ability to continue professions that involve use of ground spaces, livestock maintenance, etc. In an action research conducted by the Indian Institute for Human Settlements on comparing quality of life in occupied apartments for relocated slum-dwellers—an older site, shell and services schemes in Mysuru, Karnataka—it was found that income-poor families and slum-dwellers almost unequivocally felt that the option of individual plots, even if small, was better than apartments. Figure 4 visualises the two planning options for a redevelopment project.

Redevelopment, as mentioned earlier, requires significant investments. While under the UPA's Rajiv Awas Yojana the central government was willing to provide the bulk of the funding for approved redevelopment projects (MoHUPA, 2013), the NDA's Housing for All has reduced the allocation per unit, with the assumption that states or cities would invest in the gap-funding required (Government of India, 2015). It further encourages states

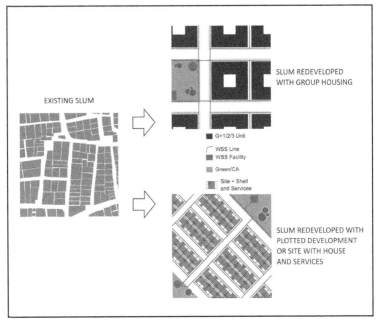

Figure 4: Options for settlement redevelopment

Source: Author.

to formulate policies that would encourage private investors and developers to redevelop slums in return for incentives, such as extra buildable areas. The developers are expected to leverage this extra area in the market and generate the funds to cross-subsidise the redevelopment scheme. While this mechanism sounds attractive in principle, it is a point of caution that such leverage may not exist in many markets in the country, especially in smaller towns or the urban periphery.

CONCLUSION

The conclusion this article draws largely reinforces certain approaches and tenets of urban development and housing provision in a limited resource environment. The two key arguments made here are for an enabling environment for increasing security of residence, and for improving existing housing through upgrading and redevelopment in situ. In a way, it supports the articulation that a resident of the Ahmedabad Slum Networking Programme responded with, when asked by this author what the key outcome of the upgrading programme was—*Parivartan,* or transformation, was the emotional response.

◆

*The Indian Institute for Human Settlements which has helped the Government of Karnataka formulate the Karnataka Affordable Housing Policy, 2016, and the Karnataka Slum Areas Development Policy, 2016. References have been made to these documents with the aim of elucidating some of their key provisions that support the arguments of this article.

REFERENCES

Agarwal, A., V. Jain and A. Karamchandani. 2013. *State of the Low-Income Housing Market: Encouraging Progress & Opportunity to Realize Dreams of Millions.* Mumbai: Monitor Deloitte.

Bhan, G. and A. Jana. 2013. 'Of Slums or Poverty: Notes of Caution from Census 2011', *Economic and Political Weekly*, xlviii (18), 2011–2014.

Census. 2011. *Census of India, 2011: Instruction Manual for House-listing and Housing Census.* New Delhi: Office of the Registrar General and Census Commissioner, India.

Deb, A. 2016. 'Viability of Public Private Partnership in Building Affordable Housing in India', *Shelter*, 17 (1), pp. 40–46.

Government of India. 2015. *Pradhan Mantri Awas Yojana: Housing for All (Urban).* New Delhi: Ministry of Housing and Urban Poverty Alleviation.

Government of Karnataka. 1973. *Karnataka Slum Areas (Development) Act, 1973.* Bangalore: Government of Karnataka.

———. 2016a. *Karnataka Affordable Housing Policy, 2016.* Bangalore: Department of Housing, Government of Karnataka.

———. 2016b. *Karnataka Slum Areas Development Policy, 2016.* Bangalore: Department of Housing, Government of Karnataka.

Government of Maharashtra. 2007. *Maharashtra State Housing Policy.* Mumbai: Department of Housing, Government of Maharashtra.

———. 2013. *The Maharashtra Slum Areas (Improvement, Clearance and Redevelopment) Act, 1971.* Mumbai: Law and Judiciary Department, Government of Maharashtra. Retrieved from https://lj.maharashtra.gov.in/Sitemap/lj/pdf/ljActs/ SLUM AREAS ACT, 1971.pdf

Government of Rajasthan. 2012. *Rajasthan Affordable Housing Policy, 2009.* Jaipur: Department of Urban Development, Housing and Local Self-Government.

Harish, S. 2015. 'Making Rental Housing Work: A Case for Slum Households and ULBs', *Administrator*, 65 (2).

Jain, V., S. Chennuri and A. Karamchandani. 2016. *Informal Housing, Inadequate Property Rights.* Mumbai: FSG.

MoHUPA. (n.d.). *Best Practices Under Challenge Fund: Slum Networking Program, Ahmedabad, Gujarat*. New Delhi: Ministry of Housing and Urban Poverty Alleviation. Retrieved from http://mhupa-ray.gov.in/wp-content/uploads/2013/09/2_1.pdf

———. 2012. 'Report of the Technical Group on Urban Housing Shortage (TG 12) 2012–17.' New Delhi: Ministry of Housing and Urban Poverty Alleviation. Retrieved from www.mhupa.gov.in

———. 2013. *Rajiv Awas Yojana: Guidelines*. New Delhi: Government of India.

MoSPI. 2010. *Some Characteristics of Urban Slums, 2008–09 (Vol. 534)*. New Delhi.

———. 2013. *Key Indicators of Household Consumer Expenditure in India*. New Delhi.

Payne, G. 2005. 'Getting Ahead of the Game: A Twin-track Approach to Improving Existing Slums and Reducing the Need for Future Slums', *Environment and Urbanization*, 17 (1), 135–146. http://doi.org/10.1177/095624780501700114

Registrar General. 2011. *Primary Census Abstract Data for Houseless*. New Delhi: Office of the Registrar General and Census Commissioner, India. Retrieved from http://www.censusindia.gov.in/2011-Documents/PCA_HL_2011_Release.xls

———. 2013a. *Primary Census Abstract on Slums, 2011*. New Delhi.

———. 2013b. *Table H1: Census Houses and the Uses to which they are put*. New Delhi.

Supreme Audit Institution of India. 2011. *Chapter II of Report No. 2 (Civil) of Performance Audit of Government of Maharashtra*. New Delhi: Comptroller and Auditor General of India.

UN-HABITAT. (n.d.). Housing & Slum Upgrading. Retrieved 22 January 2017, from http://unhabitat.org/urban-themes/housing-slum-upgrading/

———.(2012). 'State of the World's Cites 2012/2013: United Nations Human Settlements Programme.' *United Nations Human Settlements Programme (UN-HABITAT)*, 152. Retrieved from https://sustainabledevelopment.un.org/content/documents/745habitat.pdf

WIEGO. 2010. 'Approaches to Basic Service Delivery for the Working Poor/ : Assessing the Impact of Mahila Housing Trust's Parivartan Slum Upgrading Programme in Ahmedabad', *Women in Informal Employment: Globalizing and Organizing*. Retrieved from http://wiego.org/sites/wiego.org/files/publications/files/Rusling_WIEGO_PB1.pdf

WSP. 2007. 'The Slum Networking Project in Ahmedabad: Partnering for Change. Water and Sanitation Program, World Bank Group.' Retrieved from http://documents.worldbank.org/curated/en/353971468259772248/pdf/719220BRI0slum00Box370086B00PUBLIC0.pdf

◆◆

ENGINE URBANISM

HIMANSHU BURTE

Anybody returning today to Mumbai after 25 years is likely to walk (or drive) into an experience of everyday life and urban space that has changed drastically, though most of the city also stands as it is, where it is. The towers, sprouting up everywhere, repeat, everywhere, are of course the most eye-catching of additions. In a matter of 15 years, the tallest of erstwhile exceptions (like the once-legendary, 26-storied 'Usha Kiran') have been dwarfed by a new routine of towers over 30 storeys high, and growing. Flyovers and elevated rail (metro and mono) have inserted tall, long colonnades of concrete in the centre of streets, presenting a newly ambiguous public space underneath for the homeless, car owners, the Municipal Corporation and middle-class residents to covet and fight over. And driving is a different experience from as recently as the year 2000 with the Bandra–Worli Sea Link and the Eastern Freeway, for instance, speeding up north–south travel, even as the six-laning of the Jogeshwari–Vikhroli Link Road, and the construction of the Santa Cruz–Chembur Link Road enable you to even think of driving between the eastern and western suburbs. Walking, too, has changed. No more the familiar cut across the street to follow a desired line as before: footpath railings and concrete medians keep you on the straight and narrow. The extravagantly named 'skywalks'—foot overbridges from an era of desultory governmentality, now roofed and rebooted—hope to decide where you may cross the road (and, along the way, peep into the many bedrooms they graze, if you do climb up or down two storeys). Meanwhile, road widening has even taken away entire footpaths, especially on arterial roads like the Sion–Panvel highway that heads out to Pune.

What sense can one make of diverse but simultaneous changes like these? Is there a logic tying them together, one perhaps that is more generally applicable across India? I explore possible answers to these questions through this essay focused on the spatiality of urban transformation in Mumbai. I view these transformations as related to the state's increasingly definitive conceptualisation of the city as an engine of economic growth. The state has been an important player in these transformations, both through its own spatial practices as well as through new policy provisions. In Mumbai, both were unleashed dramatically in the 1990s, soon after the New Economic Policy began to make economic integration with the global economy a common sense national goal.

In spite of its distinctiveness, Mumbai's example is relevant here for two reasons. First, its urbanism has been significantly held together by informality of multiple kinds, much like that of other Indian cities. That informality appears to have no place in the urbanism that the state has sought to institute in the city. Second, many of the interventions increasingly common across Indian cities, irrespective of their actual performance—market-led slum redevelopment and elite transport infrastructure—appear to have been first tried out together, and at scale, in Mumbai. Since the interventions and outcomes have been significantly spatial in nature, this essay overviews the transformations in the built environment and spatiality. I suggest that the new spatiality also implies a way of life—encompassing space as well as the culture of everyday life, and extending into social relations—and a 'politics of forgetting' poverty, marginalisation and such other bad news (Fernandes, 2004). I call this, experimentally, 'engine urbanism'.

The image of the 'engine' recalls the idealised modernist vision of the city as a machine. This appears to orient urban policy and governance interventions more committedly than before, and is being realised in an increasingly mechanistic urban spatiality. Engine, also, because the metaphor 'engine of economic growth' is now the telos of state-authorised urbanism in bigger Indian cities. This urbanism is of interest not only as a social and cultural phenomenon, but also for the political significance of its privileging of anti-political technocracy, centralised control and the rule of the market.

THE SPATIAL GRAMMAR OF RATIONALISATION AND INTEGRATION

Two broad principles that interweave smoothly in concrete situations can be seen to underlie Mumbai's spatial transformation since the mid-1990s—rationalisation and integration. The ongoing reorganisation of urban space may be viewed innocently as a process of streamlining an unruly urban metabolism (say, through transport planning). Rationalisation may be justified on functional and economic grounds in some cases, while its substance in others might be drawn from the symbolic domain. Functional rationalisations at the city-wide scale include the upgradation of the suburban railway system (as part of the World Bank-funded Mumbai Urban Transport Project) and the construction of multiple and much needed East–West link roads. It also includes smaller details: footpath railings keeping pedestrians off the road, maximising automobile speeds reducing travel time, accidents and pollution (till 'induced travel' changes the game again). Meanwhile, the economic principle of restoring land to its 'best and highest' use may be said to drive initiatives like the Slum Redevelopment Scheme (SRS), which have been sold to the public as state generosity, eliding the fact that its recipients had asked for secure tenure, not free houses.

Perhaps the ubiquitous booster pump is a useful metaphor to understand the imperative for integration. That illegal mainstay of the urban water supply network in many Indian cities helps upper-class (and upper-storey) residents pull more than their share of scarce water from the system, at the cost of others. Cities are expected to do something similar for the nation, and pull more economic investment and activity out of an increasingly interconnected global and regional system of flows. Greater economic integration requires better (but selective) spatial integration. For goods and labour to flow quicker and in greater volumes to and from advantageous locations, cities and regions must therefore be better connected with others, even as their own internal parts are spatially better integrated than before.

As always, power decides what 'better' means specifically as well as its content (i.e., the realised or intended consequence), and involves decisions related to the grounds of rationality, the definition of costs and benefits, and the adjudication of claims of different social groups, interests and neighbourhoods.

ADJECTIVE AS VERB

The twin imperatives of rationalisation and integration are steadily transforming the spatiality of Mumbai. Its current character is instantiated in new or newly ubiquitous spatial typologies, spaces and urban elements: the flyovers and elevated metro and mono rail earlier mentioned, but also their 'underplaces' (Burte, 2016); wide concrete roads with crash barriers, concrete medians and acoustic barriers; contrasting elite and subaltern residential towers (often redeveloped low-rise, middle-class slum housing, or other either non-conforming or not 'high enough' economic uses); effectively 'permanent' and informalised, but originally formal transit housing; big buildings like malls, multiplexes, or T3, the spectacular new international airport terminal; privatised, and often ostentatiously landscaped, open spaces. These are distinct, separate spaces, some produced by the private sector and out of market dynamics, others directly by the state, while some others are enabled through new urban policies. Together, they embody a matrix of intended characteristics that constitutes the horizon of aspirational urban spatiality (with, I believe, its own corresponding way of life and world view, although I will only gesture towards those aspects here). The essence of this spatial vision is best communicated in breezy graphic visualisations of aspirational abstractions like the 'smart city' floating around in the media, in conference brochures and policy documents. Of course, that vision has a creakier landing on urban ground, as the discussion arranged around the four adjectives that follow will indicate.

Formal, *big*, *private* and *networked*: these adjectives illuminate key idealised qualities, or values, of the new urban spatiality in multiple scales. They must also be read as implying their verb forms; each describes not only a found characteristic, but also, increasingly, the orientation towards spatiality, often through state intervention or encouragement. Thus, it is the drive to *formalise* that must be noted in the spreading cult of formality in the built environment (at least in the city proper). Similarly, not only are many new constructions bigger than before, the average size of urban elements is constantly increasing vertically and horizontally with help from policy.

These tendencies, or drives, can be traced to different interacting logics of the larger social, political and economic restructuring processes underway in the country since liberalisation in the 1990s. Moreover, each of the four characteristics combines with others in specific elements and instances of the new spatiality. An equally important feature of the process is not what a drive seeks to achieve, but its often contradictory or perverse consequences, as we shall see in the discussion of the adjectives that want to be adverbs.

FORMAL

Half of Mumbai's population (approximately 12 million in 2011) has lived in informal settlements for much of the 20th century. A significant drive has been afoot to force them off the land they occupy and the settlements they have made into 'formal' housing. Lakhs of slum-dwellers have been displaced in Mumbai since the early 2000s in the course of long overdue infrastructure projects, in slum redevelopment projects, or to free reserved public amenity spaces, like playgrounds, of encroachments. The Slum Redevelopment Scheme (SRS), first introduced in 1991 and subsequently modified in 1995 by the state government, is almost explicitly a formalising device for land under informal occupation. It promises free housing (an apartment of 269 sq ft) to owners of tenements out of profits from private development of the land parcel. Infrastructure projects, notably the upgradation of the suburban railway system and a slew of road projects—many of which required the removal of informal settlements to free up land—were accompanied by a variable Resettlement & Rehabilitation (R&R) mechanism that involved the construction of minimal new housing for project-affected people, often very far from the original site of the settlement.

Thus, the ramshackle form of settlements of the poor—on footpaths, or on slums on government or private land—has been erased from many locations across the city and the tenements, replaced either on site or at a distance, by concrete towers. This brings valuable urban land, hitherto informally in the grip of 'occupancy urbanism' (Benjamin, 2007), into the formal property market (now open to Foreign Direct Investment) and, more directly, into the municipal governance system, enabling big local developers and the Municipal Corporation to encash its value through projects for the elite. On the other hand, it is also seen to 'clean' the blot of the slum from the city, step by step. Both aspects are seen to help the city's chances of integrating with the global economy by attracting foreign capital to Mumbai.

A significant percentage of those displaced have been moved into towers seven storeys and higher, as well as tower complexes that are the result of state projects or policies. Lakhs now live in R&R colonies—large collections of seven or more storeyed buildings in weakly serviced and connected locations like Chandivali, Govandi, Vashi Naka (over a lakh people in the last)—or in scattered slum redevelopment towers in better locations, pushed to a rear third of the original land parcel behind the visible, fancier towers of 'sale' flats in better locations. A smaller number have been stuffed into even less habitable 'transit camps'—temporary spaces gone nearly permanent—as at Kokari Agar near Sion.

More than anything else, the R&R colonies and many slum redevelopment towers reveal the arbitrariness of the material criteria of formality. For both, key exceptions were made through legislation to critical provisions of Mumbai's Development Control Regulations originally aligned with the National Building Code (or NBC, an advisory model of development control regulations drawn up by the Central government to help cities draft building codes to ensure efficient and healthful urban spaces). Whereas the NBC limits the number of tenements that may be housed on one hectare to 500, SRA and R&R developments usually doubled this density. This was enabled by 'relaxing' another provision: the minimum distance between buildings, which the NBC ties to the height of the building, implying that they must be placed further apart as they grow taller, so that the lowest apartments get enough daylight and ventilation. Today, the state's urgency to economise on space allocated to the urban poor has led to seven-storey towers with often just a few metres between them, which leaves most of the residents in darkness by day, and often with worse ventilation than in the informal settlements they lost. Not surprisingly, most people aware of these conditions refer to these formal developments as vertical slums that often provide worse habitats for residents than their original settlements, and push them further away from established work places and social networks. Meanwhile, in the course of genial arguments in air-conditioned cars about the fate of the city, these formal built environments are pointed out as evidence of the win-win nature of formalising approaches.

BIG

Staple urban spatial elements—all kinds of buildings and their complexes, road and rail infrastructure and allied spaces, including bridges, flyovers, railway stations, etc.,—are visibly getting bigger than before, vertically and horizontally. This is ironic in a city known—more than any other—for scarcity of space stemming from geographic limitations as a peninsular outcrop, and its peculiar political economy of land ownership.

In buildings, this enlargement represents two things: (i) the accumulation and consolidation of space as commodity which translates into (ii) a promise of larger revenue streams at lower transaction costs. There is an argument to be made that the enlargement of scale is related to the increasing supply of investable global or local capital from state- and private-sector sources for various urban projects promising high-volume revenue streams (hotels, malls), or addressing real living and business needs, and use values (residence, office space, infrastructure) as well as speculative demand. The bigger the size of the project, the lower the overheads, transaction costs, the number of risk points in processes, and the higher the profit margin. This equation is advantageous, especially for remotely controlled capital, whether global or underground. This also possibly reflects a link between the increasing scale of urban elements and the push for economic integration with a wider geography. Urban policy has enabled such enlargement of scale most transparently by increasing the Floor Space Index (FSI) which limits built-up area, as well as by less transparent modes of calculating it (as through the infamous and now scrapped provision of 'fungible FSI', which could be interpreted broadly enough to build multiple times over the limit).

One contributory local reason is the sharp rise in the price of land, urban or rural, all over the country since 2005. This is one reason for the increasing verticality of urban architecture, as more is sought to be built on the same piece of land in every city, with the blessings of state planning. Thus, a couple of years ago, I was surprised to see a horizon cluttered with multi-storeyed buildings on the outskirts of Rajkot, otherwise a city with low to mid-rise architecture. In Mumbai, and increasingly in other cities, the underlying scarcity of land prompts the elevation of transport infrastructure like flyovers, elevated roads and metro rail: existing road space everywhere is increasingly inadequate as private vehicles mushroom with explicit or implicit state sanction. The rule of the car that much of the big-road infrastructure has enforced on Mumbai's urbanism, meanwhile, has led to another manifestation of verticality: the raised 'podium' of multiple storeys of covered and enclosed car parking with a public space on top that serves as 'ground' for the residents of the apartment towers that shoot up from it.

Podium and tower also regularly reveal another important quality of largeness today: its banality. The flyovers and towers are non-monuments, or *nonuments*. Banal or monumental, verticality has an important collateral benefit from the perspective of an integration with a larger, more global economy: clusters of big urban elements or iconic structures like the Bandra–Worli Sea Link both call attention to the city, differentiating it in the presumed competition of urban branding that is the context of processes of 'worlding cities' (Roy and Ong, 2011).

PRIVATE

Privatisation is increasingly the principle of governance as well as everyday life. Everyday life is being increasingly privatised across the verticalised lifestyles of the urban poor who have been moved into resettlement housing, as well as the middle and upper classes in their newer towers (often next to each other). Where they can afford to remain in the new housing, the poor withdraw to the new luxury of privacy at relatively high maintenance costs (especially electricity bills for intermittently working elevators, and pumping water). In general, the vertical stacking of homes—of the rich or poor—elevates and disconnects the private home from the larger social sphere that the street (or slum lane) mediates. Used to the informal sociability that underpinned successful subsistence and consolidation in the slum, resettled families invest energy and (unchanged) incomes—or worse, micro-credit meant for livelihood generating micro-enterprise—in private consumption through fancy, textured painted walls and new gadgets. In any case, state-planned (hence, formal) R&R neighbourhoods have poor quality, largely unintended public spaces, and lack critical amenities such as flour mills, schools, markets and hospitals. The randomly assembled and socio-economically vulnerable households from diverse locations struggle to form communities, making public spaces threatening, especially to women. At the other end of the spectrum, elite developments too institute a new privatisation of everyday life. Increasingly, they integrate many amenities—parks, gymnasia, even shops—into ever larger complexes and townships. Travelling in cars on new roads, the middle and upper classes thus keep to a privatised city-wide network or circuit of spaces that include high-value nodes of living, work and recreation connected by the air-conditioned cocoon of the car.

As a governance principle, apart from slum redevelopment, the principle of privatisation has also spread to public and open spaces. Since the 1990s the municipal corporation has been handing over public spaces to private bodies, NGOs and citizens' groups to develop and manage, often leading to charges of elite capture or sheer land grabbing. Private security guards police public spaces developed by local middle- and upper-class citizen groups, as at Carter Road promenade in Bandra (West). Relative to the rest of public space, these privately developed and managed spaces show greater attention to design and aesthetics in the conventional sense. Confirming conservative social values (separate seats instead of benches in public gardens to try to deter canoodling couples, only to prompt more 'scandalous' positions!), these spaces are often closed to those who do not look respectable enough to private security guards at the gates.

NETWORKED

From a city with a continuous, public spatial fabric, Mumbai is increasingly becoming a collection of multiple and separated network spaces, stratified by class, religion, caste and ethnicity.[1] The large number of expensive, elite transport projects—bridges, flyovers and freeways reserved for cars, other wide link roads, the metro and mono rail—integrate and network far locations and geographies, privileging the needs of service economy and of the middle and upper classes that it favours. Fifty-odd flyovers built since the late 1990s and elevated rail enable middle and upper classes to bypass congestion on the ground and bring hitherto far (air-conditioned, securitised, and hence completely privatised) locations closer in terms of travel time.

At the same time, the widened roads fragment formal and informal neighbourhoods with fast traffic, footpath railings and concrete medians deterring easy walks across. Generations born after the 2000s will grow up to believe that extended concrete colonnades and flyovers in the centre of the street are ubiquitous features of modern Indian urbanism. They will also think it normal that one cannot see the tops of buildings on the other side of the street, or the sky, as they are regularly occluded by concrete decks of flyovers and elevated rail. These are not occasional blips. For example, three-fourths of the 13-km corridor from Fort to Sion is occupied by a total of 10 flyovers. Once a seam tying together neighbourhoods into a larger spatial fabric, the street is now an impassable and dangerous chasm that must be crossed by skywalk, itself aspiring to become another network bypassing the urban tangle, in the increasingly sorted and discontinuous space of the city.

The new infrastructure integrating wider geographies in the city and outside is an armature of emerging networks of spaces that the elite can increasingly stay within. This network is pulling away from the urban commons and the expanding world of informality (especially of labour) that it is, nevertheless, materially founded upon. Of course, it does so selectively where it is advantageous and feasible, producing a 'splintered urbanism' (Graham and Marvin, 2001).

CONCLUSION

Each of the four adjective-verbs above set out to describe a particular drive underway in the city that is steered by state and market, and is recasting urbanism by reorganising space. However, the discussion also points us to the consideration of the numerous other irrationalities and fragmentations to which the pursuit of rationalisation and integration has led: flyovers that only defer the problem of congestion to the next intersection and decade; roads that connect distant locations but fragment neighbourhoods through which they pass; R&R colonies that send people back to worse slums because they cannot afford the new costs of formal living and do not have a settled home to return to.

They illuminate the spatial telos of the world-class city in contemporary India—a city expected to act as the nation's booster pump once well integrated with the global economy. Marc Auge (1995), the French anthropologist, describes this telos as a non-place.

For Auge, the meaningful (or anthropological) place is anchored in history, which gives it and allows it to bestow identity, and is marked by a convivial and historically produced relationality. The non-place, on the other hand, is marked by contractual relations (as in an airport, freeway or hotel) and fungibility.

The telos of the non-place is clearly marked by an authoritarian politics of centralisation, and the privileging of the instrumentality of space for narrowly conceived political economic purposes over what Henri Lefebvre (1991) would call its 'lived', social dimension. Much of the lively urbanism of Mumbai has been, and still is, anchored in the lived space co-produced informally and against the grain of the law, not just in the slum, but also in the street. The much-touted spirit and resilience of Mumbai—evident in the spontaneous assistance by people coming down from safe homes with tea and snacks for the tens of thousands walking home on flooded streets as all infrastructure failed in July 2005—was possibly germinated in that informality. This is at stake as engine urbanism rolls on erasing, and exiling, informality in all its forms.

◆

NOTE

1. The politics of the interplay between trajectories of economic structures and struggles, and those of more social, and cultural, origin in the fashioning of a particular engine urbanism in any city would be interesting to study, but is outside the scope of this essay.

REFERENCES

Auge, M., 1995. *Non-places: An Introduction to Supermodernity*. London and New York: Verso.

Benjamin, S. 2008. 'Occupancy Urbanism: Radicalizing Politics and Economy Beyond Policy and Programs', *International Journal for Urban and Regional Research,* vol. 32, 3, pp. 719–29.

Fernandes, L., 2004. 'The Politics of Forgetting: Class Politics, State Power and the Restructuring of Urban Space in India', *Urban Studies*, November, 41(12), pp. 2415–30.

Lefebvre, H., 1991. *The Production of Space*. Oxford (UK) and Cambridge (USA): Blackwell.

Roy, A. and A. Ong. 2011. *Worlding Cities: Asian Experiments and the Art of Being Global*. Chichester: Wiley-Blackwell.

◆◆

POST-NATIONAL URBANISM
'Ordinary' People, Capital and the State

SANJAY
SRIVASTAVA

INTRODUCTION

U rban life is hardly new to the subcontinent. Notwithstanding
the suspicion that the term 'ancient' now arouses on the part
of those serious about lineages of the present, this part of the
world has certainly witnessed an identifiably urban life in the distant
past. Further, despite the overwhelming attention paid to the village
within Indian sociological traditions, the city as a distinct mode
of life has a significant history as a form of social consciousness.
Perhaps some part of the neglect of the city as a significant window
to Indian life can be attributed to a Gandhiesque refusal to consider
social and economic conflict as an important aspect of national life.
Notwithstanding the deep asymmetries of rural life, the village has
been relentlessly presented as a site of social harmony and a model
for the nation. The 'India lives in its villages' narrative has, however,
been shadowed by a substantial body of—primarily non-academic—
work that has addressed the meaning of urban life across a number
of registers.

Perhaps the most enduring presence of the metropolis as a
social formation occurs in Hindi cinema of the decades following
Independence. In films such as *Shri 420* (1955, Raj Kapoor), *New
Delhi* (1956, Mohan Segal), *Gateway of India* (1957, J. Om Prakash)
and *Sujata* (1959, Bimal Roy), the city is central to the struggle over
defining social life in the new nation state. Beyond cinema, urbanism
as an existential issue unfolded in contexts as varied as schooling,[1]
Hindi literature (the *Nayi Kahani* movement in general, and
Mohan Rakesh's genre-defining 1966 novel, *Andhere Band Kamre*,

in particular), planning of industrial complexes[2] and ideas around transforming villagers into urban citizens.[3] While these contexts are diverse, there is, however, a significant thread that binds them as narratives of becoming and being. This is the assumption that, beyond the webs of kinship and fraternity, the most significant relationship that individuals have is with the state. And that the state's key concern is the welfare of socially, economically marginal populations. The market and the relatively well-off did not much enter into the ways in which urban destinies and characteristics were seen to be formed. In this article, I seek to point to changes in this way of thinking about cities and urban life. The following discussion, in the context of what I refer to as post-national urbanism, is about new notions of citizenship and emergent relationships between the middle classes, the state and the market. I explore this terrain through specific ethnographies of urban life in and around Delhi.[4]

POST-NATIONALISM URBANISM[5]

In 1999, soon after being elected to office, Delhi's erstwhile chief minister Sheila Dixit 'called for an active participation of Residents Welfare Associations (RWAs) in governance'. The rationale for this was the 'failure' of 'civic agencies' to carry out their normal tasks. The chief minister's secretary noted that the call to actively involve RWAs in urban governance heralded a new era, marking as it did 'the first step towards a responsive management of the city' (Ojha, 1999). The secretary noted that various civic agencies had 'failed' in their tasks and that the 'community' should now be involved in different aspects of urban management (ibid.). Subsequently, the Delhi government decided to 'empower' RWAs to 'take certain decisions on their own'. RWAs were to be given control over the management of resources such as parks, community halls, parking spaces, sanitation facilities and local roads. A more direct relationship between the state and RWAs was also mooted through the idea of joint surveys of 'encroached' land—i.e., land that had been 'illegally' occupied, usually by slum-dwellers—with the possibility that all illegal structures would 'be demolished in a non-discriminatory manner'. Finally, it was proposed that RWAs be allowed to impose fines on government agencies which failed to carry out their assigned tasks. This was an important signpost of the changing engagement between the state and the middle classes, which has historically pivoted around the former's relationship with the poor.

In 2005, following a decision by the Delhi government to raise electricity tariffs by 10 per cent, a number of separate Delhi RWAs formed the Residents Welfare Association Joint Front (RWAJF). The Front consisted of 195 member RWAs from around the city. The increase in power rates for domestic consumers was the second one since the state-owned electricity body was 'unbundled' in June 2002 as part of power sector 'reforms'. As a result, three privately owned companies secured contracts for electricity distribution.[6] There was vigorous protest over the price rise and, in addition to the RWAJF, NGOs such as People's Action, and another group known as Campaign Against Power Tariff Hike (CAPTH) joined the campaign. Individual RWAs asked their members to refuse payment of the extra amount, while RWAJF lobbied the government and organised city-wide protests. The protests gained wide coverage in both the print and electronic media, and, echoing Gandhian anti-colonial strategies, the organisers were reported to have deployed 'the ideas of "civil disobedience" and "people's power"' (Sethi, 2005: 5). The convener of the RWAJF referred to the protests as 'non-violent *Satyagraha* (resistance)' (Sirari, 2006: 5), deftly interweaving the language of Gandhian mass politics with the concerns of urban elites. Eventually, the Delhi government backed down and the price rise was shelved. Tellingly, the head of People's Action described the success of the protest as the making of a '*middle-class* revolution' (emphasis added) (Sethi, 2005).

The deployment of ideas of 'civil disobedience', 'Satyagraha' and 'revolution', and the consolidation of the notion of a 'people' contesting the state both occur at a time of Indian modernity that might be called post-national. By this I mean a situation where the original moral frisson of these terms—provided by anti-colonial sentiment—no longer holds. Indeed, in an era of post-Nehruvian economic liberalisation characterised by consumerist modernity (Brosius, 2010; Fernandes 2006; Mazzarella, 2003), the moral universe of the anti-colonial struggle is no longer part of popular public discourse. Within this context, the earlier emphases on the ethics of 'saving' and delayed gratification for the 'national good' do not find any resonance in contemporary popular discourses on the role of the state. The term 'post-national' does *not*, however, imply that the nation state is insignificant as a context of analysis, or that we now live in a 'post-patriotic' era as is sometimes theorised (Appadurai, 1993). My usage is also different from its deployment as a mode of critique of nationalism (de Alwis, et al., 2009). Post-nationalism, in my usage, is the articulation of the nationalist emotion with the robust desires engendered through new practices of consumerism and their associated cultures of privatisation and individuation. Just as significantly, the post-national moment is also the context of a redefinition of the category of the 'ordinary person', whereby an apparently harried and taken-for-granted middle class comes to be represented as the 'common class'.

The most significant manner in which the post-national moment resonates within the politics of urbanism concerns the repositioning of the language of anti-colonial nationalism from the national sphere to the suburban one. This, in turn, also indexes the move from the idea of the 'national' family to the nuclear (gated) one, and, the translation of the notion of nationalist solidarity to (middle) class solidarity. Gated residential communities are being constructed across 300 or so Indian cities and such topographical transformations are accompanied by broader discursive shifts regarding family life, state, nation and citizenship.

It is also in this context that the figure of the consuming middle-class woman-as-citizen—a significant aspect of the imaginary of post-national urbanism—takes on particular significance. For the ideology of post-nationalism speaks of both men *and* women as having an active relationship with commodity cultures. And, the new woman-citizen is doubly significant in that not only does she take part in the (consuming) business of modernity, but is also able to withdraw from it when required in order to take on the mantle of the 'traditional' Indian woman. Through exercising 'choice', not only does she embody the logic of consumerism, but also agency. Feminist scholarship speaks of the choice women in public have of either remaining 'modest' or risk losing 'reputation' (Phadke, 2007). However, within new spaces of urban residence such as gated communities—and in line with the peculiar logic of consumerist choice—women can be both guardians of tradition *and* take part in sexualised presentations of the self. It is not uncommon to observe elaborately dressed women within gated enclaves perform the religious rituals of *Karva-Chauth* (for the welfare of husbands) at night and pace the condominium grounds on their exercise rounds dressed in skin-hugging clothing next morning. And, unlike the constraints placed on women at public celebrations of Holi, at the Bacardi-sponsored *Holi mela* in one of Gurgaon's gated communities, men *and* women dance together to Bollywood songs on an open-air stage. Here, consumerism is the grounds for the making of a 'moral middle class': one that sees itself as not determined by modernity, but able to pull in and out of it; it is both effortlessly Western as well as traditionally 'Indian'. This is also the resolution of the woman-question in the context of consumerism, where the woman as consumer—in opposition to the self-sacrificing one—has been a site of anxiety.

As mentioned earlier, post-nationalism (and post-national urbanism, in particular) is also about a redefinition of the idea of the 'people'. The making of the 'people' in a time of consumerist modernity has specific consequences: it unfolds through differentiating the 'good' consumers from the 'bad' ones, in turn identifying the 'good' citizen from his or her antithesis. The most visible signs of this are, of course, inscriptions upon urban space—the various acts of gating—that announce the presence and work of an RWA. 'Urban fear' (Low, 1997)—the slum-dweller-turned-criminal is the most frequently invoked threat—is significant motivation for the proliferation of gated communities in India. However, the RWA discourse in Delhi also acts in other ways to produce the 'uncivil' other. The 'power' agitation mentioned earlier is a case in point.

Various studies point out that the privatisation of electricity in India has had the effect of drastically reducing the already low levels of access for poor sections of the urban population, and 'reform' in the power sector has mostly benefited the well-off. With the consolidation of the idea of the consumer-citizen as the 'ordinary citizen', issues of social equity, such as those relating to access to resources, come to be evaluated in terms of the logic of consumerism; they become an issue of 'good' consumers versus 'bad' consumers. So, a frequent justification for the agitation against the increase in electricity charges was that the hike could have been avoided had the government been more vigilant against slum-dwellers who obtained power through illegal, and unpaid for, means. And, that 'power theft' meant that 'honest' and 'ordinary' citizens were subsidising 'dishonest' ones.

The remaking of the *'aam admi'* within the crucible of post-national urbanism—and through RWA activism—is particularly relevant for understanding the place of the urban poor. As the discourse of ordinariness has shifted from the poor to the middle classes, so have ideas about the nature of spaces to be occupied by ordinary citizens. The (new) ordinary citizen is increasingly identified as the resident of the 'global city' and the 'Smart City' where 'recent advancements in Information and Communication Technologies (ICT), aligned with technology cost reduction, such as cheap mobile apps, free social media...provide cities with better opportunities and tools to understand, communicate, and predict urban functions' (NIUA, 2015: 8). In line with the thinking that complex social problems have simple solutions (e.g., 'appropriate' technology), urban improvements are articulated in the language of slum demolitions. Over the past few decades, RWAs have been significant players in moving courts to demolish and remove slums (Ghertner, 2008). The 'structural exclusion' (Bhan, 2016: 234) of the urban poor 'from dignified work, access to basic services, decent housing, and core human development opportunities' (ibid.: 234) are fundamental aspects of ideas of global and Smart Cities.

It is ironic that the village has become a significant site of the urban middle-class imagination. So, discourses of leisure, aesthetics, spirituality, health, and housing, among others, draw upon romanticised images of 'village India; there are purpose-built 'ethnic villages' to experience 'authentic' rural food and entertainment, 'living museums' to watch 'tribals' producing handicrafts, clothing designed to reflect rural exuberance, and gated enclaves that promise rural idyll (Dupont, 2005). The irony lies in the fact that concurrent to the consolidation of this rural imaginary among the middle classes, actual villagers—those who migrate to cities and are forced to live in its poorest localities—face constant and brutal effacement.

Finally, and connected to the discussion of the previous paragraphs, the making of 'ordinary' citizens is part of a process that is signified by new urban relationships between capital and state. In the example that follows, capital, in effect, actively produces its own citizens, such that the notion of separate and autonomous spheres of the state, citizens and capital becomes untenable. What we are left with, in fact, is the simulacrum of autonomous spheres.

Gurgaon district in Haryana has been the site of intense real estate activity by a number of major construction conglomerates—Ansal, DLF and Unitech—since the early 1980s. Among these, the DLF corporation is India's (and one of world's) largest real estate company, and builder of the 3,500 acre DLF City. Many services within privately developed townships continue to be provided by the developers, rather than the Municipal Corporation of Gurgaon (MCG), formed in 2008. The fees that residents pay for these are known as 'maintenances charges'. These are paid to the developer responsible for the construction of the locality—residents of 'plotted' localities constructed by DLF and Unitech pay maintenance charges to DLF and Unitech, respectively.

In 1986, some residents of a particular plotted locality combined to form a Residents Welfare Association ('RWA 1'). One of RWA 1's most consistent demands was for the developer to hand over its townships to the government. According to the Haryana Development and Regulation of Urban Areas Act, 1975, the developer must hand over a privately developed 'colony' to the government after five years of its development. RWA 1 mounted considerable agitation over this issue. Its members filed court cases, petitioned the government, and even fought in assembly and council elections. An office holder of RWA 1 (the older of the two bodies) described the situation as follows:

> ...developers do not want to hand over their townships to the government and the government is not interested either: for as long as the developer has control, it can use the land within its areas in an arbitrary fashion...by simply changing original planning agreements. So, it can build a commercial building on a plot that was earlier indicated on planning documents as a community centre or a dispensary. The government does not wish to change anything because of the massive amounts of under-the-table money that it gets from private developers. If the colonies were handed over to the Municipal Corporation of Gurgaon, it would be more difficult to make money. It's easier to make money from the private sector.

In the early 2000s, another RWA—'RWA 2'—appeared on the scene. RWA 2 is an umbrella body and claimed that nearly 200 different Gurgaon RWAs were affiliated to it. RWA 2 was, in fact, created by one of the key real estate companies in Gurgaon to counter what it perceived to be an association of residents (RWA 1) that was hostile to its interests, in particular the demand that the company hand over the township to be administered by the Haryana government. The company-sponsored RWA has a comfortable air-conditioned office in the same building as many of the company's offices in a central part of 'new' Gurgaon. An RWA 1 office holder told me that in the early 2000s, the company initiated moves that led the Haryana government to appoint an administrator to oversee RWA 1's affairs. In the wake of this, RWA 1 is unable to function. The company-sponsored association, on the other hand, appears to be flourishing. It primarily acts, as an office holder put it, 'as a bridge between the real estate company and residents of the locality built by it'.

In this way, post-national urbanism—a time of significant ongoing renegotiation of the relationship between the state, private capital and citizens—is the context within which RWA activity redefines notions of 'civil society'. The term may not any longer signify a realm that either interrogates the state (Kaviraj and Khilnani, 2006), or one characterised by a series of *formal* mechanisms of law and governance (Chatterjee, 2004). Rather, contemporary discourses connected to RWA activity, such as those that relate to Delhi's erstwhile Bhagidari scheme and Gurgaon's RWA 2, tell us that 'civil society' is increasingly the realm where the idea of 'ordinary people' is being produced through the changing relationship between the state and private capital through both formal *and* informal means. And that the notion of 'ordinariness' has very specific dimensions that relate to the new cultures of corporatisation of the state and the state-like transformations of private capital in India.

CONCLUSION

The processes of new urbanism in India provide a fruitful entry into an understanding of changing relations between the state, citizens and private capital. These processes also provide a more complicated picture of the nature of the state itself. It emerges as an entity that is *part* of the informality and impropriety it seeks to banish as well as set itself apart from. These aspects can be summarised through, in conclusion, the notion of kinship capitalism (Srivastava, 2015).

When DLF began to purchase land in Gurgaon, it did not have sufficient funds to pay for the purchases, its commercial activities since the late 1950s not having generated much revenue. These purchases came to fruition through processes which can be grouped under the rubric of kinship capitalism. The following is a quote from an interview with K. P. Singh, who took over DLF from his father-in-law and was instrumental in its transformation into a real estate behemoth:

> I set about identifying myself with each family whose land I wanted to buy. A team of 70 to 80 people were deputed to find out everything about these people: the size of their families, how many children, who was good in studies, any family disputes... every little detail. I did everything it took to persuade these farmers to trust me. I spent weeks and months with their families—I wore *kurtas*, sat on *charpais*, drank fly-infested milk from dirty glasses, attended weddings, visited the sick....[7]

This is how a farmer—now a real estate dealer—from the village of Nathupur (now part of DLF Phase 3) described the situation to me in 2013:

> DLF bought the smaller plots of land on cash terms and larger plots on credit. They were very considerate: if our cattle was electrocuted, DLF paid compensation. Now the younger generation of DLF owners is not like that.

DLF purchased a great deal of land on credit, an aspect that was facilitated by the fact that K. P. Singh was able to invoke a sense of bucolic trust between caste-brethren in his dealings with the landowning farmers.[8] There was another aspect: the company also convinced the villagers to trust it with the money that was paid for the land they sold. It created a financial arrangement whereby landowners could deposit the money they had received from sale of their land into a scheme that offered a slightly higher rate than local banks. The money was utilised by the company to make further land purchases.

There was, however, one significant complication. In most areas, while the land was in one person's name, it was actually being cultivated by, and in possession of, someone else. In all these situations, the land was registered on a '50–50' basis: half of it was registered in the name of the person who was the actual owner, and the other half to the person in possession. This paved the way for legal sale of the land to DLF without any state involvement, but within a context that was facilitated by the state. For, soon after the company began to acquire agricultural land, it lobbied various levels of government and succeeded in changing land-use regulations so that such land could be put towards urban use.

Notwithstanding the absence of markers that indicate the presence of the state *beyond* the processes of private capital, it has, at different points, tried to exert its 'stateness' and the formation of the MCG is the final rung of this story.

Of the 357 sq km that constitutes Gurgaon district, about 156 sq km have been handed over to the MCG for administrative purposes. However, in these areas, the MCG is not able to levy any house tax. It is private real estate companies that levy a 'maintenance' charge upon residents. A few years ago, the MCG tried to levy a house tax in the areas where residents pay the maintenance charges to private developers. However, as one resident put it, 'we refused to pay it as we are already paying maintenance charges to the builder, so why should we pay another tax to the MCG?' So, currently, MCG is mainly in charge of older parts of Gurgaon and village areas: it is not able to levy charges in areas that have the potential to generate the largest amount of residential and commercial taxes. As one resident of DLF City put it, 'many residents do not want the MCG to take over the private townships as there was far greater trust in the administrative abilities of the private sector than the government'. And, he added, a private company such as DLF has an interest in looking after its older localities since it is building new townships and wants to maintain 'brand equity', not wanting its existing product to be sullied through poor state administration. That is why, he added, DLF will continue to privately look after its already-constructed townships. Post-national urbanism is the operation upon spaces of such significantly new processes of hybrid administration, commerce and consumer cultures. It is also a context of changing relationships between the categories we call 'the state', 'capital' and 'the people'.

◆

NOTES

1. See Srivastava (1998) for its relevance in nationalist endeavours such as the Doon School.

2. See Roy (2007) on steel cities.

3. See Bulsara (1948) for a discussion of the 'problem' with villagers in Bombay.

4. Given the constraints of space, I am unable to deal with the government's Smart Cities project as a significant aspect of rethinking urban development in India. This topic—marking an important recalibration of the relationship between the state, elite citizens and global capital—requires detailed attention on its own.

5. Aspects of this discussion are based on Srivastava (2015).

6. See Sethi (2005: 5–6). For a more benign view of privatisation, see Kanbur (2007).

7. Singh (2011: 99) notes in his autobiography that 'The acquisition of land was meticulously done over a period of time, taking every farmer or landowner into confidence. …I myself came from a rural background so I knew their realities… we spent weeks and months on building a relationship with farmers whose land we wanted to buy'…'It also helped that my parents-in-law belonged to Haryana and were a leading family in the state' (ibid.: 101). See also Radhakrishnan Swami (2005).

8. Singh (2011) alludes to this in his autobiography.

REFERENCES

Appadurai, Arjun. 1993. 'Patriotism and its Futures', *Public Culture*, 11: pp. 411–29.

Bhan, Gautam. 2016. *In the Public's Interest: Evictions, Citizenship and Inequality in Contemporary Delhi*. Delhi: Orient Blackswan.

Brosius, Christiane. 2010. *India's Middle Class: New Forms of Urban Leisure, Prosperity and Consumption*. Delhi: Routledge.

Bulsara, J. F. 1948. *Bombay: A City in the Making*. Bombay: National Information and Publications Limited.

Chatterjee, Partha. 2004. *The Politics of the Governed: Reflections on Popular Politics in Most Parts of the World*. Delhi: Permanent Black.

deAlwis, M., S. Deshpande, P. Jeganathan, M. John, N. Menon, A. Nigam and S. A. Zaidi. 2009. 'The Postnational Condition', *Economic and Political Weekly*, 44 (10): p. 35.

Dupont, Véronique. 2005. 'The Idea of a New Chic Delhi through Publicity Hype', in Romi Khosla (ed.) *The Idea of Delhi*. Mumbai: Marg.

Fernandes, Leela. 2006. *India's New Middle Class: Democratic Politics in an Era of Economic Reform*. Minneapolis: University of Minnesota Press.

Ghertner, D. Asher. 2008. 'Analysis of New Legal Discourse behind Delhi's Slum Demolitions', *Economic and Political Weekly*, 43 (20): pp. 57–66.

Kanbur, Ravi. 2007. *Development Disagreement and Water Privatization: Bridging the Divide* [http://www.arts.cornell.edu/poverty/kanbur/WaterPrivatization.pdf].

Kaviraj, Sudipta and Sunil Khilnani (eds.). 2006. *Civil Society: History and Possibilities*. Cambridge: Cambridge University Press.

Low, Setha M. 1997. 'Urban Fear: Building the Fortress City', *City and Society,* 9 (1): pp. 53–71.

Mazzarella, William. 2003. *Shoveling Smoke: Advertising and Globalization in Contemporary India.* Durham: Duke University Press.

Ojha, Abhilasha. 1999. 'RWAs will soon have Direct Control over Sanitation and Community Halls', *Indian Express,* 2 January. www.indianexpress.com/res/ple/ie/daily/19991201 (accessed 11 December 2007).

Phadke, Shilpa. 2007. 'Dangerous Liaisons: Women and Men, Risk and Reputation in Mumbai', *Economic and Political Weekly,* 42 (17): pp. 1510–18.

NIUA (National Institute of Urban Affairs). 2015. *Exploratory Research on Smart Cities. Theory Policy and Practice.* New Delhi: NIUA.

Radhakrishnan Swami, Meenakshi. 2005. 'Building on a Dream', *Business Standard,* 22 March.

Rakesh, Mohan. 1966. *Andhere Band Kamre.* Delhi: Rajkamal.

Roy, Srirupa. 2007. *Beyond Belief: India and the Politics of Post-colonial Nationalism.* Durham and London: Duke University Press.

Sethi, Aman. 2005. 'The Price of Reforms', *Frontline,* 22 (19), 10 September.

Singh, K. P. 2011. *Whatever the Odds: The Incredible Story of DLF.* Delhi: HarperCollins.

Sirari, Tanvi. 2006. 'Civil Uprisings in Contemporary India', Centre for Civil Society, Working Paper No. 161. Delhi: Centre for Civil Society.

Srivastava, Sanjay. 1998. *Constructing Post-colonial India: National Character and the Doon School.* London: Routledge.

———. 2015. *Entangled Urbanism: Slum, Gated Community and Shopping Mall in Delhi and Gurgaon.* Delhi: Oxford University Press.

◆◆

V
ECOLOGY, ENVIRONMENT AND WELL-BEING

PHOTO ESSAY
THE ART OF
EVOLUTION

HARSH
RAMAN
SINGH PAUL

During the early 1st century AD, in the time of the Romans, Vitruvius is said to have authored the oldest surviving written work of architecture. Prior to this, Imhotep in Egypt is said to have been the first to use columns as structures. However, it is undeniable that even earlier, perhaps since the time of the caveman, there has been an innate need for mankind to create and inhabit an environment of art.

Picture a caveman who studied his surroundings to find a cave. His need to repurpose this enclosure did not just end with achieving shelter, security and warmth, which are essentials of architecture, even today. We live in a time when a picture is worth a thousand words. But he lived in a time where he did not have the luxury of words. For him the picture was the default font. Perhaps this very nature is observed in children even today. Leave a child in a room and he or she inadvertently finds a way to scribble on walls. While there can be speculation on what motivated the caveman to scribble on a wall, what we have yet not questioned is if he enjoyed that experience. If so, why?

The creators of society, driven by the need to modernise and adapt technology, built monotonous structures that dulled the spirit of those who occupied it. It is no surprise that the hospitality industry realised the importance of surrounding its guests with art. Art should be for everyone. It is a beautiful tool to ignite something inside people. My public murals serve as conversation starters, and as a springboard for passers-by to question and ponder, drawn in by the colour and chaos unfolding amidst humdrum everyday life.

Erected within the landscape of the mundane, living side-by-side with countless posters selling soft drinks and cell phones, street art has the ability to crank open the mind. The art can slip through the cracks of our collective conscience and illuminate corners of thought otherwise subdued by consumerist pursuits and hedonistic distractions.

Street art for me has been a way of giving power back to the individual. It reinforces the fact that we all have the power to change the society we live in. Street art reminds us that we are not mere products of our surroundings; our surroundings are a product of our actions. We live in a consumer culture; the visual landscape of the city is filled with advertisements and messages, selling people the idea of happiness through the consumption of products. But this only leads to a never-ending race for instant gratification. True happiness is a result of a good value system. These internal values range from loyalty, hard work, love, gratitude, family, selflessness and so on. We need to communicate this to the masses for a healthy, happy and productive society. This is the role that street art is going to play in shaping the future of our nation.

In a country of high economic disparity, street art acts as a social equaliser by placing all economic classes on the same pedestal. You do not need to be rich or well-educated to interact and be inspired by public art. In that sense, street art is probably the most impactful form of art that exists today. Street art and graffiti will eventually turn into the strongest counter-culture movement in the country.

I envision street art as a tool for individual liberation and, at the same time, bringing the community together. It can trigger social change and bring media attention to the real issues that plague our community. With collaborative projects such as the Brinda Project (India+Brazil) and the Quijote Wallah Project (India+Spain), I have tried to celebrate the vast commonalities between different cultures, touching on the themes of poverty, religion, life, death, dreams, divinity, music and dance. Within these messages exists the most fundamental of them all: that we are all united by the same human experiences, regardless of race, age, creed, caste or money. This is what interests me most—talking about what it means to be a human being and our collective human experiences. This will help us not only build empathy and a connection with each other, but also help us connect to our true inner self. We seem to have lost that connection these days—we are more connected to money, fame and a distorted image of success. I think it is very important to remind people of the beautiful things in life, for which you do not need money. It is time for us as a society to detach ourselves from the transience of consumerism. My relationship with material objects is founded on appreciation as opposed to reliance or compulsion.

With the Kathakali mural in Lodhi Colony, our focus was to drive more community interaction. By leaving the bottom half of our vibrant mural empty and covered with blackboard paint, we created a canvas for the residents to fill in with their own art, using chalks. There is so much untapped creativity in people—all it needs is a trigger.

The Walls of Women (WoW) project is attempting to bridge the glaring misrepresentation of women in the mass media while addressing issues of gender equality, sexual assault and social suppression. WoW encourages women to reclaim the streets with paint by making them an active participant in the process. The power to be able to express yourself feely in public can be a liberating experience. Which is exactly what happened when we painted a mural for the sex workers of G.B. Road, Delhi. Our mural triggered such a positive psychological growth in the community that a local NGO, Kat-Katha, organised a campaign to paint 20 more murals in G.B. Road with female sex workers actively participating in the painting process.

There is a definite need for the government to join hands with artists to create an environment that is aesthetically beautiful and visually inspiring; a place where society can flourish by rediscovering the definition of happiness and success. Imagine a city where public spaces are designed for people to take over with their creativity, spaces which become the voice of its people. Where an artist does not have to fit his art into the architectural structure, but where the structure itself is designed to serve as a canvas. A noble idea of making the hard and concrete exterior of urban environments more beautiful and pleasing to live in—a future for which we must work today. There is great satisfaction in having the ability to take over your surroundings, and leaving your mark on the structures you inhabit. It can become a symbol of hope and freedom. Do we still need more reasons to cover the monotonous grey with colour?

◆

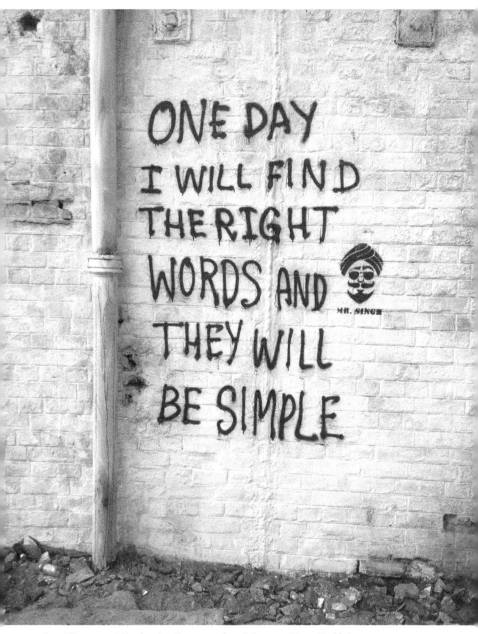

1: 'Street Wisdom', Connaught Place, New Delhi.
Photo: Harsh Raman

STREET ART:
Reclaiming Public Space

HARSH RAMAN SINGH PAUL

2: 'Brinda Project', Hauz Khas Village, New Delhi.
   Photo: Isha Chaudhry

3: 'Brinda Project', Hauz Khas Village, New Delhi.
Photo: Isha Chaudhry

4: 'Viral City Station', ScoopWhoop Office, New Delhi.
Photo: Shouvik Basak

5: 'Graffiti Baba', Rishikesh. Photo: Harsh Raman

6: 'Imagine', Haus Khas Apartments, New Delhi.
Photo: Harsh Raman

7: 'Unleash the Beast', Tihar Jail, New Delhi.
   Photo: Tarannum Singh

8: 'WOW Project Inside Out', Agrasen Ki Baoli, New Delhi.
Photo: TGKI Studio

9: 'WOW Project', G.B. Road, New Delhi.
Photo: Shouvik Basak

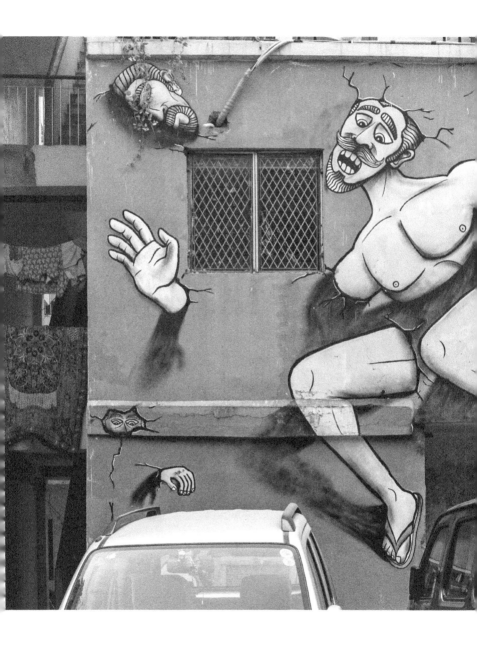

10: Shahpur Jat, New Delhi. Photo: Shouvik Basak

11;12: 'Brinda Project', Haus Khas Village, New Delhi.
      Photo: Isha Chaudhry

13: 'WOW Project', G.B. Road, New Delhi.
Photo: Shouvik Basak

1: 'Beauty and the Beast', Kingfisher calendar.
Photo: Mikhil Saluja

2: 'Kathakali Twins', Lodhi Colony, New Delhi.
   Photo: TGKI Studio

3: 'Brinda Project', Agrasen Ki Baoli, New Delhi.
   Photo: Carina Barros

4: 'Brinda Project', Agrasen Ki Baoli, New Delhi.
Photo: Carina Barros

5: 'Sadhusutra', Green Park Dental, New Delhi.
   Photo: Shouvik Basak

6: 'Jai Ho', ICD Tughlakabad, New Delhi.
   Photo: Akshat Nauriyal

NURTURING URBAN COMMONS FOR SUSTAINABLE URBANISATION

SEEMA
MUNDOLI

HITA
UNNIKRISHNAN

HARINI
NAGENDRA

INTRODUCTION

U rbanisation is an important driver of anthropogenic land use and land cover change. The spatial and demographic needs of expanding cities, as well as the imperatives of economic development, have contributed to an increase in built-up area for urban expansion. India will transition in the coming decades from a rural to a predominantly urban country. This transformation will be marked by the conversion of land and to a great extent agricultural land for urban use (Pandey and Seto, 2014: 53–66). The agricultural lands first impacted will be those located close to expanding cities in their peri-urban interface (PUI). The PUI is a complex space of mixed land use where the rural and urban coexist (Dupont, 2007). In the PUI, traditional livelihoods dependent on a natural resource base compete with more modern land use such as offices, industrial units and residential layouts. Interspersed between diminishing agricultural and increasing non-agricultural land uses in the PUI are also lands accessed as common pool resources (henceforth urban commons).

The urban commons include ecosystems such as grazing lands, wooded groves, and water bodies like lakes and ponds. These commons are interconnected social and ecological systems, characterised by close human–nature interactions. Commons were traditionally accessed by local communities for their livelihoods and subsistence, and this dependence persists even today across Indian PUIs (Narain and Vij, 2016). More recently, these urban commons have also supported the subsistence needs of migrant labour who struggle to make ends meet in a challenging city environment. Being ecological systems, commons such as wooded groves, and lakes and their wetlands, also provide key environmental functions such as the purification and replenishment of water sources, the regulation of local climate, and the reduction of the impact of pollution in cities (Nagendra, 2016).

With the projected urbanisation of India in the coming decades it is inevitable that more land in the PUI, especially agricultural land interspersed with different kinds of commons, will be increasingly converted for urban use (Pandey and Seto, 2014; Vij and Narain, 2016). This will, in turn, exacerbate the vulnerabilities faced by marginalised urban groups which depend extensively on ecological commons. These urban poor constitute practitioners of traditional livelihoods who have been long-term residents of the city, and migrant labour, who are progressively moving into cities in search of employment. The continued access of these urban poor to the commons in the context of urbanisation-related land use change is an increasing concern, raising questions for inclusiveness in cities. Equity, including an equitable access to natural resources, is recognised as an imperative for building sustainable cities. Conversions and degradations also compromise the critical environmental functions supported by urban ecological commons, contributing to a reduced quality of life for all urban residents (Nagendra, 2016).

Contributing to the degradation of urban commons in PUIs are existing models of planning that are unable to effectively address the complexities of mixed land use characteristic of a PUI. Traditional planning is marked by a clear dichotomy of rural and urban that is proving to be inadequate in the peri-urban landscape that is always in a state of flux. Conflicts in land use driven by the competing uses of land and lifestyles of the residents make governance a challenge in the PUI (Dupont, 2007).

This article examines land use changes taking place in urban commons in the rapidly expanding metropolis of Bengaluru. It is part of ongoing research in this city in which we evaluate land use changes to commons such as conversions, degradation or encroachment, and the resulting consequences of the loss of commons for urban residents in the PUI who depend on them for their livelihood and subsistence. We further highlight the implications for the environment of cities as a result of the loss of commons as a major concern. Based on our findings, we discuss gaps in current modes of planning for mixed use spaces such as the PUI, and potential ways forward for re-envisioning the models proposed for future city planning and policy.

METHODS

The study began in February 2015 and involves documenting the status of commons in Bengaluru East *taluk* (administrative boundary). We present preliminary findings focusing on five types of commons in 44 sites: lakes, ponds, wooded groves (known locally as *gunda thopes*), grazing lands and cemeteries.[1] In all, there are 291 commons of these five types in the 44 sites, of which 241 commons could be located in the field till date. Of these 241, 31 were lakes, 21 were ponds, 75 were wooded groves and grazing lands each, and 39 were cemeteries. Among the sites selected, 19 fall within the Bruhat Bengaluru Mahanagara Palike (BBMP), i.e., the municipality boundary, while 25 come under the gram panchayat. All the sites are located in the PUI, but within it they occupy a spectrum from the more urban to the more rural. Field visits were conducted to assess the status of the commons, i.e., whether they were converted, degraded, encroached or in good condition. Where possible, this information was cross-checked by interaction with local residents.

CHANGING LAND USE AND THE RESULTING LOSS OF URBAN COMMONS

Bengaluru's history is closely linked to the ecology of the region, and the creation of its landscape has been influenced considerably by human interactions with nature. From a tiny settlement in the 16th century, the city has expanded demographically and spatially. Nature in the city, including the urban commons, has been an important contributing factor shaping the transformation of Bengaluru into the metropolis that it is today (Nagendra, 2016). One of the biggest challenges faced by the city has always been access to water. Located in a semi-arid region, with no perennial water sources, rulers from successive dynasties constructed rainwater reservoirs—tanks or lakes—to meet the city's water needs. Hundreds of lakes were built across the plains and elevated ridges that were characteristic of Bengaluru's landscape, giving it the sobriquet, 'city of lakes'.

The undulating topography of the region was effectively harnessed to create interlinked water bodies connected by channels, around which settlements expanded steadily (Rice, 1897; Nagendra, 2016). Thus, lakes were in a sense the essential nodes around which the city was built.

Contiguous with the landscape of the lakes were other commons situated in the vicinity of the settlements. Ponds were located closer to the village centre and supplemented the water needs of residents. Wooded groves were planted adjacent to lakes to meet the local communities' needs for wood, fodder and fruit. The groves were once scattered across the countryside and Bengaluru district itself in 1894 had 2,118 groves containing 106,103 trees (Rice, 1897). The preferred species of fruit trees planted in groves were that of jamun (*Syzygium cumini*), mango (*Mangifera indica*), tamarind (*Tamarindus indica*) and jackfruit (*Artocarpus heterophyllus*). The mowra butter tree (*Madhuca longifolia*), from the seeds of which oil was extracted, was also planted in these groves, as were several species of ficus (*Ficus sp.*). Grazing lands ringed the village settlements, extending across several acres, and were an important source of fodder for livestock. In addition, fuelwood from trees and shrubs growing on these grazing lands were accessed by local residents. Cemeteries for different castes were also important commons. Often situated adjacent to lakes, they were accessed sometimes by grazers, and where trees were present, dried branches were collected as firewood. This mosaic of commons is still visible, especially in the more rural sites in the PUI of Bengaluru. However, there have been considerable changes to the land use of these commons as the city expanded and sprawled into the PUI, a process that is still underway.

Lakes and ponds have been subjected to considerable changes with the development of the city. Additionally, an increased reliance on external sources of water, from the river Cauvery situated more than 100 km away, has reduced the importance of local water bodies. Over the years, many lakes have been converted, others have been encroached, and still others have become cesspools. These changes were especially exacerbated in recent decades when the city witnessed rapid urbanisation. As a result, both the quality and quantity of water in these lakes have been adversely affected

a.

b.

c.

d.

e.

Multi-use commons of peri-urban Bengaluru that provide food, water, fuel-wood and fodder:
(a) lakes; (b) ponds; (c) wooded groves; (d) grazing lands; (e) cemetries
Photos: Manjunatha (b,d,e); Seema Mundoli (a, c)

(Nagendra, 2016). This was clearly visible in the field visits. Lakes were once seasonal water bodies, dry in summer but overflowing into the wetlands after the rains. However, several of the lakes in the study sites were silted, with little water, and locals interviewed mentioned that it had been years since the lakes had filled to their full capacity. Land use changes around the lakes, e.g., increase in the built-up area around the lakes and building over inflow channels in the lake vicinity, have all contributed to reducing waterflow into the lake. Wetlands are being extensively built over with high-rises looming over lakes in many sites, and impacting inflow and outflow from lakes. In other sites, sewage flowing into the lakes has turned these once seasonal water bodies into perennial but polluted pools. Garbage and construction debris, wastes generated by an expanding city, are dumped into the water and around the lake. A few instances of partial encroachments of lakes were also observed in the study sites, where houses had come up on land that once was part of the lake. While degradations predominantly contributed to adversely impacting quality and quantity of water, there was also one instance of a lake converted to an approved layout in the study sites. Some of the lakes were in the process of being rejuvenated with fencing and the construction of pathways, indicating a prioritisation of recreational needs. Ponds too faced a similar fate. Nearly 70 per cent of the ponds were filled and the land reclaimed was used for constructing buildings, such as schools and government offices, while 14 per cent were degraded with little water, overgrown with weeds and dumped with garbage.

The wooded groves in the study sites were a sad reflection of their past state. Of the 75 groves, only four were in good condition. Sixteen were degraded, and a couple of mango and jamun trees, or a solitary ficus, were all that existed in these groves. Fifty-five groves—73 per cent—were converted to roads, schools, bus stops, government offices, markets and temples to meet the growing needs of local development. Housing for disadvantaged groups has come up where groves once stood and only memories shared by the local residents indicate that the site was once a grove. In one of the relatively more urbanised sites in the PUI, a grove was acquired for industrial use: this was located close to one of the information technology hubs in an area that has seen rapid urbanisation in just the last two decades. Many groves have increasingly been converted to cemeteries owing to the lack of space in existing burial grounds, while two of them were converted to parks.

Cemeteries seem to be least affected in terms of land use change, although three of the 39 were no longer burial grounds as they were converted to a school, covered over and encroached. Grazing lands have been parcelled out and extensively converted, and many more acres have been marked for future conversions. Acres of land have been converted to layouts and slums, both authorised and unauthorised, and for schools, government offices and cemeteries. Even more land has been allocated for industry use. Bengaluru is known as the Silicon Valley of India, and the infrastructure for the information technology industry comprising roads, offices, hotels, malls, hospitals and residences has been supported considerably by conversions of these grazing lands.

ALIENATION: A RESULT OF CHANGED LAND USE OF COMMONS

The landscape of commons in the PUI of Bengaluru is clearly witnessing rapid transformation. But how have the changes to the land use—visible in the conversions, degradations and encroachments—impacted those who depended on these commons?

Food, water, fodder and fuelwood were some of the critical resources accessed by local communities and, more recently, by migrants from these urban commons. Lakes and groves contributed to the household food basket. The wetlands watered by the lake were where food was grown for household purposes and for sale. Water from the lake was used to grow paddy, millets and a variety of vegetables. The produce was used for household consumption and also sold in markets from where it was distributed to houses across the city. Indigenous varieties of fish once contributed to the protein requirements of the local residents, while some species of leafy vegetables and tubers collected from the lake bed were consumed for their high nutritional value. Fruit from the groves was eaten by children and adults alike, and mango was harvested for household consumption.

In addition to agriculture, water from the lakes and ponds was used for domestic purposes such as drinking, cooking, washing clothes and vessels, and bathing. More recently, water from the lakes has become critical for migrants who reside in temporary shelters adjacent to them. In the absence of alternative sources of water, the migrants are forced to depend on the lakes even when the water is polluted. The lakes also helped recharge groundwater and in turn replenished wells accessed by the villagers. Grazers used water from the lake for washing and watering their livestock. Livestock rearing was an important traditional livelihood for many residents. Cows, buffaloes, goats and sheep were reared, and the milk and meat sold contributed to incomes. The land around the lake was an important grazing site, and fodder growing on the water's surface and around the lake was collected for stall feeding. Grazers took shelter in the groves to escape the hot afternoon sun while their herds grazed there. Branches from trees were also loped as fodder for their animals. The groves, along with the extensive grazing lands, meant that fodder could be sourced relatively close to their habitation. Before many families shifted to cooking gas as a fuel source, wood for cooking and heating water was collected from around the lakes, groves, cemeteries and grazing lands. Today, for the increasing migrant population living in hutments, fuelwood from these commons is still critical for cooking.

The land use changes to urban commons have, however, compromised the livelihoods and subsistence uses for locals and migrants alike. Local sources of water, food, firewood and fodder have all been eroded with the loss of the commons. Water, once readily available for multiple household uses from lakes and ponds, is now accessed via pipelines and tankers from distances much further away, but the supply of which is both inadequate and intermittent. In the absence of adequate water, the cultivation of paddy has been discontinued and that of millets reduced. Vegetables are grown using sewage water. Fishing has moved to a tender-based system and locals are no longer allowed to fish as before in lakes. Several lakes are extremely polluted, and those living around them do not buy fish caught in these water bodies. Indigenous species of fish have progressively been replaced by catfish, not normally preferred by locals. Local greens that were once collected in abundance to include in daily meals have become harder to source from the degraded lakes. Less water in the lake, and polluted water, have both meant that grazers have difficulty securing water for washing and watering cattle, and are often forced to purchase water from tankers. The decreasing water levels and mounds of debris dumped around the lakes have affected fodder sources for the grazers as well. Fodder grass is not available as abundantly as before, and this has adversely impacted herd size and the quantity of milk. Some grazers are forced to purchase fodder, reducing their profit margins from the sale of milk. Many are considering shifting to alternative livelihoods but do not always possess the necessary skills for doing so. The difficulties in accessing fodder have been further exacerbated with the conversion of grazing lands and groves. Cemeteries are perhaps the only commons that have survived, but these serve little extractive uses except for grazers and, to some extent, as a source of firewood. Degraded and converted groves are no longer a local source of fruit and plant material for consumption.

The loss of the commons has also resulted in the erosion of key environmental functions that these ecosystems supported. According to the interviewees, with lakes drying up, the water table adjacent to them has also been falling. Wells, which once supplied water throughout the year, have turned dry. Wetlands perform several regulatory and purification functions, but by being built over extensively these functions have been lost. Groves were planted close to the bunds to prevent soil erosion and the shade provided by them helped cool the surroundings. In the peri-urban, these groves are now located close to roads and could help mitigate the harmful effect of air and noise pollution from vehicular traffic. However, the groves are today increasingly devoid of trees and are thus unable to provide these important regulatory functions.

POLICY IMPLICATIONS

While Bengaluru is used as an illustrative case, similar uses of, and alienations from, commons exist in other Indian cities as well. The emphasis on developing more cities necessarily requires a policy to guide land use and management that is able to recognise the diverse uses of commons, to ensure equitable access to vulnerable urban groups, and to protect them for the environmental functions they support.

India's National Land Utilisation Policy, 2013, which is expected to serve as a guiding framework for states in the preparation of their land utilisation policies, is still in the draft stage. This policy recognises the need to balance land use to support the needs of development—be it agriculture, industry or urbanisation. It acknowledges that there is a lack of integrated land use planning for the country. Competing land uses in the context of peri-urban development, along with the haphazard development of the PUI also find mention, as do the adverse impacts of urban expansion on agricultural land and the environment, especially the water bodies. The policy divides land into Land Utilisation Zones based on land use, and the peri-urban is categorised as an 'area under transformation', where conversion from agricultural to non-agricultural land use is in progress. The recognition of the PUI as a challenging space, and the need for regional planning extending beyond the municipal boundaries of expanding cities by draft policy, is a step in the right direction. However, the use of land by marginalised communities is mentioned only in the context of rural and tribal populations; the urban poor in the PUI and their dependence on natural resources that are commons do not find any mention. While the policy continues to languish in its draft stage, proposed models for cities, such as smart cities, are expected to induce further land use changes by the redevelopment of cities and Greenfield development around existing cities. A sustainable environment is one of the core infrastructural elements of smart cities, but the emphasis is on the development of technology for the management of water, waste and energy. Open and green spaces are mentioned purely for their recreational use as parks and playgrounds (MoUD, 2015). There is no mention of the importance of ecological systems in cities as multi-use urban commons or for their environmental functions, both of which are important for the sustainable and inclusive development of cities.

According to the Sustainable Development Goals (SDGs), sustainable cities matter because at present half of humanity lives in cities, and the solutions to problems faced by humanity necessarily need to be found in cities. The SDGs' goals emphasise that cities need to be inclusive, safe, resilient and sustainable. The rapidly urbanising cities in India require a similar ethic guiding their growth. For inclusive and sustainable urbanisation, this requires an understanding of how urban residents use different spaces within the city. As outlined here, ecosystems in Bengaluru city have traditionally been viewed as multi-use commons, accessed for livelihood and subsistence, especially by the urban poor. An emphasis on only developing physical infrastructure for cities, or perceiving these spaces purely for the recreational use of wealthier residents is detrimental to these vulnerable groups and is a concern for developing equitable cities (Nagendra, 2016). The loss of commons also has implications for the larger environment of cities; commons support important ecological functions such as flood control, maintaining microclimate, replenishing water tables and so on, underscoring their importance for the resilience and sustainability of cities. Planning for dynamic land use changes in the PUI, where much of urban growth is predicted, will require the unlearning of traditional models for planning that sees the urban and rural as binaries. Urban commons in the PUI need to be recognised as interconnected social and ecological systems serving multiple functions, and not merely as readily available land for further infrastructural development. Urbanisation may be inevitable today, but the kind of urbanisation that promotes sustainable and inclusive cities can still be of our choosing.

◆

ACKNOWLEDGMENTS

The authors acknowledge the following funding sources: research grant at the Azim Premji University, Bengaluru, and a USAID PEER grant to Harini Nagendra at the Ashoka Trust for Research in Ecology and the Environment (ATREE), Bengaluru. B. Manjunatha is especially acknowledged for his invaluable help with field research.

NOTE

1. The RTI file also lists other types of commons, e.g., rock, submerged land, *kharab*, to name a few, but for this article we have limited the analysis to the five commons—lakes, ponds, grazing lands, wooded groves and cemeteries.

REFERENCES

Dupont, Véronique. 2007. 'Conflicting Stakes and Governance in the Peripheries of Large Indian Metropolises: An Introduction', *Cities*, vol. 24 (2), pp. 89–94.

MoUD (Ministry of Urban Development). 2015. *Smart City Mission Statement and Guidelines*. New Delhi: Ministry of Urban Development.

Nagendra, Harini. 2016. *Nature in the City: Bengaluru in the Past, Present and Future*. New Delhi: Oxford University Press.

Pandey, Bharatendu and Karen Seto. 2014. 'Urbanization and Agricultural Land Loss in India: Comparing Satellite Estimates with Census Data', *Journal of Environmental Management*, vol. 148, pp. 53–66.

Rice, Lewis B. 1897. *Mysore: A Gazetteer Compiled for Government, Volumes 1 & 2 (revised edition)*. Whitehall Gardens: United Archibald Constable and Company.

Narain, Vishal and Sumit Vij. 2016. 'Where have all the Commons Gone?' *Geoforum*, vol. 68, pp. 21–24.

◆◆

THE UNSUSTAINABLE URBAN WASTE ECONOMY

What is to be Done?

BARBARA
HARRISS-
WHITE

WASTE AS A PROBLEM IN SUSTAINABLE DEVELOPMENT: REGULATION, POVERTY AND DISCRIMINATION

Human society has always produced waste, and always will. Waste—materials and substances without value—is constantly generated in all production, all distribution and all consumption. Waste is even generated in the handling of waste itself. The moment it spends without value may last a few minutes or for all effective eternity. The provider of resources—nature—is not simply a tap. In subjecting waste to the physical laws of decomposition and recomposition, nature is also a sink. The roles of sinks are poorly recognised in the study of sustainable development: only those of gaseous sinks in the atmosphere have political urgency. Many biophysical processes act almost infinitesimally slowly compared with the rapid physical cycles of the developing economy with which they co-evolve. My fieldwork in 2015–2016 on the waste economy of a small town in south India[1] indicated that about half the waste cannot be recycled and is left to nature's sinks: riverbeds, lakes (and the sea), subsoil and, increasingly, socially produced land surfaces including verges, tracks and dump-yards.

In the production of waste globally, India ranks third after the United States and China. A 2013 paper in *Nature* also describes India's waste production as among the fastest growing. Urban India is reckoned to emit 62m tonnes of solid waste per year—160,000 TPD. This quantity is predicted to increase by a factor of 2.7 by 2030, and by 7 by 2050. Even harder to imagine, 'peak waste' is reckoned as at a century into the future (Hoornweg, et al., 2013). Seventy per cent of urban waste is collected, of which 30 per cent is currently 'treated'. At present, just 12 per cent of urban faeces is treated.

Waste is classified in many different ways by its economic agents and regulators, by engineers and international development agencies. The official, national Total Sanitation Campaign (*Nirmal Bharat Abhiyan* [NBA]) classifies waste through many management technologies, while the World Bank stresses the fact of it not being wanted after productive use. Urban human waste is cast as a network engineering problem intimately bound with water supplies. Waste is liquid and solid (gaseous is not recognised and is a separate 'field'); hazardous vs. non-hazardous; according to (bio)toxicity; wet/dry; by origins (e.g., medical waste, meals hotels, streets); by significant (recyclable) materials (e.g., plastic, glass, paper, cardboard, metal); by site (e.g., the Railways); by commodity (e.g., motherboards, bottles); by types of degradability (e.g., edible [by animals], biodegradable, non-biodegradable); by human vs. non-human waste; human and non-human disposal (e.g., animals, nature); and by the kind of exchange involved (e.g., gathering, barter, sharing, buying and selling, gifting for second-hand reuse and sale, recycling or disposal involving public expenditure); and abandoning. So one of the most important characteristics of waste, both for our understanding of it and for urban development policy, is its discursive incoherence. The wide range of principles and the incoherence resulting from their daily use defeats the concept of a 'system' of waste.

The nameless small town whose waste I studied in 2015–2016 in south India is a one-lakh town, slipping over into surrounding villages. A central place for administration, construction, wholesale and retail trade, and its finance, it is a hub for communications, public and private health care, school and college education and culture (e.g., cinemas and marriage halls). Its waste is not only understood through incoherent categories, it is too costly to control, and by afternoon engulfs all open spaces irrespective of property rights—a public-health catastrophe showing signs of starting to happen.

INFORMALITY

At an all-India level, roughly equal volumes of waste are generated from agriculture, industry and households. Waste in agriculture and villages is relatively ignored, although agriculture contributes to greenhouse gas emissions, and the perimeters of villages often stink and are surrounded by heaps of plastic waste. Here, we focus on formality and informality in commodity exchanges and labour contracts in relation to waste generated through the town's economic circuits: in urban production, distribution, consumption, the production of human labour and the reproduction of urban society. The concept of formality denotes the status of the commodity and money transactions that are recorded and subject to state regulation/taxation, and of labour contracts that are written and accompanied by workforce rights (e.g., provident fund, pension, medical entitlements, etc.), and entitlement to social protection. Informal activity is generally taken to be the opposite.

WASTE FROM URBAN PRODUCTION

The town has an industrial distillery, foodgrains processing and clothing accessories factories, all registered. But that is where formality meets its political frontier. Registered receipts for commodity exchange are imperfectly confined to heavily regulated sectors, long-distance trade and documents marking the passage of some industrial waste from zero to positive value. Formal contracts for labour are confined to those keeping records of transactions or accounts, or to skilled workers whom employers wish to keep. ('We're bonded', said one mill engineer, not entirely in jest). The handling of waste is a specialised activity inside these industries, whether waste is heaved over the compound wall, deposited in a river bed, or sold as raw materials. Compared with total labour forces, waste workers are disproportionately casualised and Dalitised, sometimes as an expression of open social contempt. For example, Dalits are about 5 per cent of one factory's main labour force but 50 per cent in its waste department, none with formal contracts, work rights or work-related social protection.

WASTE IN DISTRIBUTION

Distributive activity can be seen in two forms: physical and economic. As case studies, we took the movement of people by Indian Railways and the movement of vegetables through a large wholesale market. Together, they generate a great range of waste as well as of formal–informal economic behaviour. Indian Railways is a public-sector undertaking, extensively and strictly regulated.

Even as a service, it generates commodity contracts, which tend to take on a formal expression. Licenced and registered companies transacting with Indian Railways deposit trails of formal records. Large quantities of waste are generated by Indian Railways passengers, not only human waste on tracks but also consumption waste in and around stations ('Ours is a dustbin', commented a sanitary inspector). By contrast, the vegetable market is dominated by a dozen registered wholesale firms, family businesses, some of whose transactions are formally recorded, and a market auctioneer who collects private fees from hundreds of unregistered retailers. Distance, scale, inspectability and consequentiality drive the registration of commodity contracts.

When it comes to the workforces, since 2005, in a process of slow diffusion throughout India, Indian Railways' cleaning labour force has been dismissed from the payroll, subcontracted and privatised. In the station we studied, this happened in 2012. At a stroke, waste workers/station cleaners have been stripped of formal status, their earnings halved or reduced to a third and their benefit entitlements destroyed. Although the private company, whose rate of profit well exceeds the average for India, has mechanised certain operations, changes in labour productivity have not resulted in the displacement of any labour because the total quantity of waste generated by stations is rising fast. Given that wages have dropped to levels at which families cannot be provisioned, the already casualised labour force—disproportionately Dalit—is forced to supplement long shifts with additional informal work segregating, bulking, transporting (in huge and heavy re-sized cement bags) and selling waste to a private waste wholesaler. In this 'side-work' they compete with a further, wholly informal, labour force (disproportionately tribal) which gathers and segregates waste from the same station waste heaps. By contrast, the significant amounts of biodegradable waste generated by the vegetable market have never been regulated and are removed by the work of animals and of an army of informal self-employed, which shifts raw food waste from the market and cooked food waste from meals hotels, to a large number of micro-enterprises rearing milch cows, pigs and poultry in the town's residential quarters. In addition, hundreds of feral dogs, together with privately or communally owned flocks of goats and small herds of cows, roam the town, feeding directly on its edible waste and generating their own waste. Fear of swine flu has forced the municipality to banish the hundreds of pigs from the streets to household compounds, and created informal supply chains for their feed and their waste.

CONSUMPTION WASTE

Waste from consumption is deposited on roadside verges and spare plots of land. In principle, consumption waste is comprehensively regulated and is the responsibility of the municipal government, which employs a set of 130 sanitation/'conservancy' workers on relatively decent salaries with full work and social security rights, and access to municipal housing. This workforce is also unionised. Over time it has become caste-cosmopolitan: 40 per cent Dalit; 30 per cent Adivasi; and the rest Backward Castes (BCs), Other Backward Castes (OBCs) and Most Backward Castes (MBCs). Over the last quarter-century, while the volume of consumption/household waste has increased by a factor of 8 to 10 and shifted decisively to being non-biodegradable, the municipal sanitation labour force has declined in numbers by 60 per cent. Technologies have hardly changed, so this trend is not the result of growing productivity. Tax evasion starves the local state of resources; municipal budgets for waste are capped at 49 per cent of total revenue; supervision is seriously inadequate and corrupt; and payments are delayed. The municipal workforce has no changing-rooms or toilets; it regularly has to pay from private pockets for work-related equipment (e.g., gloves, shoes or even diesel for the tractor-trailer), thereby privately subsidising the public sector.

The crisis in public-sector jobs in waste with full ILO-style work rights at ₹15–25,000 per month is being both resolved and exacerbated by progressive downsizing and casualisation. In one-third of the urban wards, decent work in consumption waste has been formally displaced by a subcontracted private firm employing migrant wage-workers on verbal contracts, sometimes involving labour bonding. This fetches ₹4–7,000 with no rights and very few discretionary welfare favours. Not only is this work informalised in itself but—as with Indian Railways—further informal side jobs are essential to supplement this pay. Recyclable waste is siphoned off, sorted and bagged at the end of long shifts, to be taken to a wholesaler. In addition, rounds of entirely informal self-employed gatherers scour the town mostly on foot, sometimes by cycle or (bonded) cycle carts, before dawn and after municipal labour forces have finished their shift. Many of these people live in flimsy shacks and are constantly vulnerable to eviction. A significant proportion has forfeited the right to be dependent on their kin or their village by virtue of disease, crime, cross-caste elopement or addiction. Others present themselves as 'transient workers': some 'transient' for six years in this town. They also supply the wholesale scrappers who sort, bulk up and supply a massive depot, a joint-family monopoly, where another workforce of bonded migrant labour, several hundred strong—working, eating and sleeping in primitive physical conditions—redefines recyclable waste into hundreds of categories for onward reprocessing. Small fortunes are made by the few wholesalers dominating the local waste economy.

FORMALITY AND INFORMALITY IN HUMAN WASTE

As biological beings, humans produce waste. As with consumption waste, urine, faeces and menstrual waste are in principle carefully regulated. In the early 1990s, the formal abolition of manual scavenging carried the implication of abolition of jobs reserved for female scavengers. By now, half the town's houses have septic tanks. But the Dalit and tribal owners of small fleets of septic tankers report that very few households void them regularly—they might be cleared once in a generation or when they break down. And there are no facilities for the treatment of faecal sludge when it is pumped out: it is dumped, untreated, in a nearby lake and river bed, and the lorry drivers are fined by the police when caught in the act. Meanwhile, human waste from the other 50 per cent houses and almost all commercial buildings finds its way into open drains and urban gullies, where it joins general consumption waste. De-reserving and disinheriting this kind of municipal sanitation work now means these distasteful, but comparatively well-paid, jobs are increasingly casualised. Entry depends on official patronage and discretion. The municipal labour force is ever more male and the disposal of 'wet waste'—faecal waste mixed with consumption waste—is now men's work. Privately subcontracted municipal waste disposal requires the bonded migrant labour force attached to the private company to deal with human waste too. Impossible to separate, this unrecyclable waste comes to rest in the dangerously toxic dump-yard managed by the municipality. But there, entire families of indigent gatherers and their children also survive on a pittance from sifting the putrid surface for recyclables. Someone contains and compresses the mass of waste by systematically setting fire to quarters of it, week by week (it is illegal, but the tribal families who are generally blamed have no interest in adding fiery temperatures and dioxin-laden smoke to their already disgusting work conditions). These problems of a dangerous and informalised system of disposal of human waste are not recognised in public discussions about defecation.

INFORMALITY IN THE WASTE GENERATED BY THE REPRODUCTION OF SOCIETY

Society cannot reproduce from one generation to the next if it is not healthy. In this town, the vast majority of women and men disposing of waste, on whose labour the population of the town depends, will also not work without alcohol. Liquor steels the workforce for the disgusting experiences of wastework and is said to help 'unwind' workers' bodies racked by pain at the end of long and strenuous shifts. And 90 per cent of municipal waste workers—let alone the army of informal labour—die of diseases of aging, before the age of retirement.[2] So in our case study we studied waste generation and formality and informality in waste disposal in the sectors of health care essential for a healthy society, and liquor—essential to the workforce dealing with day-to-day waste.

Through a multiplicity of institutions and organisations the state regulates both health and liquor, both public sector and private. Most waste from hospitals and clinics is not dangerous and enters the general consumption waste circuit, but waste from operating theatres and maternity wards, drugs, wound dressings, syringes, etc., are dangerous and strictly regulated. Segregated and bulked through a separate private disposal system, medical waste is supposed to head for incineration and burial. In a nutshell, what actually happens is that while medical waste from government hospitals follows this route, the incinerator has been closed down following local public outrage at the pollution it causes, and medical waste is currently buried untreated. Some private medical waste also follows this route. But the fact that syringes, dressings and body parts appear on the dump-yard implies that some medical waste joins the spaces and practices of general consumption waste, already mixed with faeces. Apart from regulation, the state also formally subsidises private health (allowing senior staff from government hospitals to moonlight at their private clinics, underwriting the training of medical and paramedical staff which leak to the private sector, and acting as a last-resort safety-net when private health care fails). In both the public and private health sectors, as also in liquor retailing, some records are maintained for inspection. In practice, in both sectors, leakages occur into informal private practice or black markets.

Turning to the labour involved in processing medical waste, as in the cases of Indian Railways and the municipality, the government hospital has privatised and subcontracted hundreds of 'housekeepers', with the same deterioration in work conditions and earnings, and the same pressure to add informal self-employment to informal wage-work after very long housekeeping shifts. Meanwhile, in the registered private sector, there exists a flexible continuum between full formal contracts at one extreme, via permanent verbal contracts to casual verbal contracts, the content and privileges of which depend upon discretion, patronage, loyalty and the worker's own needs. Housekeeping in private hospitals is characterised by informal contracts, low pay, very long hours and flexibility in tasks, with illiterate housekeepers moving between cleaning and segregating waste, nursing and theatre tasks, and even the dispensing of drugs.

In state-owned liquor retail outlets, where consumption has increased by a factor of 30 times during the previous decade, staff is retained on minimal salaries and permanently casual contracts. These are expected to be supplemented up to 10 times informally through 'commissions' on sales (and further supplemented by black marketing). Huge quantities of glass waste are generated by liquor. Unbroken bottles embossed with their factory names create informal livelihoods in sorting, cleaning and recycling to breweries and distilleries. Broken glass may be aggregated and recycled, but may also be deposited with general consumption waste, increasing the danger of the dump-yard's landfill.

We see that informal activity cannot be ignored as of residual or marginal importance. It is hardwired into the economy of waste, which itself is hardwired into the urban economy. For one formal livelihood with full rights, it is estimated that there must be 10–15 informal livelihoods with entitlements grounded in discretion, loyalty, imperfect citizenship—or none at all. Informality is essential to, and positively encouraged by, the state. In the municipality, the principle of private enterprise is overdetermined by the theory and ideology of neoliberalism, by compulsions of fiscal starvation, by the convenience of new public management, and the practicalities of a socially segmented labour market where costs can be minimised by the import of destitute labour from other regions of India. The state ignores the inadequacy of informal wages paid from the companies to which it subcontracts its own municipal waste work, which forces deprived workers to supplement their livelihoods and long shifts by further informal work. As long as waste proliferates, livelihood niches are generated for a massive sponge of self-employed people. In the public discussion of technological change in waste 'systems', the costs of displacement and of the economic relocation of the informal labour indispensable to the waste economy is never mentioned.[3] Nor are the active and passive roles of the urban animal economy and the human livelihoods dependent on animals in turn dependent on waste.

POVERTY

Despite the protective entry barrier of disgust (the stench, the physically and socially offensive nature of the substances handled), most waste workers' earnings are low. Informal self-employment and wage work yields between ₹4–6,000 per month. The urban minimum wage for the relevant state (₹180 per day) would generate ₹4,500 for 25 days (₹5,400 for a no-rest month), so waste livelihoods hover above and below the minimum. As the minimum wage is not set to provision a family, these incomes require a minimal ratio of dependents to workers, which explains the appearance in the waste economy of labouring children and the aged.

By contrast, the urban Poverty Line has been revised upwards on CMIE (Centre for Monitoring Indian Economy Pvt. Ltd.) data by the Rangarajan Committee from the Tendulkar Planning Commission's ₹33 per day (₹990 per month) to ₹47 per day (₹1,400 per month) (Jitendra, 2014). By this yardstick, earnings in this essential part of the economy are mostly in excess of the revised poverty line. But, clearly, for people to reproduce at this level of income, their basic needs have to be available and subsidised, which is not the case here. In the past, waste workers have had to beg for food. Some formal municipal waste workers still report accepting gifts of food from householders (though they no longer take it in their hands or pick it up from the ground when householders place it there). However, in addition to food and shelter, and time-consuming searches for fuel and water, private health, education and dowry costs are now well established to eat into the conventions of 'essential expenditure' of even the lowest status and poorest labouring people (Heyer, 2000). In this town, the neediest people work in the informal waste economy and the neediest waste workers are the most imperfectly entitled to social protection. The public distribution system was frequently praised by workers as their nutritional lifeline and its rations are sometimes shared with the many households without ration cards.

STIGMA

Most waste work is hard, dangerous, stinking and oppressive. Waste work is stigmatised throughout the world but, in this respect, India is exemplary. Many educated people consider waste as uniquely a domain for the lowest of Dalit castes, but in the case I studied, the municipal workforce is growing cosmopolitan among lower castes because being labelled as 'municipal labour' does not cause shame. The informal waste economy, by contrast, consists almost entirely of Dalits and Adivasis. It is socially stratified. Indeed, one tribe is shunned as 'animals' and actively socially expelled, as are the 'transient' people who have forfeited the social right to be dependent upon others.

The social structure is experienced as one of violence that consigns people who have lowest social status and the least choice to work in the waste economy without options of exit. While few of those we interviewed experienced discrimination among themselves at work, more instances were reported in their work-related contact with the rest of society (e.g., passengers expressing annoyance at Indian Railways' subcontracted cleaners if they even touch the inside of compartments; and abusive commands by medical patients to hospital housekeepers). But there is a long way to go before discrimination is eliminated from what the then RBI Governor described in early 2015 as people's 'preparation' for the economy: in housing, school, access to health, transport, temples, etc. In what we describe here as the reproduction of society, discrimination against waste workers is rife. Although one tribe was routinely abused as a group, many other waste workers are now experiencing discrimination, not as a result of 'ascribed' group-based identity (their caste, tribe, gender), but rather as the product of socially 'acquired' characteristics such as poverty, illiteracy, the dirt of this work and the need to drink alcohol to which it inevitably leads. Individual discrimination exists alongside group-based discrimination and may be replacing it—or may be a modern mask for persistent ritual pollution. In India, waste is rarely discussed as a problem of caste discrimination (Rodrigues, 2009).

WHAT IS TO BE DONE?

Swachch Bharat has awakened India to its metropolitan waste. Unavoidable as a process, waste generation is variously problematised not as a problem of caste, but of technology, management and planning; of land use and the need for the permanent sequestration of spaces; of costs (and benefits) to the economy; of growing threats to public health and of aesthetics.[4] For Isher Ahluwalia, 'garbage is a personal threat to all of us and the challenge will only become greater in future as more people move to the cities as urbanisation and rising incomes bring changing lifestyles which usually means more waste' (2016).

The problem of waste control and governance is being addressed through two conspicuous policy approaches. First, Swachch Bharat has the dual aim of making India free from open defecation and achieving clean streets. In this urban case study, the latter is more urgent because the problem of defecation is not so much where people defecate (mostly privately), but what happens to their faeces afterwards. Second, the Atal Mission for Rejuvenation and Urban Transformation (AMRUT) is tasked with installing drainage and sewage networks, and waste water treatment—an ambition which the Bangalore-based Indian Institute for Human Settlements (IIHS), after serious evaluation, has concluded is physically and financially not possible to extend to all Indian towns. Meanwhile, policy approaches from environmental economics scope urban waste producers' willingness to pay for segregated waste disposal, and their own willingness to segregate (Khati, 2016). And guidelines for urban waste management grounded in engineering promote and cost technology without the ongoing costs of labour, and without the opportunity costs of displaced labour, let alone the unknown numbers of informal labour trapped in waste work with no alternatives, whose livelihoods may be threatened by technological upgrading. Over and above the problems of each of these approaches, there is the fact that in the small town we studied, none of these approaches were mentioned by municipal officials, PWD engineers, planners and politicians responsible for waste. A scour of the town generated one advertisement for Swachch Bharat near the station.

In this part of the article, we therefore summarise local stakeholder research from 2016 on the policy question, 'what is to be done with the town's waste' according to two groups of stakeholders: (i) officials responsible in some way for waste, and (ii) municipal waste workers responsible for its disposal.

Local officials explained that waste was out of their control but they also lacked basic knowledge about it. Conceiving waste variously as an epidemic of plastic and/or packaging, or irresponsible human defecation, they even lacked a consensus about the amount generated. Estimates varied from 25 to 60 tonnes a day. As a problem, waste was driven by the uncivil behaviour of citizens and of the 'floating population' around transport infrastructure: compulsive littering and people's inability to segregate waste. Problems were exacerbated by insufficient engineers and municipal funds. This narrative was not challenged by municipal sanitation labour, but they focused instead on waste in terms of public toxicity, mismanagement and, like Ahluwalia, threats to health and well-being. 'Waste production and disposal is dangerous to our workforce' (male municipal sanitation worker). 'Inadequate workforce strength, inadequate technology, inadequate enforcement of laws and rules, disgusting work conditions, delays in pay and entitlements all make it intolerable' (female municipal sanitation worker).

The agenda of solutions to the problems of waste also reflected the standpoints of stakeholders. 'What's the use of planning without revenue?' (municipal official). All officials had heard of the best practice of vermicomposting (which would displace the urban animal economy). Otherwise, officials volunteered projectised responses such as compressed waste briquettes, biogas, incineration—ideas possibly got from TV. Even so, the town had but one proposal (composting), and that too at an early stage of formulation, stalled since 2014 and unfunded. In the discussion of waste, one official volunteered that outside funding had supported a bicycle hearse for unidentified corpses, a slaughter house and crematorium, the last two of which were unused because of informal alternatives. One of 15 officials had attended a short course in waste in Singapore but regarded the skills he had acquired as inappropriate and irrelevant. Municipal sanitation workers identified revenue reform as vital, through a hike in property taxes, and exemplary punishment for evaders. With an increased budget, the most disgusting and dangerous tasks would be mechanised, the workforce enlarged and re-trained, only after which public education would result in enduring improvements. However, 'investment in labour is not considered as development'.[5]

'Waste is not a political issue' (politician). The low political and bureaucratic salience of waste can be understood from both the architecture and the practices of urban governance.

THE ARCHITECTURE OF GOVERNANCE

Responsibility for waste is dispersed across departments of the municipality and field stations of the state government, resulting in lack of communication, complex coordination and fractured lines of reporting/decision making. Waste is a small, unspecialised part of wide-ranging official job specifications and heavy work burdens. Political responsibility for waste is unclear and easy to shift. The town's low status and revenue stress is exacerbated by high turnover, short working days, poor motivation, understaffing and double jobs, officials' unfamiliarity either with the town's character or with practical aspects of waste, which require site visits, and their inability to conceive consultations with the workforce as relevant to their responsibilities. Last, policy jurisdictions may be territorial (Town and Country Planning) or networked (Public Works Department). Neither kind of jurisdiction is systematic. Outside authority must be invoked to deal with mismatches of territorial responsibility (as in the planning of a sewage treatment plant), or the development of new networks spanning rural and urban territory (the costs of routes when relocating the dump-yard).

THE PRACTICES OF GOVERNANCE

While the architecture of waste leads to the increasing incoherence and neglect of the state's waste work, practices of governance that are not confined to waste further compromise its capabilities. The local state has formal power over decisions, standards, technologies, the uses of territorial and networked infrastructure, part of the labour force and disciplinary regulation. While the legal and procedural framework for governance is well-developed, enforcement capacity is severely constrained. When the Pollution Control Board has but one officer to serve an entire district without an official means of transport, the intentionality of policy has to be questioned.

Despite its low priority, some aspects of waste are party politicised and in this case lead to stalemate. Urban open drains started to be capped under Party A, but investment was halted when Party B was elected to power in the state. A new round of municipal elections put Party C in command locally. The state minister for urban development from Party B has no interest in investing in political benefits for Party C.

The lack of coordination and conflicts of political interest between jurisdictions of local and state government are intensified by the gradient in status between office work and practical activity. Plans may be approved but construction is not supervised. Specifications, scales and purposes can be changed with impunity in construction and implementation, with or without bribes. Buildings encroach onto drains and wasteland, and water bodies become dumping grounds for waste.[6] While 'waste is a low-rent sector' (engineer), budgets are regularly appropriated and shared between officials and politicians. These practices result in workers being paid at least a third less than formally accounted, and equipment being cheaper than planned and of poor quality, affecting capacity utilisation as much as the costs of wear and tear—mediocre outcomes that range from municipal tractor trailers to state-subsidised septic tanks.

CONCLUSION

Waste is becoming a major urban development problem. In this case study, it is out of control and much is uncollected. An informal economy has ballooned—now indispensable to the waste system— and so to the rest of local society and economy. This informal waste economy is necessary to the state and encouraged by it, despite widespread official ignorance of its character and significance. Its governance is politically disorganised through a mass of informal practices: tax evasion and the acute lack of revenue, which hobbles municipal expenditure; the architecture and practices of governance, including fractured responsibilities and routine corruption; lack of political and bureaucratic capabilities and knowledge; and short-term party-political conflict.

This can all happen because waste—especially dirty waste and the spaces of dirty waste—lies below the social radar. It is the lowest status sector of the economy, socially invisible and disregarded. The negative value of waste (its private and social costs) is contained by a huge informal labour sponge in which an uneducated, unasseted, socially stigmatised, poorly organised and politically fractured workforce finds livelihoods, some of which approach starvation levels. While trade unions claw limited gains for the elite waste workers from the municipality, other acts of resistance and empowerment work on the general problems of caste and ethnic identity and not the specific problems of waste work, let alone of the generation of waste.

Whatever is or is not done about small-town waste, some implications for policy can be learned from this case study. First, new policy needs a thorough analysis of the institutional conditions under which it might work as intended. Second, policy analysis needs to attend to the costs of policy proposals. Third, as well as beneficiaries, victims and enemies of policies need identifying prior to policymaking, and the means to neutralise them need mainstreaming and costing. Fourth, implementation needs credible enforcement capacity. Last, when new policies are made without destroying previous policy and political economy arrangements, they lie like geological sediments, leaving a pre-existing underlying structure of interests intact, and adding to dysfunctional bureaucratic complexities.

◆

ACKNOWLEDGEMENTS

This paper is one of the fruits of my role as co-investigator on LSE's EU/ESRC-funded programme of research on 'Poverty and Inequality', directed by Professor Alpa Shah, whom I wish to thank, as much as I thank my co-researcher in the field. The views expressed here are my own.

NOTES

1. Using a snowball method, over 80 formal and informal waste workers were interviewed, together with 15 local officials responsible in some way for dealing with waste, seven local politicians, two business association presidents, caste

associations' presidents, Dalit lawyers and legal activists, trades unionists and civil society activists—about 110 people in all.

2. Human Rights Watch (2014).

3. Beswada Wilson has been a notable exception but is a campaigner rather than an engineer.

4. See Government of India (2014).

5. CITU official. Confederation of Indian Trade Unions (CITU).

6. For examples of other deviations from official municipal plans, the planned community hall is a bank; the cricket ground is a bus stand; a crossroad has become a petrol station.

REFERENCES

Ahluwalia, I. 2016. 'Cities at Crossroads: Can't Sweep it Under the Carpet', *Indian Express,* 28 September.

Government of India (GOI). 2014. *Guidelines for Developing State Policies on Solid and Liquid Waste Management (SLWM) in Rural Areas.* New Delhi: Ministry of Drinking Water and Sanitation, Asian Development Bank and CEE, pp. 9–11.

Heyer, J. 2000. 'The Changing Position of Agricultural Labourers in Villages in Rural Coimbatore, Tamil Nadu, between 1981/2 and 1996', *QEH Working Paper Series* 57. Oxford: University of Oxford.

Hoornweg, D., P. Bhada-Tata and C. Kennedy. 2013. 'Waste Production Must Peak this Century', *Nature,* vol. 502, pp. 615–17.

Human Rights Watch. 2014. *Cleaning Human Waste: 'Manual Scavenging', Caste and Discrimination in India.* https://www.hrw.org/report/2014/08/25/cleaning-human-waste/manual-scavenging-caste-and-discrimination-india (accessed on 30 March 2016).

Jitendra C. 2014. 'The New Poverty Line', *Down to Earth.* http://www.downtoearth.org.in/news/new-poverty-line-rs-32-for-rural-india-rs-47-for-urban-india-45134

Khati, P. 2016. 'Municipal Solid Waste Management in Kalimpong Town: An Economic Analysis', paper for the Indian Society for Ecological Economics (ISEC) Conference, January, Bangalore.

Rodrigues, V. 2009. 'Untouchability, Filth, and the Public Domain', in G. Guru (ed.), *Humiliation: Claims and Context.* New Delhi: Oxford University Press, pp. 108–23.

THE CANAL AND THE CITY
An Urban–Ecological Lens on Chennai's Growth[1]

KAREN
COELHO

THE BUCKINGHAM CANAL AS URBAN HERITAGE

U rban waterways are eloquent sources of urban history. The scapes that they provide—of settlement and land-use, built and open spaces, nature and infrastructure—carry narratives of the city's pathways to its present. Some waterways are more equal than others. Large rivers often assume an emblematic status, closely associated with the city's identity. Canals, on the other hand, may barely make it to the consciousness of urban residents. Struggling through backstreets and backyards, choked with sewage and waste, they are often not even recognisable as waterways.

Chennai's Buckingham Canal, viewed in these terms, is a paradox. An engineered waterway, conceived and built in phases through the 19th century as a navigation channel to transport commercial cargo through the eastern districts of the Madras Presidency, it is an important figure in Chennai's history. It is also a central feature of the city's geographic and ecological landscape. The canal runs like a curving spine down the length of the city for about 35 km, veering close to the coastline in parts, and intersecting with the city's three major rivers—the Kosasathaliyar in the far north, the Cooum in the north-centre and the Adyar in the south. Its antiquity and geographic centrality have earned it recognition in the historical lore of Madras/Chennai. The Chennai Heritage Week celebrations, held annually in late August to commemorate the founding of Madras in 1639, have come to include photo exhibitions on the canal, comprising nostalgic representations of locks, sluice gates and wharves, most of which are currently in disrepair. Representations of Madras are rarely complete without old images of wooden boats on the canal. Despite its decrepit condition, then, the Buckingham Canal remains emblematic of Madras/Chennai.

On the ground, however, the canal in the city has followed a rather typical urban trajectory from a buzzing navigation canal to a sluggish stream of sewage. While its flow through most of its 796-km length down the Coromandel Coast is challenged by various factors, including siltation, tidal surges and damage from storms and floods, the canal is all but killed within the city. For most of its career through Chennai, it remains invisible, hidden behind or buried under the accumulated hardware of urban development. In its northern-most urban sections, thick deposits of fly-ash and silt obstruct its flow as it runs through heavy industrial landscapes of thermal power plants and coal yards. In its central sections, railway and road bridges and dense built-up neighbourhoods obscure its presence, offering piecemeal glimpses of a fragmented, much-abused and diminished waterway. It is only in its southern reaches, as it leaves the city, that the canal flows broad and serene, although it is even here a polluted carrier of untreated sewage and effluents.

As heritage, then, the Buckingham Canal functions ironically, throwing a rather dark light on the city's urban–ecological trajectories. Its ongoing struggle to survive is telling testament to the city's choices and patterns of growth. In 2004, the Inland Waterways Authority of India (IWAI), which proposed to revive the larger Buckingham Canal for navigation as a part of National Waterway 4, found that the Chennai segment of the canal was 'totally in abandoned condition' and not salvageable (2010: 10). This was partly due to sewage pollution, but also to the profusion of bridges within the city, reflecting the priority that had been accorded to road and rail. The report recommended 'multi-modal cargo transfer' for the stretch of the canal inside the city.

What can the Buckingham Canal tell us about Chennai? This article argues that the canal offers novel heuristics on two aspects: first, the way that large hydraulic infrastructures figure in urban governance, and, second, the socio-spatial formations and transformations of the city since the early 19th century.

THE CANAL AS FAILED INFRASTRUCTURE

As infrastructure, the canal presents several ambiguities and conundrums. First, although an engineered navigation channel, it is also a tidal waterway intersecting with rivers and backwaters, playing an important but complex part in the drainage of the eastern coastal plains. Hydrologists have reported on its contribution to absorbing and mitigating the impact of cyclones, floods and the 2004 tsunami on the city, and in channelling and draining eastward flows of monsoon waters to the sea. This has made it part of the 'natural' ecology of the city, along with the city's three rivers and smaller drainage canals. However, its drainage functions have been compromised by a severe reduction in depth and width, and by encroachments of various kinds.

Second, the canal offers an 'anti-dam' understanding of hydraulic installations, a counterpoint to the typical profile of colonial and postcolonial engineered water infrastructures such as dams, reservoirs and irrigation canals. Such projects have been presented as grandiose, monumental interventions into the landscape, serving multiple projects of state formation, from transforming land use to generating revenue, to promoting economic activities, providing employment and legitimating rule. The Buckingham Canal has historically fulfilled some of these functions. And when the canal was completed at the end of the 19th century, British engineer A. S. Russell (1898: 40) noted that it had dramatic effects on the landscape:

> The construction of the Buckingham Canal has placed the town of Madras in cheap and easy communication with no less than five districts, and with the large and important towns of Cocanada, Bezwada, Masulipatam, Ongole and Nellore....It passes through what was, before its construction, a dreary waste of sand, but much of this barren and arid country has been greatly developed and improved owing to the remarkably cheap means of communication afforded by the canal; cultivation has been brought into existence or extended, owing to the facilities given by the canal for the drainage of low-lying land; numerous casuarina and other plantations have been formed along its entire length ...; and a great increase in the wealth and prosperity of the population has taken place.

Yet, the canal was not planned and built as a single grand project or as part of a major state engineering scheme. Rather, it was patched together over about 75 years, from segments—scraps of excavated channels, links, junctions, and other existing canals—built at different times by different actors, both public and private, from British entrepreneur Basil Cochrane who made the first cut in 1804, to the Public Works Department (PWD) that took it over in the mid-1800s. Large segments of the canal were, in fact, constructed as a food-for-work scheme, providing employment to thousands of workers after the severe famine of 1877.

Once completed, the Buckingham Canal was, and remained, a low-key, plebeian infrastructure. It served to transport small wooden craft with cargoes of basic essentials such as firewood, salt, lime and locally grown agricultural produce. While it was heavily used in certain periods and certain stretches, historical evidence suggests that its navigational function had always been under stress. Russell, in the late 19th century, had highlighted obstructions to navigation on the canal caused by chronic siltation, partly from tidal action and partly from sewage discharged into it inside the city. By the 1960s, the navigation potential of the canal was clearly on the decline. Despite periodic efforts by the PWD to deepen, widen and desilt its bed and augment its terminal and wharfage facilities, the canal remained a challenge to maintain and operate. By 1962, the PWD concluded that while the canal served to provide low-cost freight services to the public, it would never yield direct returns, as annual expenditure on its maintenance significantly exceeded the revenue earned from its operation.

As processes of urbanisation were peaking in Madras city in the 1960s, there was considerable ambivalence in official and political circles about the functions and future of the canal in the city, including proposals to close it up and reclaim the land for other infrastructure. S. Krishnamurthy, Mayor of Madras in 1964, expressed some of this when he wrote:

> it has to be considered (i) whether it would be practicable to preserve the canal entirely free from the pollution from the slums along its banks, or (ii) whether the closure of the canal and replaced [sic] by railway line would seriously affect the drainage system in the city.

In the 1990s, the construction of the elevated railway of the Mass Rapid Transit System (MRTS) to follow the canal along most of its length in the city was perhaps the final blow to the canal's survival as a waterway. The project was planned in the 1960s and its first phase was completed in 1996 with funding from the central Ministry of Railways. The Tamil Nadu government, tasked with providing land for the project, identified the canal alignment as a corridor of cheaply available land. Today, most of the canal in the city lies shrunk and shadowed under the pillars and bridges of the MRTS, emblematic of a class of failed urban infrastructures that live on uncertainly in the urban milieu, their original purpose buried under, or overwritten by, other forms and functions.

THE CANAL AS VANTAGE POINT ON CHENNAI'S GROWTH

The canal also offers a perspective on the formation of Chennai as a city that runs against the grain of dominant histories. Chennai's history has mostly been told from statist or elitist angles, which emphasise its origins and trajectories as a colonial trading post and military/administrative hub centred around Fort St. George (and its factory and White Town) established in 1640 on the north-eastern coast of the present city. The social geographies of these accounts also focus on the early urban centres of Black Town, Purasawakkam and Chintadiripet that were created by colonial industry from the late 17th century onward, on the suburban settlements of colonial and Indian elite that arose around the Choultry plain from the early 18th century, and on the temple towns and *mirasi* villages of the Tondaimandalam region, all of these dispersed across the territory that was in 1798 bounded as Madras city.

Almost entirely neglected in these histories are accounts of settlements and movements of working-class populations, and how they shaped and formed the city. Notable exceptions are works by historians Susan Neild and Ravi Ahuja, which describe lower-caste spatial dynamics in the 18th and 19th century. The early morphology of Madras was shaped by processes of what can be termed 'expansion through in-filling'. Existing villages and towns were coopted into the sprawling urban formation along with the larger urban centres; all of these were separated by vast tracts of open lands, which became slowly joined by '*paracheris*'—settlements of 'untouchable' Paraiyars—that attached themselves to the edges of these centres throughout the 18th century (Neild, 1979; Ahuja, 2001). Neild estimates that by the early 1800s, Paraiyars may have accounted for about a fifth of the population of Madras. They constituted the majority of the unskilled labour force, initially working in mirasi village lands, but increasingly, through the 19th century, opting for wage labour in the towns, or jobs as servants in suburban estate homes. Prohibited from settling in the villages, and unable to afford accommodation in the urban centres, they created hamlets of their own which grew over time into distinctive settlements, drawing Paraiyar migrants to the city (Neild, 1979). The paracheris were, thus, an important and ubiquitous settlement type in the unfolding of the city's urban form. According to Neild, they were the most numerous of the non-mirasi villages in the city, numbering at least 40 by the 1830s.

A SPOTLIGHT ON 'SLUMS'

Madras/Chennai has often been dubbed a city of slums. This reputation is not without basis. Well into the 20th century, Madras was marked among Indian cities for its large concentration of Dalit settlements. Writing in 1938, C. W. Ranson remarks on the 'relative importance of the Adi Dravidar in Madras. This community occupies a more prominent place in the life of the city than the "outcaste" in Bombay and Calcutta' (1938: 3). He noted that the Adi-Dravidars in Madras tended to move in with their families and establish themselves 'in mud and thatch huts and to retain [their] own form of community life, within the larger city community' (ibid.: 3).

The banks of the Buckingham Canal were key spaces for these processes of urbanisation through spontaneous in-filling. The canal cut through some of the oldest and most densely settled urban centres of Madras: Chintadripet, Triplicane, Mylapore, and later Adyar, where squatter settlements and paracheris were widely prevalent. This social geography persisted into recent times. By 1960, a Census study found that the banks of the canal were the single most concentrated site of slums in Madras, accounting for 10 per cent of the city's slums.

The perspective from the canal illuminates an alternate corridor of urban development to that delineated by Mount Road, an old military roadway that has been highlighted as pivotal in consolidating the extensive urban formation of Madras

(Hancock, 2008). This road extended south-west from the Fort, linking Madras to the cantonment area of St. Thomas Mount, and forming the axis along which colonial residential suburbs and concomitant municipal services developed from the 1700s onwards. Mount Road has remained the dominant corridor of Chennai's urban development and is still regarded as the city's Central Business District (CBD). Indeed, part of the stated rationale for selecting the alignment of the Buckingham Canal for the MRTS railway line in the 1960s was to redistribute urbanisation and development away from the CBD.

AN URBAN–ECOLOGICAL LENS

The canal as vantage point also highlights the shifting morphologies of land and water, and the associated dynamics of value ascription implicated in Chennai's histories of urbanisation and settlement. Historians of Madras concur on the uniquely agrarian character of this 'city of villages' into the late 18th century, wherein even Paraiyar families, customarily deemed landless, cultivated fruit and vegetable gardens in and around their urban settlements to supplement their income from labour. Until the late 18th century, according to Ahuja (2001), the labouring poor and low-caste settlers enjoyed relatively easy access to land for settlement and garden cultivation. Of the large number of paracheris scattered around the city, some were squatted, typically on lands of marginal quality and low value like river banks, low-lying swamps and sandy shores, where no titles were asserted (ibid.; Neild, 1979). In others, residents paid occupancy fees to local landlords 'who could find no better use for their least attractive and usually swampy pieces of property' (Neild, 1979: 227). The paracheris, thus, inscribed value into these marginal lands even as they drew their subsistence from them.

However, a consolidation and valorisation of these lands as property began to occur by the late 18th century, when, as Ahuja notes, claims (customary, use and proprietorial) over land became more 'volatile', and an urban property market had begun to emerge. By the end of the century, the colonial administration had tightened its control over urban lands within the just-established municipal boundaries, and had begun to impose more stringent requirements for proof of purchase. Accommodation became 'rare and dear' in Madras even as the scope for informal appropriation of low-value lands was curtailed (ibid.). The process of property-creation entailed evictions of unauthorised occupancies. For instance, in the 1770s, the Company cleared several houses and huts of fisherfolk and Muslims off the beach near Black Town. In this period, then, 'private property rights clashed with plebeian use rights: the one was created by the colonial administration to invalidate the other' (Ahuja, 2001: 95). This formalisation of property rights was accompanied by a 'normalising' discourse of Paraiyars as unpropertied people (ibid.). Ahuja argues that the expropriation of land from low-caste and working-class groups reinforced and perpetuated urban poverty and closed off avenues of mobility that had earlier been available.

Much of the reclamation of squatted swamplands and floodplains, and their revaluation as landed property in the early 19th century, took place in what Ahuja describes as an arch of territory stretching from Tondiarpet in the north to Santhome in the south. This arch broadly corresponds to the tract of land through which the Buckingham Canal was dug a few decades later in the 1870s. This waterway, cut through parcels of landed property, once more created large areas of 'open lands' on its banks, which attracted new waves of Dalit and other squatters and settlers, both from outside and other parts of the city.

EMERGENT URBANISMS ALONG THE CANAL

Utilitarian narratives of the canal as a failed navigation route and a dubious drainage channel have obscured other important ways in which this waterway crafted or transformed urban space in Chennai. The building of the canal drew a large migrant population to service its economies as boatmen, watchmen, loaders, wharf and warehouse labour. Many settled with their families close to, or along, its banks. While the canal's navigational function declined from the middle of the 20th century, settlements on its banks continued to expand, offering the urban poor an affordable space within the city to live and work. These settlements underwent a variety of changes over time: some entrenched themselves, were upgraded by the state, and have morphed into developed neighbourhoods. Others were cleared and resettled; still others remained informal, un-serviced and constantly vulnerable to threats of eviction. Many settlements along the canal have also served as staging grounds for movements, voluntary or forced, of populations to other areas of the city. In all these ways, these settlements have played important roles in shaping the socio-political and economic geography of Madras/Chennai.

The canal, as it snakes slowly down the city, offers a map—albeit rather schematic—of the changing economic geography of Chennai's urbanisation. Different moments of the city's economic development can be tracked along its path: from the older heavy industries of Ennore and Manali in its far northern reaches; through the small-scale informal manufactories, commercial, administrative/institutional and service-sector economies in its central parts; to, finally, a landscape of real estate urbanism in its southern reaches. This spatio-temporal map is schematic and even, perhaps, coincidental. The chronology of Chennai's economy was neither planned in this manner, nor does it follow such a linear progression. There are loopbacks and intersections as different economies negotiate their way into the contemporary urban. Yet, the canal corridor provides a broad spatial profile, from north to south, of the economic trajectories that have shaped the urban character of the city.

Colonial Madras had relatively little industrial activity, apart from a large textile mill, a railway coach factory and a few tanneries. However, with the post-independence thrust on heavy industry, a batch of oil refineries, fertiliser and petrochemical factories, and a thermal power plant, were established in Madras in the 1960s. Following colonial geographies they were located in the northern edges of the city in Manali and Ennore. Here, the Buckingham Canal flows close to the coastline, merging in parts with the Ennore Creek, and supporting the livelihoods of fisherfolk from the surrounding villages who fish in the creek and the canal as well as the sea. However, like the creek, the canal in these parts has been nearly killed by heavy deposits of silt, fly-ash and slurry from the power plants, and by inflows of effluent, sludge and sewage from the Manali Industrial Area and nearby municipalities. In a classic enactment of the tragedy of 'development' (some) fisherfolk were promised factory jobs in compensation for the takeover of their lands and the destruction of their livelihood by the industries. In the rare instances where they materialised, however, these jobs turned out to be insecure, poorly paid casual contracts, casting these families into the ranks of the urban poor.

Further south, near Wall Tax Road and Central Station in north-central Chennai, the neighbourhood called Wood Wharf, exemplifies the small-scale informal manufacturing industry that grew rapidly in Chennai from the 1970s. Wood Wharf as a settlement emerged directly from the Buckingham Canal's operations, where wharves were built in the early 1900s to offload firewood, salt and other material transported from northern parts of the Madras Presidency. Dalit families, who came to the city to work as loaders, boatmen or watchmen, pitched tents or built huts on open lands slightly inland from the canal. In the 1950s, the PWD, to supplement revenues from the canal's operations, leased out land on the canal banks to entrepreneurs who established warehouses, firewood depots and salt godowns. In the 1970s, with capital from the Marwadi community residing in the nearby trader precincts of Sowcarpet and Purusawakkam, these godowns were converted into small manufacturing units, fabricating a range of aluminium and stainless steel products for sale in local wholesale markets and in neighbouring states.

The neighbourhood of Wood Wharf is now a vibrant manufacturing hub, directly employing thousands of unskilled and semi-skilled workers, both local and from other parts of Chennai, and indirectly provides livelihoods to hundreds of local families through a proliferating support economy of logistics and meal supplies. As none of the residents have titles to their homes, there is minimal vertical extension of houses and living conditions are congested. Yet, large numbers of families have moved in and few have moved out. The residents of Wood Wharf almost unanimously declared that this place had provided for them across two or three generations and had given them access to education and mobility for their families. Several residents owned flats in other parts of the city, but would not leave despite the congestion and squalor here. However, the precariousness of the settlement was highlighted by periodic threats of eviction and by the demolition of a set of homes on the edges of the canal in 2014.

The middle section of the canal between the Cooum and the Adyar, comprising Chepauk, Triplicane and Mylapore, is a heavily residential stretch, hosting a large number of small and self-contained neighbourhoods, each with its distinctive origin stories, cultural character and social dynamics. Here, too, the 1960s generation of unskilled manual labourers had achieved socio-economic mobility, in this case through their secure foothold in the centre of the city which allowed them access to educational opportunities and employment in the commercial, trading and service economies of the area.

Once the most concentrated slum corridor of the city, this stretch of canal banks was transformed from the late 1970s into a dense corridor of low-cost housing for the city. This was achieved through the dialectic action of state slum clearance schemes and incremental auto-construction by settlers. In 1975, soon after the Tamil Nadu Slum Clearance Board (TNSCB) was formed with a mandate to resettle slum-dwellers in tenements constructed in situ, a special action plan was drafted to clear 40 slums comprising about 6,000 households from the central section of the Buckingham Canal banks and resettle the residents in tenements constructed on adjoining land, at a total cost of ₹6.8 crore.[2] The PWD identified parcels of land belonging to various government departments and private trusts at 15 different sites along the canal to be transferred to the Slum Clearance Board. The scheme was approved in 1976.

However, these well-made plans did not materialise as envisioned. Many of the slum communities flatly rejected the tenement schemes and instead demanded titles to the land and houses they had built and occupied. Meanwhile, in the late 1970s, came an official shift in the state's slum clearance policies. The World Bank's entry into the urban housing sector of Tamil Nadu in 1972, and its substantial funding support for the Madras Urban Development Projects (MUDP) I and II, implemented between 1977 and 1988, introduced considerations of financial sustainability and replicability in state housing and slum clearance interventions. This provoked a shift in approach from expensive tenement construction to in situ slum upgrading and Sites-and-Services schemes as part of an emerging global consensus on best practices. The MUDP schemes offered tenure security, basic amenities and loans to slum-dwellers to enable them to incrementally develop their housing. This policy shift, as well as the slum-dwellers' resistance to the tenement scheme, impelled the TNSCB and the state's Housing Department to drop the tenement plans in several canal settlements.

Thus, in 2014, our field research on settlements along the canal found a landscape vastly different from that envisioned by the neat, rational and mathematically balanced proposals sanctioned in 1976. The planned tenements were in evidence in only eight of the

40 slums named in the proposal. Several others had been improved under MUDP schemes, receiving No Objection Certificates as tenure security and support to build their own housing. These settlements, along with numerous others not officially recorded under MUDP schemes, are today vibrant, dynamic, solidly built lower-middle-class neighbourhoods, comprising multi-storeyed buildings of varying shapes and sizes, water facilities and community infrastructures such as schools, temples and meeting halls. Built residential spaces are enmeshed with livelihood spaces, shops, saloons, warehouses and small enterprises. Rental housing is a major source of income and a significant part of the housing stock that these neighbourhoods contribute to the city.

A third category of settlements found along the canal in its southern sections as it leaves the city are resettlement sites for slum-dwellers, either voluntary or forced. These sites index the new imperatives of real estate urbanism that have shaped Chennai since the 1990s. In the late 1980s and early 1990s, several settlements were moved out of high-value central canal bank localities to make way for beautification projects or infrastructure like the MRTS, and were resettled on undervalued marshlands in the southern parts of Chennai. One such site along the canal banks is the notorious mass resettlement site of Kannagi Nagar.

However, there were also households—primarily renters, but also squatters—that voluntarily moved out of central city slums and went south looking for land that they could settle on and eventually own. Arignar Anna Nagar in Neelangarai along the southern banks of the canal is one such site, where groups of pioneers arrived with their families in the mid-1980s. This represents a second-generation encroachment, where urban working-class families exchanged one kind of urban foothold—that of shelter in proximity to livelihoods— for another—that of property and real estate. This move called for a re-enactment of the squatter cycle of taming rural lands for urbanisation, clearing undergrowth, fighting snakes and feral dogs, and building up urban infrastructure from scratch. Thirty years later, Arignar Anna Nagar appears to have fulfilled at least some of the settlers' aspirations. Despite none of the residents having obtained titles and thus remaining officially squatters, the settlement is a far cry from a slum. It is a well-ordered neighbourhood, comprising neat rows of concrete houses inside walled yards, many built up with an extra floor, a few provisions stores and several temples along a road running beside a quietly flowing, if polluted and malodorous canal. Years of collective action and incremental efforts have ensured that the neighbourhood is well equipped with electricity, street lights, water facilities and transport. Culturally, the neighbourhood is diverse, even cosmopolitan, comprising settlers from various religious and caste groups, including a cohort of recent migrants from the north-eastern states who rent rooms from the locals.

These workers, like thousands of others from the resettlement colony of Kannagi Nagar further south, provide informal labour to the 'new economy' establishments—IT companies, multinational electronics and automobile manufacturing firms, and gated residential and commercial complexes—that have arisen since the late 1990s on the southern and western fringes of Chennai. This traffic of informal workers between canal-bank settlements and the new economy corridors exemplify one more way in which the settlements and economies of the canal have shaped the urban character of Chennai.

CONCLUSION

Describing Chennai's urbanisation and growth from the vantage point of the canal corridor offers a range of new perspectives on the city's processes of urban formation. First, it highlights the overlooked but substantial contribution of low-caste and working-class settlements to the making of the city. The canal space was catalysed by the urban working classes to build up housing, livelihoods and communities through informal, incremental and largely independent means, creating one kind of heritage of the city. This account shifts attention from the flow of the canal to its banks, from a north–south orientation to the east–west, to crossings, connections and communities. It also challenges mainstream representations of 'slums' as a unitary category, revealing the diversity of social, economic and cultural forms of 'settlement' found along the canal banks. And, finally, the canal as a dubious waterway speaks eloquently of the legacies of engineering and governance of both urban nature and urban socio-economic opportunity in Madras/Chennai. It reveals shifts in the state's relations with urban land, nature and the poor, and yields insights into the ways by which dominant 'developmental' metrics have produced a corridor of undervalued spaces and people along the canal.

◆

NOTES

1. This paper is based on a case study of settlement along the Buckingham Canal commissioned by the Indian Institute of Human Settlements (IIHS) in Bangalore. My thanks are due to Gautam Bhan of IIHS, and to the team of researchers in Chennai that contributed most of the ethnographic material in this study: T. Venkat, Meghna Sukumar, Anusha Hariharan, Madhura Balasubramaniam, M. Subadevan, and R. Vaishnavi.

2. G. O. 1004, Public Works Department, 17/7/1976. Obtained from Tamil Nadu State Archives.

REFERENCES

Ahuja, R. 2001. 'Expropriating the Poor: Urban Land Control and Colonial Administration in Late Eighteenth Century Madras City', *Studies in History*, 17 (1), pp. 81–99.

Ranson, C. W. 1938. *A City in Transition: Studies in the Social Life of Madras*. Park Town, Madras: The Christian Literature Society of India.

Hancock, M. E. 2008. *The Politics of Heritage from Madras to Chennai*. Bloomington: Indiana University Press.

Inland Waterways Authority of India (IWAI). 2010. 'Final DPR for Development of Navigation in Kakinada–Puducherry Canal along with Rivers Godavari and Krishna'. WAPCOS Limited

Krishnamurthy S. and A. A. Kabalamurthy. 1964. *Greater Madras*. Chennai.

Neild, S. 1979. 'Colonial Urbanism: The Development of Madras in the Eighteenth and Nineteenth Centuries', *Modern Asian Studies*, 13 (2).

Russell, A. S. 1898. *History of the Buckingham Canal Project, With a Descriptive Account of the Canal and its Principal Works, and a Guide to its Future Maintenance*. Compiled for the Government of Madras.

◆◆

CITIES
Changing the Metaphor
to Quality of Life

VIKRAM
SONI

I f over a third of the living planet has been decommissioned by the affluent and conspicuous standard of living practised by less than a billion people of the developed world, imagine what would happen if all six billion people on the planet were to rise to such living standards. If we accept that the living planet cannot support such a scenario, then where do we go from here?

This article develops the common sense that the First World standard of living is an impossibility for all global citizens. However, we shall explore if an alternate but far more sensible, subtle and perhaps satisfying, index—quality of life—can be possible for all. Thus far we have identified progress with a crass, increasingly devastating high standard of living.

The city design we propose works out a new philosophy and template to build self-organised, non-invasive cities that 'conserve and use' their living natural resources, and are self-sufficient in water, food and milk. They are low on consumption but integrate living natural resource in an essential way into the scheme of living and yet provide an impeccable quality of life.

The millennium report indicates that in the last 50-odd years, 60 per cent of the world's ecosystems have degraded significantly and are showing terminal stress, as over 60 per cent of the wild species on land, rivers and the sea are on the verge of extinction. Yet more alarming is that in the last two years, over 12 per cent of species suffered this fate. Not so coincidentally, this was accompanied by a rather alarming accumulation of wealth by the richest 1 per cent of the world, which now holds almost 60 per cent of the world's wealth. It must be considered that it is in the last half-century that this has come to pass, which is the span in which urbanisation has really intensified. Much of this has come from the heightened consumption that identifies with the high standard of living of the more urban developed world.

This brings us to the cultural compulsion that leads the rest of the world to chase the American dream. After the last war, the United States became the ultimate index of prosperity. Powered by heady technology and a consumer boom, it became a magnet for migration. The fascination was so strong that the rest of the aspiring world was lulled into the facile assumption that all you needed was to invent and consume. Most nations are still chasing this dream, oblivious of the fact that it has curdled and given us climate change, ozone holes, slick seas, species loss and insatiable appetites. The American dream is actually the American anomaly—the Americans happened to be one-time beneficiaries of this consumer binge. For the rest of us, it will continue to remain a dream or, more likely, become a nightmare. It has not yet sunk in that the planet just does not have the larder for another freak event like the American dream party. It seems that the human appetite for acquisition and consumption has been firmly entrenched by market forces. The media, a product of technology, takes it further by connecting from a local audience of a few hundred to a global one of several millions. Love thy neighbour has become love for whatever thy neighbour has. The difference is that TV and travel have brought into the neighbour fold Moscow and Tokyo and Washington, Beijing....

QUALITY OF LIFE

Good air and water are so basic to not just the quality of life but to life—no amount of luxury can compensate for them. Cities need nature to regulate their climate and pollution to provide health for their citizens. Cities cannot exceed their carrying capacity or they become invasive. They should be self-sustaining, like other living systems, and not prey on their environs. They need to conserve and use their local, living natural resources.

The one thing that does not square up in all this is that conspicuous consumption does not necessarily mean a better quality of life. Quality of life is not an entirely material thing—it is far more subtle and sensitive. Just what do we do with our money? Go to faraway places in search of natural getaways when we have ample in our own neighbourhood. We seek health and peace at health spas and retreats when they are present in natural areas everywhere. More luxury does not necessarily bring pleasure; on the other hand, it makes happiness and fulfilment seem more elusive. Often we find beauty in simplicity. We see this in everything from architecture to painting and garments. A nature walk by a river or a lake or in a forest is more poetic and romantic than the claustrophobic luxury of a five-star hotel.

A remarkable example of this is the universal appreciation for the minimalist aesthetic of the Japanese, who—ironically—are anything but minimalistic in their lifestyle. Perhaps we need to simplify our lifestyle and learn the art of living from nature. In what follows is provided an actual realisation of the design for such a living scheme.

CITIES

Cities have a chronology that may be worth visiting. The first human settlements were perhaps caves and other such insulated shelters in the early times of hunter gatherers. Then came agriculture, and the settlements changed to walled habitation and huts on stilts. This was followed by tribal society, which also ushered in a time of fighting for dominion over fertile land by competing clans. Then came Empire and imperial capitals, which announced wealth and power by building the grand and imposing. Along with this came temple cities, and crusading religions founded papal cities and caliphates with the grand architecture of palaces and forts.

The colonial city emerged with the ascent of the European colonial powers. These were apartheid cities with separated status-defined quarters. For example, Calcutta had an elitist British quarter, a separate Indian civilian quarter, a separate workers' quarter, and so on. The colonialists wanted to exhibit their dominion with grand buildings and avenues. They built imperial cities like Delhi and Buenos Aires.

In India, we have had new capital cities like Chandigarh, which was designed by the architect Le Corbusier, based on the earlier work of Maciej Nowicki and Albert Mayer, and which had excellent drainage and so-called rectilinear sectors with 'Soviet'-style architecture. Another such new capital is Brasilia, designed by architects Lucia Costa, Oscar Niemeyer and Roberto Marx.

Brasilia is grander than Chandigarh but cut from the same cloth. None of these cities, though, is self-sustaining in, for example, water, vegetables and milk, or lean in energy use.

In the last several decades, we have had numerous high-rise skyscraper cities, beginning with New York and Chicago in the United States. But now many cities have transformed into megacities.

In the developing world, the city never stops growing; the gravity of the city is like matter—the larger the mass, the larger its gravitational attraction. But then we know that beyond a certain threshold, matter can collapse to a black hole, or explode. Examples take us across continents, from Mexico City to Sao Paolo and Rio de Janeiro, Lagos, Delhi, Mumbai, Beijing, Shanghai and Jakarta—the list goes on.

INVASIVE CITES

Over time, urban living has transformed the landscape of life. The change has been wrought by human development moving to larger and larger human settlements—cities, and now megacities. Often, such cities defy the idea of limits to growth. Much like monopolistic capital appropriation by a few individuals or corporations, megacities hold a monopoly over the rest of the planet. Yet, while we are glibly racing to greater urbanisation, we also find that this fabric is becoming frayed and strained, tearing the larger landscape of the planet. So much so that now the planet has a 'technosphere' that has been added to the living planet that now encompasses not just the biosphere, but also the lithosphere, geosphere, hydrosphere and atmosphere. The technosphere is the combined mass of building material and non-biodegradable waste added onto the biosphere, and is estimated to have a mass of 30 trillion tons or about 50 kg for each square metre of the planet's area. It would be misleading to forget that, actually, this concrete mass is not spread democratically but is concentrated in and around cities, industrial townships and mining sites.

Urbanisation is the order of the day. Whereas the developed world has stable cities, landscapes and populations, in the developing world they are anything but. We are getting infra cities with ultra-structures. Big cities are conspicuous consumers—it takes several times more resource to service a megacity resident, with the same standards as in a small town.

These megacities are fast becoming unliveable. Take the example of a 20-million city like Delhi or Beijing. They have toxic air and sometimes even killer air, exceeding six times the allowed health safety limit of microscopic particulate matter. Such cities now have a very large and expanding water footprint; Delhi gets water from 300 km away—the Tehri dam, which has permanently scarred the great Himalayas—whereas Beijing's water is brought by bulk long-distance transfer from the leaching of a great river—the Yangtze—the consequences for its river ecology, which are yet unknown, but cannot be anything but adverse.

Not only do commuting distances inflate in a big city, but so do traffic jams and, consequently, travel time. Particularly in developing countries, big cities exhibit enormous medical problems from air pollution and dust and stress, and therefore need a huge medical infrastructure. They also need an inordinate transport infrastructure. These cities need huge storage for supplies and they generate huge quantities of sewage; they can have large shanty populations (even 40 per cent) that makes life intolerable for half the population.

Often democracy is blamed for this. Can one stop people from migrating to a megacity to find employment? One can. Migration is induced by investment. We have invested unilaterally in big cities and if the 'news' is an indicator, more investment in the form of mass housing for the shanty or *jhuggi* dwellers is imminent in Delhi. This is in total violation of the carrying capacity—it is a thoughtless populist measure.

True, you cannot force anyone out of the megacity regardless of their abject living condition. But you can move investments to smaller towns in the form of schools, universities (IITs and IIMs), good transport and green areas. Citizens of smaller towns can be seduced further by giving them tax cuts in personal income tax, in property tax and in car registration, and in so many other ways. The bad air, traffic and often water problems in megacities will induce people to move to a better place.

There are many small towns that are an easy commute from Delhi—Meerut, Mathura, Panipat, Alwar. It does take a little empathy and cooperation between the Delhi government and the Union government to do this but, sadly, that is not happening. And now with the antipathy between these two adversarial governments, it is even less likely. Any such proposition individually by the state or the centre will be greeted with a populist cacophony of protest against eviction. Here is a case where common sense must override political rhetoric.

Take note of the trend that the Chandigarh gentry, who once were drawn to Delhi like a moth to a candle, no longer want to get singed by Delhi's toxic air—they prefer to move events to Chandigarh. And the people of Delhi enjoy the reprieve of breathing good air for a few days. As a universal responsibility for our future, we therefore need to move to less invasive, self-sustaining 'natural cities'.

PERENNIAL WATER FOR CITIES

From being blessed countries that had plenty of water 50 years ago, India and China are now moving towards terminal water stress. All the rivers of northern China have been polluted, and it has also gone into overdrive on groundwater. As a matter of fact, it may be heading for a bigger disaster in undertaking an unwise and unnatural long-distance bulk transfer of water from south to north.

Equally serious, India has unconcernedly pulled out most of its groundwater in the north-west and the central-south in working its celebrated green revolution. If natural wisdom prevails, there is a whisper of a chance to recover this in 40 years, but only if the agricultural map of the country is redrawn. And in the water-short half of the country, expectedly, rivers are overdrawn and polluted, which means another long and painful haul to restore them. A huge and irreversible water problem has been created by lack of foresight.

Many cities of the world depend on rivers for their water. How can a city by a river be self-sustaining for water now that the rivers are polluted? The only way out is to discover a new perennial local source of water and protect it with one's life. To this, we turn.

THE HIDDEN TREASURE: FLOODPLAIN AQUIFERS

The Himalayan rivers and their tributaries flow down from the Himalayas into the plains of north India and China. They have been flowing for millions of years, overrunning their banks during the monsoon, swollen with water and depositing sand on their floodplain. This sandy layer on top can be anywhere from 50 m to even 100–200 m deep, which is a lot. Sand and gravel are excellent for water storage.

SAND AND WATER

Take an equal amount of dry river sand and water in two identical glasses and start pouring the water into the sand glass, watchfully. Not surprisingly, half the water glass can empty into the sand glass because sand and gravel are excellent for water storage—they are aquifer material.

NATURAL UNDERGROUND STORAGE

The Yamuna river floodplain in Delhi is about 100 sq km in area and on average 50 m deep, and runs for a river length of 50 km in the National Capital Territory. Even after gravity compactification, it holds a lot of underground water—about 35–40 per cent of this volume is water. Approximately one-third of this, about 12 per cent of the total volume of the aquifer, can be withdrawn. This is called the specific yield. Can we use this?

One may think that if we pull out all this water from the floodplain, we will end up leaching out all the water. But, the floodplain is an extensive aquifer that runs the whole length of the river—over 1,000 km. If we take out the water locally for the city, the rest of the floodplain will recharge it by gravity, even when there is no rainfall recharge. This has been seen to be true from the hydrographs of the floodplain. Experiments on local withdrawal of water show that if there was no recharge from outside the local area of withdrawal, groundwater levels would have diminished by 10 m, whereas, actually, in the floodplain they diminish by only 2 m. This shows that the floodplain is an exceptional and extended aquifer, where any withdrawal is compensated by gravity flow from a large surrounding area. And, unlike other aquifers, the water supply from the floodplain wells never runs out. This is optimal natural underground storage with the advantage of no land (reservoir) and no evaporation losses as for surface storage.

While this sounds too easy, we must remember that ecology demands that we only pull out no more water than the annual recharge.

NATURAL RECHARGE

But there are clear limits on how much recharge can occur naturally. On carefully working out the natural recharge from rainfall (60–70 cm a year for Delhi) and flooding, we found that the withdrawal has to be considerably scaled down. Even so, about 50 km of river length can take care of the yearly water requirements of almost three million people, i.e., 200–250 MCM (million cubic metres). It is non-invasive and perennial. It can be preserved and used every year—nature's gift.

The Mahanadi, in Cuttack and Bhubaneshwar, has 300 sq km of quality floodplain that is about 40 m deep. Its rainfall, which is 160 cm per year—almost three times that of Delhi—can provide a non-invasive perennial water supply for seven million people.

The recharge takes place from rainfall and flooding that comes late in the season when the river has washed out the pollution. Naturally filtered floodplain water is of drinking water quality—far better than polluted river water.

ECONOMIC VALUE

It is quite straightforward to set an economic value on this water. The highest slab tariff on water for commercial use charged by the Delhi Jal (Water) Board (DJB) is ₹1,500 for 10,000 L (10 m³). At this tariff, the value of the annual sustainable yield of the flood plain, about 200 MCM, is over ₹3,000 crore a year. Recycling the same volume of water for drinking costs much more.

This scheme is not a pie in the sky but is working on the ground. This project is a pioneering and a path-breaking one for the world. The scheme is working in Delhi on the northern (Palla) half of the Delhi Yamuna floodplain, which has the capacity to deliver a sustainable water yield of 100 MCM a year. It is already yielding half its capacity, 50 MCM, while it awaits a new pipeline. But at the highest commercial water tariff of the DJB it already amounts to ₹750 crores of annual revenue for the DJB.[1] This scheme is perennial and sustainable while being very low cost; an annual yield of 100 MCM would cost about ₹100 crore for the installation of all the borewells, a pipeline and a SCADA (supervisory control and data) system, which will have sensors for all parameters of quality, and computerise all operations for optimal pumping.

PERENNIAL, NON-INVASIVE AND GLOBAL

Is it not absurd to recycle water with more technology and dispense more waste in the environment, with costs over ₹3,000 crore a year, rather than access a natural and perennial source of water that does the same practically for free? Such a creative scheme can be of immense value in hundreds of cities that have a river flowing through. Cities which have populations of less than three million, like Mathura, Agra, Allahabad and Benares to name a few, can source all their water from the floodplains. Delhi will need other sources as its population is very large. It is a pity that it is yet to be adopted by numerous other cities. It can be hugely useful for China and the Middle East as well.

The uniqueness of this novel and creative scheme is that it employs only natural storage and natural recharge. Such non-invasive use ensures sustainable and perennial water solutions which strictly conserve the ecological integrity of the water resource. Such 'preserve and use' schemes are the guarantor for holding these natural resources that were created over millions of years, for future generations—something that has been regrettably absent from most human inventions and interventions in the last century. It would allow us to move to a new template for city design.

NATURAL CITIES

We therefore need a new blueprint for cities that will be self-sustaining and minimally invasive. It is here that we depart from our earlier narrative on the historical evolution of cities. The contemporary dilemmas of urbanisation call for a radically new idea to design cities on the basis of self-sustainability. By happy 'coincidence', this runs parallel to our starting proposition that we must provide *quality of life* with minimum consumption, and habitat wear and tear.

How can cities be self-sustaining and not prey upon their environment? This led us to think of cities in a different way. With some daily 'bread' as the input, all natural organisms maintain a steady state that is reflected in their physical parameters—temperature, pressure, trace elements, blood or plant plasma—holding steady. We have a word for this principle of life—*homeostasis*—but science is yet to find an explanation for this. We do not understand homeostasis even for a single living cell. As a matter of fact, this year's Nobel Prize for medicine was given for revealing a part of this mystery, the recycling function of a single cell—that is how far we are.

At the largest scale, the living planet uses sunlight to do the same—it is self-sustaining and keeps the composition of the atmosphere and the salt in the seawater constant over cosmic time. So, perhaps, this could be the natural organising principle at the intermediate scale of a living city.

There is another principle to guide us: *conserve and use*—of being non-invasive to nature. And, finally, it has ears and feet on the ground—it is not just an idea.

The river floodplains are still intact and happen to be possibly the only new source of city water on the horizon. We have found that a new urban civilisation of a million people can be watered by about 20 km of floodplain along the river course. This can happen by locating the city by the river floodplains, and marking out a 3–4 km-wide floodplain across a river length of 20 km as a water sanctuary.

Now we shall move on to one of many possible templates for city design. Bordering the floodplains, we can set the city on a 15 km × 15 km square chessboard pattern, with white squares as built areas and black squares as green areas, which could be parkland, organic vegetable gardens, orchards or pasture. The 3 km-wide floodplain aquifer that runs along for 20 km has to be protected to provide a local and perennial quality water supply. Above ground, the floodplain can be used to grow (only) organic vegetables.

Downstream and transverse to the river, a 15 km × 3 km-wide strip can treat the sewage and be kept as pasture for cows. The cleansed water can either be used in pastures or sent back to the river. Of the green area in the city, we will use a third for parkland, a third for vegetable gardens and orchards, and a third for pasture. This will make the city self-sufficient in vegetables, fruit and milk. Essentially, this integrates farming into the city design and will deliver fresh, quality organic vegetables and fruit to the residents.

In the summer months in India, the built areas get a little hot—over 40°C. The hot air will rise, pulling in the cool air from the green areas—green convection. The city also pulls in cool air from the river—blue convection. Add insulating, hollow brick walls for housing, and reflecting roofs and solar panels. Put together, this can bring down ambient temperatures by over 4–6°C and in-house temperatures by 7–10°C, saving much energy that would have been consumed by air-conditioning.

Now the city is so designed that bicycle paths will run along the green diagonals and be non-stop—all less than 7–8 km from the city centre. This will make it an easy and shady bicycle ride, which will be shorter in time than driving and parking, encouraging people not to use cars. Such smaller traverses and non-hydrocarbon pathways will cut transport costs. Reducing commuting distances and the open green nature of the city will reduce pollution by a factor of eight with a similar improvement in the health index, compared to a megacity like Delhi. This will greatly improve the quality of life of the city almost at no cost.

This city will cut down dramatically on fuel costs for transportation and energy for cooling. We find that by factoring in all the costs, including cheaper rentals, the cost of living will diminish to a third of that in the big city. Moreover, the sustainability index, based on these parameters, would be hugely better.

There are many local forested hills in the neighbourhood. Rain seeps through the humus and organic matter on the forest floor, gathering nutrients, and then percolates through the rocky terrain underground to pick up minerals. Such forest hill tracts can provide mineral water for the inhabitants at almost no cost. Add a final flourish and run a picturesque blue canal from the river, through the city and back to the river. So, here it is—the design for a sustainable city that provides an exceptional quality of life for a million people.

We call such a city a 'Natural City'. The idea of a self-sustaining natural city has evolved as a counter to the ongoing practice of invasive urbanisation that destroys nature and its right of way—rivers, floodplains, waterways, lakes, reservoirs, marshes, etc., making it highly unsustainable. Amravati, the future capital of Andhra Pradesh, offers an excellent opportunity to have a self-sustaining natural city. Such a vision is presented in the monograph 'Amaravati: Natural City'.

A natural city conserves living natural resource like river floodplains, but uses them non-invasively. It also uses natural ways to regulate the climate of the city and the health of all its residents. It is energy lean and can use renewable solar energy for its modest needs. A feature of such cities is that they must reside within their carrying capacity or they cease to remain self-sustaining. This is being violated in the present scenario of uncontrolled urbanisation. Carrying capacity is an obvious non-invasive principle in nature that applies to our weight, consumption, population and cities as well.

Let me emphasise once more that we need to exchange the metaphor for conspicuous consumption 'world-class' standard of living that will bring us to a nasty end with that for the 'quality of life', which is low on consumption but integrates living natural resources in an essential way in to the city scheme of living—this is the basis for the Natural City Scheme.

Such cities will provide quality of life to people belonging to all strata of society at minimal cost and consumption. This vision was first presented by the author at an invited talk in November, as a template for the HABITAT III conference in Ecuador in October 2016. It was carried forward to the conference and has since become an attractor.

However we decide to design urban habitats for the future, we must adhere to the principle that it will be self-sustaining and in symbiosis with nature if it is to endure. This will preserve the quality of life for all. It will also bring the rural and the urban into seamless natural congruence. Such self-sustaining cities are the ones that can secure the planet and habitat for future generations.

◆

ACKNOWLEDGEMENT

I thank Romi Khosla, Arvind Virmani, Satya Bolishetty, Diwan Singh, Kapil Mishra, Sachin Jain, M. Devasahayam and others for their collaboration. Natural Cities literature can be found on the Internet and on YouTube, and in the *Economic and Political Weekly* and *Current Science*.

NOTE

1. See the Delhi Government press release, 1 June 2016.

◆◆

For Product Safety Concerns and Information please contact our EU
representative GPSR@taylorandfrancis.com Taylor & Francis Verlag GmbH,
Kaufingerstraße 24, 80331 München, Germany

Printed and bound by CPI Group (UK) Ltd, Croydon, CR0 4YY
01/05/2025
01858419-0001